Truth and the Unconscious in Psychoanalysis

What is the truth of the unconscious? *Truth and the Unconscious in Psychoanalysis* explores the intersection of these two concepts within a Bionian framework. Giuseppe Civitarese maps out the unconscious in psychoanalysis, and focuses on the differences between the Freudian, Kleinian, Bionian and Lacanian schools of thought on this topic, as well as drawing on findings from neuroscience.

The book explores topics including the inaccessibility of the unconscious, dreams, body issues, issues of personality, the influence of field theory and the clinical implications of this theorizing. It contains innovative comparison between Freudian metapsychology and the Bionian theory on thinking, and novel use of Bion's hallucinosis as an important new technical tool. An internationally recognized author, Civitarese provides fresh ideas throughout on a challenging subject, supported with vivid clinical material.

Truth and the Unconscious in Psychoanalysis will be of interest to anyone following the growing post-Bionian movement within contemporary psychoanalysis, enabling them to familiarize themselves with some of the most important current issues in psychoanalytic research. *Truth and the Unconscious in Psychoanalysis* will appeal to psychotherapists, psychologists and psychoanalysts, as well as undergraduate and postgraduate students studying in the field.

Giuseppe Civitarese is a training and supervising analyst in the Italian Psychoanalytic Society (SPI), and a member of the American Psychoanalytic Association (APsaA). He lives in Pavia, Italy. He has published several books including the Routledge titles *The Intimate Room* (2010) and *The Violence of Emotions* (2012).

THE NEW LIBRARY OF PSYCHOANALYSIS
General Editor: Alessandra Lemma

The New Library of Psychoanalysis was launched in 1987 in association with the Institute of Psychoanalysis, London. It took over from the International Psychoanalytical Library which published many of the early translations of the works of Freud and the writings of most of the leading British and Continental psychoanalysts.

The purpose of the New Library of Psychoanalysis is to facilitate a greater and more widespread appreciation of psychoanalysis and to provide a forum for increasing mutual understanding between psychoanalysts and those working in other disciplines such as the social sciences, medicine, philosophy, history, linguistics, literature and the arts. It aims to represent different trends both in British psychoanalysis and in psychoanalysis generally. The New Library of Psychoanalysis is well placed to make available to the English-speaking world psychoanalytic writings from other European countries and to increase the interchange of ideas between British and American psychoanalysts. Through the *Teaching Series*, the New Library of Psychoanalysis now also publishes books that provide comprehensive, yet accessible, overviews of selected subject areas aimed at those studying psychoanalysis and related fields such as the social sciences, philosophy, literature and the arts.

The Institute, together with the British Psychoanalytical Society, runs a low-fee psychoanalytic clinic, organizes lectures and scientific events concerned with psychoanalysis and publishes the *International Journal of Psychoanalysis*. It runs a training course in psychoanalysis which leads to membership of the International Psychoanalytical Association – the body which preserves internationally agreed standards of training, of professional entry, and of professional ethics and practice for psychoanalysis as initiated and developed by Sigmund Freud. Distinguished members of the Institute have included Michael Balint, Wilfred Bion, Ronald Fairbairn, Anna Freud, Ernest Jones, Melanie Klein, John Rickman and Donald Winnicott.

Previous general editors have included David Tuckett, who played a very active role in the establishment of the New Library.

He was followed as general editor by Elizabeth Bott Spillius, who was in turn followed by Susan Budd and then by Dana Birksted-Breen.

Current members of the Advisory Board include Giovanna Di Ceglie, Liz Allison, Anne Patterson, Josh Cohen and Daniel Pick.

Previous members of the Advisory Board include Christopher Bollas, Ronald Britton, Catalina Bronstein, Donald Campbell, Rosemary Davies, Sara Flanders, Stephen Grosz, John Keene, Eglé Laufer, Alessandra Lemma, Juliet Mitchell, Michael Parsons, Rosine Jozef Perelberg, Richard Rusbridger, Mary Target and David Taylor.

TITLES IN THIS SERIES

Impasse and Interpretation Herbert Rosenfeld
Psychoanalysis and Discourse Patrick Mahony
The Suppressed Madness of Sane Men Marion Milner
The Riddle of Freud Estelle Roith
Thinking, Feeling, and Being Ignacio Matte Blanco
The Theatre of the Dream Salomon Resnik
Melanie Klein Today: Volume 1, Mainly Theory Edited by Elizabeth Bott Spillius
Melanie Klein Today: Volume 2, Mainly Practice Edited by Elizabeth Bott Spillius
Psychic Equilibrium and Psychic Change: Selected Papers of Betty Joseph Edited by Michael Feldman and Elizabeth Bott Spillius
About Children and Children-No-Longer: Collected Papers 1942–80 Paula Heimann. Edited by Margret Tonnesmann
The Freud–Klein Controversies 1941–45 Edited by Pearl King and Riccardo Steiner
Dream, Phantasy and Art Hanna Segal
Psychic Experience and Problems of Technique Harold Stewart
Clinical Lectures on Klein & Bion Edited by Robin Anderson
From Fetus to Child Alessandra Piontelli
A Psychoanalytic Theory of Infantile Experience: Conceptual and Clinical Reflections E Gaddini. Edited by Adam Limentani
The Dream Discourse Today Edited and introduced by Sara Flanders
The Gender Conundrum: Contemporary Psychoanalytic Perspectives on Femininity and Masculinity Edited and introduced by Dana Birksted-Breen

Psychic Retreats John Steiner

The Taming of Solitude: Separation Anxiety in Psychoanalysis Jean-Michel Quinodoz

Unconscious Logic: An Introduction to Matte-Blanco's Bi-logic and its Uses Eric Rayner

Understanding Mental Objects Meir Perlow

Life, Sex and Death: Selected Writings of William Gillespie Edited and introduced by Michael Sinason

What Do Psychoanalysts Want?: The Problem of Aims in Psychoanalytic Therapy Joseph Sandler and Anna Ursula Dreher

Michael Balint: Object Relations, Pure and Applied Harold Stewart

Hope: A Shield in the Economy of Borderline States Anna Potamianou

Psychoanalysis, Literature & War: Papers 1972–1995 Hanna Segal

Emotional Vertigo: Between Anxiety and Pleasure Danielle Quinodoz

Early Freud and Late Freud Ilse Grubrich-Simitis

A History of Child Psychoanalysis Claudine and Pierre Geissmann

Belief and Imagination: Explorations in Psychoanalysis Ronald Britton

A Mind of One's Own: A Psychoanalytic View of Self and Object Robert A. Caper

Psychoanalytic Understanding of Violence and Suicide Edited by Rosine Jozef Perelberg

On Bearing Unbearable States of Mind Ruth Riesenberg-Malcolm

Psychoanalysis on the Move: The Work of Joseph Sandler Edited by Peter Fonagy, Arnold M. Cooper and Robert S. Wallerstein

The Dead Mother: The Work of André Green Edited by Gregorio Kohon

The Fabric of Affect in the Psychoanalytic Discourse André Green

The Bi-Personal Field: Experiences of Child Analysis Antonino Ferro

The Dove that Returns, the Dove that Vanishes: Paradox and Creativity in Psychoanalysis Michael Parsons

Ordinary People, Extra-ordinary Protections: A Post Kleinian Approach to the Treatment of Primitive Mental States Judith Mitrani

The Violence of Interpretation: From Pictogram to Statement Piera Aulagnier

The Importance of Fathers: A Psychoanalytic Re-Evaluation Judith Trowell and Alicia Etchegoyen

Dreams That Turn Over a Page: Paradoxical Dreams in Psychoanalysis Jean-Michel Quinodoz

The Couch and the Silver Screen: Psychoanalytic Reflections on European Cinema Andrea Sabbadini

In Pursuit of Psychic Change: The Betty Joseph Workshop Edited by Edith Hargreaves and Arturo Varchevker

The Quiet Revolution in American Psychoanalysis: Selected Papers of Arnold M. Cooper Arnold M. Cooper. Edited and introduced by Elizabeth L. Auchincloss

Seeds of Illness and Seeds of Recovery: The Genesis of Suffering and the Role of Psychoanalysis Antonino Ferro

The Work of Psychic Figurability: Mental States Without Representation César Botella and Sára Botella

Key Ideas for a Contemporary Psychoanalysis: Misrecognition and Recognition of the Unconscious André Green

The Telescoping of Generations: Listening to the Narcissistic Links Between Generations Haydée Faimberg

Glacial Times: A Journey through the World of Madness Salomon Resnik

This Art of Psychoanalysis: Dreaming Undreamt Dreams and Interrupted Cries Thomas H. Ogden

Psychoanalysis and Religion in the 21st Century: Competitors or Collaborators? David M. Black

Recovery of the Lost Good Object Eric Brenman

The Many Voices of Psychoanalysis Roger Kennedy

Feeling the Words: Neuropsychoanalytic Understanding of Memory and the Unconscious Mauro Mancia

Constructions and the Analytic Field: History, Scenes and Destiny Domenico Chianese

Projected Shadows: Psychoanalytic Reflections on the Representation of Loss in European Cinema Edited by Andrea Sabbadini

Encounters with Melanie Klein: Selected Papers of Elizabeth Spillius Elizabeth Spillius

Yesterday, Today and Tomorrow Hanna Segal

Psychoanalysis Comparable and Incomparable: The Evolution of a Method to Describe and Compare Psychoanalytic Approaches David Tuckett, Roberto Basile, Dana Birksted-Breen, Tomas Böhm, Paul Denis, Antonino Ferro, Helmut Hinz, Arne Jemstedt, Paola Mariotti and Johan Schubert

Time, Space and Phantasy Rosine Jozef Perelberg

Rediscovering Psychoanalysis: Thinking and Dreaming, Learning and Forgetting Thomas H. Ogden

Mind Works: Techniques and Creativity in Psychoanalysis Antonino Ferro

Doubt Conviction and the Analytic Process: Selected Papers of Michael Feldman Michael Feldman

Melanie Klein in Berlin: Her First Psychoanalyses of Children Claudia Frank

The Psychotic Wavelength: A Psychoanalytic Perspective for Psychiatry Richard Lucas

Betweenity: A Discussion of the Concept of Borderline Judy Gammelgaard

The Intimate Room: Theory and Technique of the Analytic Field Giuseppe Civitarese

Bion Today Edited by Chris Mawson

Secret Passages: The Theory and Technique of Interpsychic Relations Stefano Bolognini

Intersubjective Processes and the Unconscious: An Integration of Freudian, Kleinian and Bionian Perspectives Lawrence J. Brown

Seeing and Being Seen: Emerging from a Psychic Retreat John Steiner

Avoiding Emotions, Living Emotions Antonino Ferro

Projective Identification: The Fate of a Concept Edited by Elizabeth Spillius and Edna O'Shaughnessy

Creative Readings: Essays on Seminal Analytic Works Thomas Ogden

The Maternal Lineage Edited by Paola Mariotti

Donald Winnicott Today Edited by Jan Abram

Symbiosis and Ambiguity: A Psychoanalytic Study Edited by John Churcher, José Bleger and Leopoldo Bleger

Psychotic Temptation Liliane Abensour

Supervision in Psychoanalysis: The Sao Paulo Seminars Antonino Ferro

Transference and Countertransference Today Robert Oelsner

Living Psychoanalysis: From Theory to Experience Michael Parsons

Imaginary Existences: A Psychoanalytic Exploration of Phantasy, Fiction, Dreams and Daydreams Ignês Sodré. Edited and with an Introduction by Priscilla Roth

The Pioneers of Psychoanalysis in South America: An Essential Guide Edited by Nydia Lisman-Pieczanski and Alberto Pieczanski

Minding the Body: The Body in Psychoanalysis and Beyond Alessandra Lemma

Inquiries in Psychoanalysis: The collected papers of Edna O'Shaughnessy Edna O'Shaughnessy and edited by Richard Rusbridger

Torments of the Soul: Psychoanalytic Transformations in Dreaming and Narration Antonino Ferro

Frances Tustin Today Edited by Judith Mitrani and Theodore Mitrani

Formless Infinity: Clinical Explorations of Matte Blanco and Bion Riccardo Lombardo

Murdered Father, Dead Father: Revisiting the Oedipus Complex Rosine Jozef Perelberg

The Work of Psychoanalysis: Sexuality, Time and the Psychoanalytic Mind Dana Birksted-Breen

Truth and the Unconscious in Psychoanalysis Giuseppe Civitarese

Psychoanalytic Education at the Crossroads Otto Kernberg

TITLES IN THE NEW LIBRARY OF PSYCHOANALYSIS TEACHING SERIES

Reading Freud: A Chronological Exploration of Freud's Writings Jean-Michel Quinodoz

Listening to Hanna Segal: Her Contribution to Psychoanalysis Jean-Michel Quinodoz

Reading French Psychoanalysis Edited by Dana Birksted-Breen, Sara Flanders and Alain Gibeault

Reading Winnicott Lesley Caldwell and Angela Joyce

Initiating Psychoanalysis: Perspectives Bernard Reith, Sven Lagerlöf, Penelope Crick, Mette Møller and Elisabeth Skale

Infant Observation Frances Salo

Reading Anna Freud Nick Midgley

Reading Italian Psychoanalysis Edited by Franco Borgogno, Alberto Luchetti and Luisa Marino Coe

TITLES IN THE NEW LIBRARY OF PSYCHOANALYSIS 'BEYOND THE COUCH' SERIES

Under the Skin: A Psychoanalytic Study of Body Modification Alessandra Lemma

Engaging with Climate Change: Psychoanalytic and Interdisciplinary Perspectives Edited by Sally Weintrobe

Research on the Couch: Single Case Studies, Subjectivity, and Psychoanalytic Knowledge R.D. Hinshelwood

Psychoanalysis in the Technoculture Era Edited by Alessandra Lemma and Luigi Caparrotta

Moving Images: Psychoanalytic Reflections on Film Andrea Sabbadini

Reflections on the Aesthetic Experience: Psychoanalysis and the Uncanny Gregorio Kohon

THE NEW LIBRARY OF PSYCHOANALYSIS

General Editor: Alessandra Lemma

Truth and the Unconscious in Psychoanalysis

Giuseppe Civitarese

Routledge
Taylor & Francis Group
LONDON AND NEW YORK

First published 2016
by Routledge
2 Park Square, Milton Park, Abingdon, Oxon OX14 4RN

and by Routledge
605 Third Avenue, New York, NY 10017

Routledge is an imprint of the Taylor & Francis Group, an informa business

Previously published in Italian as *I sensi e l'inconscio*, 2014, by Borla, Roma, Italy

British Library Cataloguing in Publication Data
A catalogue record for this book is available from the British Library

Library of Congress Cataloguing in Publication Data
Names: Civitarese, Giuseppe, 1958– author.
Title: Truth and the unconscious in psychoanalysis / Giuseppe Civitarese.
Other titles: I Sensi e l'Inconscio. English
Description: New York, NY : Routledge, 2016. | Series: New library of psychoanalysis | Includes bibliographical references and index.
Identifiers: LCCN 2015037706| ISBN 9781138954939 (hardback) | ISBN 9781138954953 (pbk.) | ISBN 9781315666662 (e-book)
Subjects: LCSH: Subconsciousness. | Psychoanalysis. | Bion, Wilfred R. (Wilfred Ruprecht), 1897–1979.
Classification: LCC BF315 .C5813 2016 | DDC 616.89/17—dc23LC record available at http://lccn.loc.gov/2015037706

ISBN: 978-1-138-95493-9 (hbk)
ISBN: 978-1-138-95495-3 (pbk)
ISBN: 978-1-315-66666-2 (ebk)

Typeset in Bembo
by Keystroke, Station Road, Codsall, Wolverhampton

Translations by Adam Elgar, Ian Harvey and Philip Slotkin

For my parents

Contents

Acknowledgements

Chapter 1 is based on 'The inaccessible unconscious and reverie as a path of figurability', in H. Levine, D. Scarfone and G. Reed (eds), *Unrepresented States and the Construction of Meaning: Clinical and Theoretical Contributions*, Karnac, London 2013, pp. 220–239; *Psicoterapia Psicoanalitica* 18, 1, 61–75 (2011); *Quaderno dell'Istituto di Psicoterapia del Bambino e dell'Adolescente* 36, 2, 109–124 (2012).

Chapter 2 is based on 'Campo incarnato, rêverie corporea e pazienti con blocchi della simbolizzazione', *L'Educazione Sentimentale. Rivista di Psicosocioanalisi* 20, 25–31 (2013).

Chapter 3 is based on 'Poesie du rêve et dépersonnalisation'. *Revue Française de Psychanalyse* 77, 1066–1081 (2013).

Chapter 4 is based on 'Transformations in hallucinosis and the analyst's receptivity', *International Journal of Psychoanalysis* 96, 1091–1116.

Chapter 5 is based on 'The unconscious. What is your theory of unconscious processes? What are other theories that you would contrast with your conceptualization?', *International Journal of Psychoanalysis* 92, 277–280 (2011); *Revista de Psicoanálisis* 68, 1, 29–32 (2011); *Rivista di Psicoanalisi* 57, 2, 401–405 (2011); *Revue Française de Psychanalyse* 75, 3, 839–842 (2011); *Revista Brasileira de Psicanálise* 45, 2, 63–66 (2011).

Chapter 8 is based on 'La Griglia di Bion e la pulsione di verità', *Rivista di Psicoanalisi*, 58, 2, 335–360 (2012); *The Italian Psychoanalytic Annual* 7, 91–114 (2013); *Revista de Psicanálise* (SPPA), 21, 1 (2014).

Chapter 9 is based on 'L'intermedietà come paradigma epistemologico in psicoanalisi', *L'Educazione Sentimentale. Rivista di Psicosocioanalisi* 17, 40–55 (2012).

Chapter 10 is based on 'Bion's "Evidence" and his theoretical style', *The Psychoanalytic Quarterly* 82, 3, 615–633 (2013); *Revista de Psicoánalisis* 11, Mayo, 11–26 (2013); and in F. Bazzani, R. Lanfredini and S. Vitale (eds), *La questione dello stile* II, Clinamen, Firenze 2013, pp. 109–123.

INTRODUCTION

For Bion, truth is the food that makes the mind grow. Not only that: what moves humans is a real drive to truth. But what are the truths of the unconscious? How can we grasp them? What attitude must we adopt if we wish to comprehend the facts of the unconscious? And which unconscious are we talking about? Freud's repressed unconscious or Bion's 'aesthetic' unconscious? And lastly, what does psychoanalysis have to say about the concept of scientific truth?

This book attempts to formulate some answers to these questions, questions which have become even more fundamental in an age such as ours characterized by the deconstruction of positive reason and in which all values are seen as relative. It should be emphasized, however, that while I consider it essential to expand the horizons of psychoanalysis to embrace the most topical issues of the contemporary world and, with all due caution, to incorporate other approaches, I remain faithful to the Freudian principle of *Juntkim*, the indissoluble binding together of method, theoretical reflection and clinical practice. In my view, indeed, it is the cognitive and ethical dimension of therapy that makes psychoanalysis unsurpassed.

The occasion that prompted the writing of this book was the IPA Congress in Mexico City in 2011. I was asked to participate in the inaugural session on the unconscious. I felt a great responsibility and put in a lot of preparation. I soon realized with a certain apprehension that the familiar concept of the unconscious was becoming more and more alien to me. The closer I came to it, the more it seemed to elude me. Indeed, it is true: the more we study the unconscious, the darker the picture becomes, and the tangle of various conceptualizations becomes almost impenetrable. Already in Freud we have the problem of the transition from the first to the second topography. Then there are also its major reformulations to consider, from Lacan to Laplanche, passing through Klein and Bion, not to mention the various hybrids that combine psychoanalytic theories and the various models of brain function current in neuroscience.

The attempt to map some of the essential nodal points of the conceptual network that developed from the key notion of psychoanalysis cost me no little effort, but in the process I was able to draw up a small atlas of the unconscious. However provisional and imprecise, this atlas will I hope be helpful to readers in continuing explorations I would like to think of as being cautious but also courageous in spirit.

The first place we come to on this notional map is 'the inaccessible unconscious', as Bion puts it, an unconscious that dates back to foetal life and whose effects can be felt powerfully in adulthood. The question I address in the opening chapter is how we can confer figurability on the primitive traumas inscribed in an unconscious that is not made up of representations. My idea is that a possible way forward would be to adopt a theory of the analytic field and for the analyst to use reverie. But it can also be helpful to 'dream in the body', and in the next chapter I theorize this idea through the notion of body reverie. Unlike Ogden's concepts of 'sensory reverie', which is perceived as such almost immediately, and 'interpretative action', which is characterized by obvious intentionality, body reverie is neither intentional nor conscious. Rather, it is an action or sequence of actions to which the meaning of an acted out performance can be attributed only in retrospect: a performance that is a kind of understanding through the body or of dreaming in the body what is unconsciously going on in the analytic field at a given moment or over a longer period of time. I would not even use the term *enactment*, a word too closely identified with the idea of the unreflective offloading of instinctual drives or proto-emotions, and not necessarily through behaviour. Moreover, the concept of *enactment* is still framed within a theory that sees two separate subjects in interaction and that strictly speaking is not authentically intersubjective in nature.

In the next chapter I try to explain why we should trust dreams, and how this reflects a different idea of the unconscious from the classical one. The human capacity to dream both at night and while awake can be seen as the task of creating a film of meaning that functions as a para-excitatory screen against the traumatic nature of reality. The psychic skin that dreams produce is a mask of self-deception or pretence (*finzione*), in the etymological sense of 'pretend' (*fingere*; imagine/think), which enables us to become persons. In Latin, 'persona' does in fact mean mask. Dreaming thus expresses the poetic ability of the mind. Like a poem, the dream-text seeks each time to restore harmony between body and mind, to give the body back to the mind or to reinstate the mind in the body – as Winnicott puts it, to 'personalize'; in other words to propel the process of subjectivation.

The theme of the fourth chapter is also connected to dreaming. Here I look at Bion's concept of transformation in hallucinosis. Bion describes transformation in hallucinosis as a psychotic defence, as the hallucinatory activity that infiltrates perception physiologically and allows us to know reality by contrasting it with a background of familiarity, and finally, surprisingly, as the ideal state of mind the analyst must enter into in order to grasp the facts of the analysis. If the analyst knows how to use his negative capability, he can come close to the state of passivity that makes him permeable to reverie. When he then wakes up from hallucinosis, in other words when he regains a sufficient critical distance, a transformation is produced that will inevitably be transmitted to the analytic field and to the patient.

At this point – after describing the new conceptual tools that we can use in clinical practice: reverie vis-à-vis the inaccessible unconscious, body reverie, the dream understood as a poetic creation of the mind and transformation in hallucinosis – I try to reformulate, more broadly and on a purely theoretical level, the differences between Freud's conception of the unconscious and Bion's. To do this, I start from a neologism introduced by Bion: 'unconscioused' – a term that expresses the idea that the point of therapy is not so much to make the unconscious conscious but the opposite, that is, to make the conscious unconscious, to 'make/produce' unconsciousness. For Bion 'making unconscious' means admitting the infant into the area of symbolic signification, making its mind grow – in essence, helping it to see the world using the rhetoric of dreams that Freud had already highlighted. Giving meaning to experience and dreaming experience become synonymous.

We then immerse ourselves in clinical practice to rediscover the continuity between conscious and unconscious experience. The unconscious is no longer seen as an area in which repressed representations are restricted because they are incompatible with the ego, but as a psychoanalytic function of the personality that has been given the task of creating meaning. Unconscious and conscious experience interpenetrate with each other continuously and seamlessly. The unconscious is no longer beneath or behind the conscious, but rather *inside* conscious experience. To realize this, however, we must be receptive – a skill that cannot be taken for granted, even in an analyst.

Then we venture into some places that are even more inaccessible, albeit fascinating: the puzzle of the transition from body to mind and the difficulties presented by the metapsychologies that try to explain it. We look at Freud's metapsychology, based on a psychology of the subject as isolated and studied in his intrapsychic functioning, and that of Bion, which on the other hand starts from a radically social theory of how subjectivity comes into being. But if we want to clarify our ideas about how therapy works, we cannot avoid taking this path, starting from the study of how the mind takes up position in the body for the first time.

Another place that at first glance may seem inhospitable is Bion's Grid. But even here it is worth pausing long enough to look from this unusual and indeed surprising angle of vision at the themes of truth and the drive to truth. Conceived as a tool designed simply for scoring sessions, the Grid is revealed as extraordinarily stimulating when viewed as an updated map of the psyche.

Leaving the Grid behind us, we enter into a psychoanalytic area par excellence. Psychoanalysis is concerned specifically with intermediate processes; Freud called this area *das Zwischenreich*, the middle kingdom, something between, rendered in the English translations as 'in-between' or 'halfway region'. In psychoanalysis, what we might call 'the paradigm of intermediacy' is absolutely central. The theory of the analytic field represents its most recent, coherent and radical version. Saying intermediacy is like saying the field of the symbolic: what distinguishes us from animals is the gap that we interpose between stimulus and response, the time-space of the symbol.

The route along which we have ventured in our exploration of the unconscious finally comes to an end with a re-reading of a brief but intense paper by Bion (1976), 'Evidence', which is absolutely crucial to the question of the senses and the analyst's receptivity to the derivatives of the unconscious. The central question addressed by this text – which in the account it gives of two sessions also lets us see Bion at work – is what constitutes the evidence of the analysis, the facts we are concerned with; whether we can be sure that we really grasp what is going on; how to intuit the facts, given that the senses are of little help – but the 'senses' of the title also alludes to the plurality of meanings that the unconscious generates. These are events that cannot be seen and are not felt *directly*.

Intertwined with the theme of receptivity is that of style. How can one convey to the patient the understanding that has been reached and speak to him in a language that touches him emotionally? Bion suggests that in some cases style is really a matter of life or death. In his discourse, writing, reading and interpreting converge on one point: all are significant if they are directed at understanding what is true and if they reflect an ability to learn from experience. Here I continue the investigation I started in particular with *The Violence of Emotions* and *Losing your Head*; namely, an exploration of the aesthetic unconscious. What do I mean by this term? Why do I use it? Not so much to refer to the theory or space of art, but in the more purely Heideggerian meaning of mode of sensibility in general (*aisthesis*) and reflection on experiential processes. What is 'aesthetic' about the unconscious is the expressive-creative aspect as reflected, for example, in the rhetoric of the dream. It is also true that from the very beginning this theme also refers to aesthetic experience in the proper sense of the term, in other words as a felicitous model of the creation of meaning and significance.

The aesthetic experience in art, the experience of immersion in a dream world, the miraculous moment in analysis when the evidence/truth of the unconscious emerges or the event occurs are thus brought together into the essential unity of the psyche. Sensibility and intellect, intuition and concept, semiotics and semantics, meaning and significance all coalesce.

It is no coincidence that, in an attempt to transcend the caesuras of these pairs of opposites, the most recent psychoanalytic research has been moving towards the body and the here and now. Familiarity with the unconscious, the cornerstone of Freudian theory and practice, becomes an opening up to the world, learning to see, the vision that transmutes into image and nourishes the faculty of imagination. Nor is it a coincidence that at the heart of Bionian and post-Bionian psychoanalysis lies poetic reverie. The emphasis on the truth of the lived moment recalls some lines by Rilke which in one of his poems depict us as ignorant and astonished before the starry sky of our life. It is better, Rilke urges, to experience this vertigo rather than take refuge in an inauthentic life.

1

THE INACCESSIBLE UNCONSCIOUS AND REVERIE AS A PATH OF FIGURABILITY

The treatment of patients with serious difficulties in symbolization is a riddle. How can we find a way to communicate with someone whose representational function is seriously impaired, to the extent that he is not able to give a personal meaning to experience? How can we begin to build some threads from experiences, however small, of sharing emotions, and then weave them with and for the patient into a fabric of thoughts? If repairing deficits in symbolization and representation depends upon intersubjective relationships and the patient is tenaciously avoiding every kind of contact, how can treatment go forward? It is my belief that an emotional connection can only be born out of living – or better, out of suffering – the same things, out of a moment of intersubjective connection between two separate subjects. But what is to be done when the patient – and sometimes the analyst, as well – has no language at their disposal with which to build this connection?

These difficulties are evident in overtly psychotic patients, but in this paper I shall deal with another category of patients who can be very difficult to treat: neurotic patients who possess autistic barriers or autistic nuclei (S. Klein, 1980; Tustin, 1986). These patients do not present the severe symptoms of the most serious cases, and their cognitive functions are in some areas usually well preserved. Nonetheless, the challenge they pose is that they suffer from a deficiency in their capacity for thinking, which originates in traumas that are filed in the so-called 'inaccessible unconscious'.

Although limited, this deficiency is significant enough to determine subtle situations of impasse in the analysis.

Bion (1997) maintained that alongside conscious and unconscious states of mind, there is a third psychic category, which he calls the 'inaccessible'. He relates this mental category, which has never been psychically represented or conscious, mainly to intrauterine life and a conjectured type of primitive form of projective identification. However, the notion of a non-repressed, non-representable unconscious goes far beyond Bion's 'imaginative speculations' on the nature of foetal life in the womb and the persistence in the adult's mind of embryonic vestiges of 'thalamic' or 'sub-thalamic fears'. It was implicit in Freud (1915, 1923) and, indeed, its significance may extend to all forms of procedural, implicit or nondeclarative memory which are currently being discussed in contemporary psychoanalysis.

We now know that implicit and explicit memories are stored in different neuroanatomical structures, respectively subcortical and cortical. The former is the only memory 'available' in the first two years of life. This means that the most archaic mnestic traces, including those related to earliest traumas, can be registered only in a non-representational form. I propose to use Bion's term, 'inaccessible unconscious', to refer generally to all these systems of basic and primitive memory. My aim is to highlight both Bion's idea of a possible continuity between foetal and post-foetal life (Bion, 1976) and, above all, the link, which the term he employs suggests, between the traumas that we hypothesize have been inscribed in this inaccessible memory/unconscious and inaccessible patients who are difficult to reach.

Since these mnestic traces cannot be verbalized or ever become conscious (as memories that can be represented and recalled as 'thoughts'), the question emerges as to how they can be evoked within the analytic setting, so that we may help our patients to work them through. Mancia (2003), following Freud, has noted that some traces of these very remote events can be found in dreams and of course in the transference. But what can be done when a patient does not dream or there seems to be no transference at all? What can we do in contexts where, rather than commenting on the film being screened and working on its plot, we first need to repair the actual device that projects images on the screen of the mind, that is, the alpha function of the patient?

It is my assumption that representational deficits connected with preverbal traumas that generate autistic or psychotic nuclei in the patient's personality 'force their way' towards a stage of pre-representability via projective identification, action and enactment. In particular, I believe that they speak 'semiotically': unlike ordinary repressed memories, they can emerge almost exclusively in the form of disturbances in the setting.[1] While such disturbances are most commonly thought to involve enactment and forms of action, they can also present themselves in a general feeling of blankness and deprivation; in a poverty of discourse or the relative incapacity to think or express emotions. Such patients appear frozen and stuck.

But this may be only half of the story. After a time, this void may reverse itself into a fullness of emotions, which overflows and overwhelms analyst and patient, as the terror that hides behind autistic nuclei breaks through. When this occurs, what will prove decisive is the analyst's capacity for containment and reverie. If this proves sufficient, these tensions may take root in the subjectivity of the analyst and translate into particularly vivid images (an occurrence, however, that is not a *sine qua non*). It is the specificity and distinctive nature of these images that leads me to conjecture that they are triggered by projections of the inscriptions of early traumas ingrained in the inaccessible unconscious. I further believe that this vividness conveys the particular violence of their attendant emotions and at the same time bears witness to the genuine oneiric quality of the analyst's reverie – i.e. that these images speak with the authenticity and truthfulness of the unconscious.

A parallel could be drawn between these analyst's reveries and Freud's (1937) description of *überdeutlich* or ultra-clear, quasi-hallucinatory memories, which may occur in patients in response to a construction.[2] In my experience, the analyst's reverie connected with autistic nuclei in the mind of adult patients – and psychotic elements as well – is characterized by a certain powerful, 'hallucinatory' sensorial quality. The working hypothesis of this article is that the reverie of the analyst as conceptualized within the theory of the analytic field (Civitarese, 2008a) may represent not only a crucial tool in order to access these negative areas of the mind, but also an opportunity to produce a transformation in the patient.

From the perspective of a post-Bionian theory of the analytic field, I will attempt to show in a detailed clinical vignette how the analyst's reverie can gradually lead to figurability (Botella and Botella, 2001) in the patient and that the more sensorial the quality of the analyst's reverie, the higher the degree of thinkability achieved by the patient in relation to traumas originating in the non-verbal stages. Reverie is the place where the patient's partially obstructed capacity to dream and the (hopefully more available) oneiric space of the analyst overlap – it is where the analysis actually *takes place*. The analyst's core intervention in this context is therefore not so much an interpretation (i.e. a de-coding or putting into words), even if, from the point of view of the classical psychoanalytic theory, it could be described very much as an interpretation *in* the transference. Rather, it reflects the often silent, spontaneous, internal working through of the patient's projected emotion and the analyst's own emotion induced by the patient's projections, which push us to tend towards fantasies and/or enactments of basic assumptions – i.e. a bipersonal unconscious phantasy.

Rather than *reflect* like a mirror, the analyst must try to *be reflective* by introducing *his own mind as a function or locus of the analytic field* and *trying to detect its unconscious dimensions*. In fact, reverie may be considered the equivalent of the slightly uncanny feeling whereby, as the unconscious comes to the surface, we may sense it as something situated not 'underneath' or 'behind' (as if in some sort of storage room/reservoir/sack/container) but *inside* consciousness. It is by creating a deep (somato-psychic) connection with the patient that the analyst can help the patient to expand both the area of 'thinkability' and that of his own psychic container (i.e. the process of weaving emotional threads which will be able to hold floating psychic contents), with container and contained understood as standing in a dialectical relationship with each other, comparable to the reversible dynamic figure/ground.

Step-down transformers

Some patients who protect themselves by building autistic barriers may, at times, make use of a mechanism comparable to what Meltzer et al. (1975) have termed 'dismantling'. When this occurs, their senses follow different perceptual paths and no longer work in coordination with each other. At such moments, patients may, for example, focus exclusively on the sheer sound of the words they utter, rather than their meaning, like Beckett's character,

Krapp, who loses himself in the endless repetition of the word 'spool', drawing out the 'oo' sound in sensuous preoccupation and delight. In so doing, they reach a state in which they avoid thought and suspend their attention by hyper-attaching it to some form of sensorial self-stimulation. By scotomatizing their experience, they retreat from reality, make the object disappear and exorcise their terror of separation and loss.

The capacity to coordinate the senses is not fully developed at birth, but is strengthened through the introjection of a positive relationship with the caregiver and the process of somato-psychic integration that follows. When the senses are dismantled, these patients retreat to an illusory sense of continuity of their Self, which has not yet been confronted by the awareness of the separateness of the other – an experience that for them would trigger an unbearable feeling of dread. They thereby attempt to escape from their hypnotic fascination with the object, an entity which on the one hand could restore the dispersed fragments of their Ego, but on the other is perceived as a dangerous monster that could swallow or engulf them.

These patients almost never bring dreams to their sessions, and tend to endlessly and monotonously repeat the same stories from their daily lives. They drain words of their meaning, turning them into mere sensorial elements – dull, empty tones devoid of affective significance. Due to their extreme fragility, attempts to introduce something new into their arid mental landscapes may be experienced as painful. They perceive closeness as a threat and only allow emotions in on a Lilliputian scale. They seem lost in a two-dimensional reality, a grey-coloured world with neither stories nor characters (and when they do, on occasion, speak of characters, they are not engaging). The stage of their mind seems empty. Confronted with such desolate scenes, the analyst's predominant feeling is that of conducting a dreary, hopeless analysis devoid of the living images that move us. All emotion feels as if it is being sucked into a black hole.

Like black holes, autistic nuclei create zones around themselves that defy contact and exchange. Here the trapped light is the emotions, and the radiations that reflect and reveal the existence of the autistic nuclei are the turbulences produced *in the analyst*. These turbulences – invariably occurring at moments where a new balance is about to be set – allow us to see things. However, they differ from turbulences developing in the treatment of borderline or psychotic disorders: in fact, they almost seem to be the opposite. Here, everything that occurs is characterized by negativity: 'Nothing' seems to be happening. And yet despite this, the analyst comes to feel a strong and almost intolerable tension. Sessions may become pervaded by a sense of stasis or death. While the analyst's mind is powerfully solicited as container, it is as if we were present at the catastrophe of the collapse of time or a building suddenly imploded due to an abrupt increase in pressure on its surface. What instrument, then, should be used to make the terrible forces acting on the surfaces of the psyche visible? How may we reduce them to a bearable level? The answer is that the analyst must in some way experience (suffer) this collapse and, through reverie, try to transform this negativity into images and thoughts, restoring continuity, temporality and meaning.

In the autistic areas of the mind, the pressure I am trying to describe is connected with the tantalizing and dangerous nature of the object. The subject despairs of existing in the other's desire and thus of being recognized and becoming alive. It is for this reason that, even though relationships are vital to the patient, he refuses all offers of them. The internal suffering is extremely intense, yet well hidden. It is comparable to a state of agony or near-death, but it is one which the patient barely feels, at least at first, and that the analyst personally perceives as boredom, uselessness and claustrophobic sensations. The analyst may be haunted with doubts, with the fear of finding himself trapped, empty and without resources, struggling to maintain composure, to stay still, alive or alert. Time never passes. It stops, melts away like the clock in Dali's famous painting.

But even these feelings may be seen as a translation and representation of the indistinct, yet crushing, threat troubling the patient – who, as it were, senses the paralyzing presence of Godzilla without seeing him, because the monster is huge and towering above him. These experiences may also prove threatening to the analyst, who must resist the temptation to shut himself in a mirror-image state of autism of his own, turn off his attention, reset the tension and withdraw to his own private thoughts in order to survive.

What is therefore required of the analyst is a great deal of patience and the knowledge that transformations – if they do occur – can be painful and, for long periods, barely perceivable. The analyst needs to stay constantly and very closely in touch with these patients in the sense of sustaining, enhancing and strengthening their fragile narcissism, while being respectful of their self-protective need for stasis to avoid over-stimulation. Thus, the hypersensitivity of such patients, protected by the shield of autistic functioning, is best approached when the analyst painstakingly strives to detect the most minute signs of movement where everything seems to be still, looking for elements of growth where there only seems to be arrested development – granting hope and trust even when scepticism may seem the most sensible attitude.

As the analyst exposes the patient to his own capacity to tolerate frustration, to his 'faith' that it is possible to give things a meaning, and to his 'thinking method', this offers the patient the chance to internalize the transformational experience. The image used by Ferro (2006) to describe the analyst's intervention in autistic states is that of 'voltage'. If the voltage of an interpretation is too high, it may infuse an unsustainable tension into the relational field, incurring the risk that the field will collapse. When this happens, it implies that the analyst has failed to use an adequate 'step-transformer' to reduce the intensity and impact of his intervention.

Consequently, it is always necessary to activate the 'security device' of a second look (Baranger and Baranger, [1961–1962] 2008) or of an internal 'monitor' to try to catch the signals of the field and the moment to moment clues to its suffering. The voltage must be indirectly proportional to the extent of the patient's deficiencies in alpha function or in the capacities of his thinking (and dreaming) apparatus. Sometimes, as in situations of massive trauma, the problem is an excessive sensorial influx, which may overwhelm the accepting and transforming capacity of even a sufficiently developed mind.

Less despairing than the image of a 'black hole' and with more room for potential positive movement, the metaphor of voltage points to the differential the analyst activates each time he introduces his opinion on what is happening. The points of view of two separate subjects can never completely overlap. If, however, they are similar enough, a fruitful interplay of identity and difference may occur – to be sure, in terms of psychic development, difference is no less important than emotional attunement – patient and analyst may share an emotional experience and the patient's mind as container may become more elastic and expand.

The puma

I see A., a quiet and melancholic girl, once a week vis-à-vis. She is always on time. She puts her bag on the floor and sits up straight in the armchair, her head slightly tilted to one side, a shy and elusive look on her face. Then, she remains silent for three-quarters of an hour. Each time, I am immediately overwhelmed by a sense of oppression. Time seems to stand still. Perhaps A. needs to slow down until she stops time altogether. Perhaps too often, she went through traumatizing situations, events which have made her feel not really alive and without any control over things. Her nanny, whom A. considered her true mother, died when she was nine years old. Could this occurrence also represent the re-opening of an older wound?

Gradually, similar to the way in which when we turn off the sound of the TV and become more aware of the small details to which we were previously oblivious, I realize I am paying more attention to my own sensations and what is entering my visual field. I am getting more in tune with my own body and posture, as though A. wanted to draw my attention to these primitive levels of somato-psychic (non)-integration; as though she herself needed to entertain a purely fusional and sensorial relationship in the safe womb of the setting. I am reminded of Winnicott's (1945) distinction between Id needs and Ego needs and think that perhaps here words would only be appropriate if they were in tune with the latter, otherwise they could be hurtful.

A. seems to be really far away, yet at the same time she is totally aware of my every move. During each session I try to get in contact with her, but to no avail. I resign myself to silence. Pure Beckett, I say to myself – but then I think that I do love Beckett, and this thought leads me to consider the possibilities offered by analysis to stage even the most extreme situations. I become more hopeful. I know that even my feeling this way is useful to her; at times, she has managed to tell me so herself. Feeling me a witness to her suffering makes her feel more at ease. Each time she integrates a bit more, thanks to the space I reserve for her both physically in the room and symbolically in my mind. It helps me to follow to my own flux of ideas, as though they were a commentary on what is happening. It is the negative of a dialogue which cannot exist yet, as in the novel *Mr Mani* by Abraham Yehoshua, where the reader only finds out what is said by one of the two interlocutors in a telephone conversation.

By following my stream of thought, I once found myself fantasizing I was at a pool with A., who did not yet feel up to going in the water. The image transformed into a beautiful Sardinian beach, similar to a tropical setting. I remembered though, the day I had been there, the sea was infested with jellyfish – yet to me, this is tantalizing. I understand that A. is diffident and paralyzed by fear. But then I begin to think there must be something else that she can see and I cannot. Perhaps it is something even more terrifying than jellyfish. I think of those who go swimming where only a coral reef stands between them and the sharks. I would not feel very safe in those waters. Does A. also 'see' or sense sharks? Perhaps her coral reef has gaps which could let in terrible things, the disturbing presences living deep in her unconscious. And the gaps, opened in the 'aesthetic of being' – the basic frame of the personality provided by the mother as a transformational object (Bollas, 1978) – were caused by traumas suffered in her earliest life, prior to the construction of the 'Ego' and subsequently inscribed as sensory-motor schemes in the inaccessible unconscious.

I then make an association with another patient, B., who went on a boat holiday with friends in the period when, after years of solitude, he was again attempting to build an emotional relationship with a woman. On his return, B. told me how they used to dive in to see the sharks. He explained that when they did this, the sharks were no longer aggressive as they had already eaten (!). We laughed for a long time, having both understood that he had feared women (actually an intensely haunting mother imago) more than sharks. Through this reverie, I realize that I have transferred a quantity of emotions from one scene (with B.) to the other (with A.), offering tentative meaning to something which could seem to be nonsense from the outside and perhaps putting the clock back into motion. I am now able to reformulate the situation with A. in these terms: the problem is how to feed the sharks or tame the wolves (like St Francis) in order to make them less dangerous. But at this initial stage I still know very little about pumas.

Weeks and months go by. One day, the orange bag that she brings to each session reminds me of Little Red Riding Hood lost in the woods. I suppose to a certain extent she sees me both as the grandmother-nanny that brought her up and the wolf disguised as the grandmother. Then, as I walk her to the door, she turns, and I at once notice a figure on one side of her bag and the word 'puma'! I am surprised – but start to see a glimmer of light in the dark. I tell myself that inside her there is something primitive, ferocious, maybe very angry. Here come the sharks, rather the wolves – nay the pumas! For A., keeping still and quiet might be a way of representing herself as both mortified by a cold and distant maternal gaze and paralyzed in a defensive reaction, such as 'playing dead' when faced with terror. It may also be a way of trapping the explosive puma-emotions inside.

A. compresses these feelings until they are totally 'flat', then she curls up inside an invisible, yet resistant autistic shell. However, this time I have perhaps found a way of saying what she has been unconsciously trying to tell me about what is going on! Difficulties aside, despite our near-total silence, we are starting to write a script, which is beginning to have a small cast. The 'casting' (Civitarese, 2011a) has begun, as we try to find actors good enough to play the role of the (proto-) emotions that have not yet found their place in the scene of the analysis. I do consider these 'actors' not only as *my* associations or reveries, but as *co-created* in the analytic field by the crossing of reciprocal projective identifications. In this instance, I interpreted to her the meaning I assigned to the figures on her bag and she *silently* agreed to play this game! In this way, she started to communicate even *consciously* with me.

A few sessions later I discover that the other side of her bag features the image of two rabbits cuddling each other, drawn in a childish manner. They join the tiny pair of red pumas that are part of the famous logo of the brand of athletic shoes – that she is wearing – as 'actors' in her unfolding story. Could it be that A. is showing me that she is slowly conquering small shares of emotional ambivalence: two tiny pumas, one on each shoe, next to two large playful rabbits on the bag?

This is how A. begins to recruit my alpha function to begin to formulate and structure a psychic device that will allow her to represent (and possibly pierce) the 'bubble' of grief she has been living in for so long. Through a narration that develops without words, she is now able to put a number of fragments of herself and her life on the stage that analysis offers her. Thus, she manages to express her intense urge to reveal herself, even in complete silence. When this need is satisfied by a suitable response of the object, the sense we have of ourselves and the continuity of our existence is strengthened.

At a certain point, A. swaps bags. This time the writing says 'legami', which in Italian means both 'relationships' and 'tie me up'. So perhaps in this way she is expressing the fear of and the yearning for a connection which, as seen in Almodòvar's film *Tie Me Up! Tie Me Down!* (*Legami* in Italian), is a mutual kidnapping and a reference to a Sadian world of abjection as the primary repression of the maternal body. Then still another new bag arrives, camouflage in design and colour, which shouts 'fight, danger, ambush, hiding, guerrilla'. Moreover, I notice some time later that on this bag the word 'energy' has been written many times in tiny letters. Is A. informing me that her energy is being robbed by the relative disconnection between intelligence and emotion? An energy which must nonetheless exist, or else it would be very hard to explain how she manages to pass her arduous maths exams at university?

Thus I begin to draw maps of the emotions activated in the field of analysis and consequently of A.'s internal world. At the same time I see we have found a way to communicate and give a shape to her emotions that she is as yet unable to express in words. So sometimes I tell her what comes to my mind. Indeed I think that if at times the analyst feels free to express doubts or to confess he is uncertain about how to behave with respect to some facts of the analysis, then the patient may enter a state of ambiguity, which might prove useful. Indeed, by introducing the analyst on the scene in a new role, a third or alternative space is created through self-revelation, favouring self-reflectivity and thus subjectivation.

Of course, from the analytic point of view, self-revelation does not escape the paradigm of the setting and of the oneiric in the session. In this respect, self-disclosure might be introduced and understood less as the irruption of the analyst's life fragments and more as the entrance of a new unconventional kind of actor, very aware of his role and committed to disclosing it to the audience. From the field perspective, *all* references to past or present private life events (made by patient or analyst) are immediately virtualized, becoming fictional characters of the analysis or loci in the analytic field.

The moment eventually arrives when we begin to talk of everything above tactfully and delicately. 'Which bag is it today?

The one with the cuddles or the combat?' I ask her. A. laughs about it. Then a few more steps as – on my suggestion – we begin talking about films and books, discussions seemingly going nowhere. She tells me her favourite film is *Amélie*, the story of a young motherless waitress from Monmartre, who finds a small box containing childhood souvenirs and toys. She asks her neighbour, the glass man, to help her find the box's owner. Seeing how happy she has made him, she decides to dedicate her life to 'fixing' the things that are wrong in the lives of those around her.

Another time, A. tells me of her favourite book, *The Number Devil*, by Hans M. Enzensberger. It is the story of Robert, a ten-year-old boy, who keeps having nightmares about maths. But then a wizard begins to show up in his dreams: a funny looking little man who slowly helps him to overcome his fear of maths in the course of eleven nights. The silent bag game has turned into the book game. Each week, A. would read something, be it a story or a chapter from a novel, which we would then discuss.

Another book was *The Solitude of Prime Numbers* by Paolo Giordano. To talk about himself in the novel, the narrator uses prime numbers (dividable only by one or themselves) as a metaphor. These numbers sometimes appear in twos, though always separated by another number. Thus they are a pair that can never really be together. A.'s next choice, also very appropriate, was *The Daydreamer* by Ian McEwan (the Italian title is *L'inventore dei sogni*, the dream inventor). This is exactly what my efforts were directed towards: the creation of space for dreams. The child protagonist of the book, Peter, has various dreams: first he imagines a magic dust which makes his mum, dad and sister disappear; second, he envisions giving the school bully a sort of interpretation, reducing him to tears only by using words, and making him feel ashamed of his misdeeds. Finally, Peter dreams of turning into a cat. At this point of her account, much to my surprise and gratitude, A. turns around and says 'Kind of what should be happening here'. Due to my/our constant attempts at creating dreams, it seems as though the puma is slowly turning into a housetrained cat! I mean by this that violent unmanageable emotions were now on the verge of being transformed into thoughts. I continue to listen for new images to surf, either coming from A. or from myself, that *après coup* might confirm – or not – that we were in contact.

Silence played a significant role in A.'s treatment, and returned even after the most fertile moments. It was the necessary insulator that kept tensions activated during every session at a tolerable level. Faced with A.'s silence, I could only keep track of my own emotional reactions, stay alert and be ready to dream A.'s interrupted and undreamt dreams (Ogden, 2005), mindful that the analyst should not try too hard to push the patient out of an autistic shell. On the one hand, such pushing might neglect recognizing that silence may be necessary as a protective device to 'reduce the voltage'. Or, pushing might reflect the analyst's attempt to escape from contact with the more dead/depressed parts of the patient's mind, or a refusal to let himself be treated transferentially as the patient's depressed/despairing internal object.

Such moments require that the analyst pay careful attention to his own emotional reactions, physical impressions and the images arising in his mind, presumptively assuming that each element in his stream of associations represents a private, non-verbal(ized) comment about what is going on. On some occasions elements of this stream of consciousness can be verbalized: for instance, like the psychologist played by Bruce Willis in *The Sixth Sense*, dealing with an isolated, dumb boy, the analyst can simply describe what he sees or what he thinks is happening.

What A.'s treatment illustrates is that in order to acquire or strengthen the ability to represent, it may be essential to first relive the earliest stages of life, when sensoriality was paramount, and repeat the primitive process of strengthening the indwelling of the psyche into the body as described by Winnicott (1949). With patients like A. who have been so seriously wounded, the anonymous, pre-reflexive, and pre-personal tapestry of intersensoriality/intercorporeality representing the foundation of the subject when there is still no actual self-awareness shifts from pre-categorical background – endowed with significance, albeit an obscure one – to figure. Indeed, as persuasively argued by the French philosopher Merleau-Ponty (from whose writings Willy and Madeleine Baranger drew inspiration in developing their notion of the analytic field), at this stage subject and object are not separate: rather, they stand in a dialectical relationship to one another.

Subject and object are not definite, autonomous entities, pure presences-to-self, but continuously mould each other through a fluid process of transactions regulated by the 'porosity of the flesh'.

In fact, they co-originate from a primordial medium to which they both belong. In this archaic context, to touch also means simultaneously to be touched. Our sense of the world is mediated not only intellectually: it is also informed by the direct experience of the body. This sense of reality stems from incarnated existence, and is already – though rudimentally – developed even before a form of self-awareness is established. Accordingly, Merleau-Ponty affirms: 'I am a field, an experience' (1945, p. 473), that is, a system of relationships. It is worth pointing out that, as the Ego will never completely free itself from the constraints of the environment that surrounds it and of specific life situations, this primordial stage is destined to establish itself as a constant form of experience also throughout adult life.

It is precisely this intersubjective relational framework that Melanie Klein strives to illuminate with her obsessive, dramatic observations on how the fragile Ego of the baby is not a separate entity in the way a 'subject' will be separate from an 'object' in later life. In fact, in her account, this early Ego 'incessantly consumes the breast from within and ejects the breast into the outside world by constructing-vacating itself while constructing-vacating the Other' (Kristeva, 2000, pp. 62–63). In turn, Bion approaches the same issue through his notion of 'proto-mental system':

> The proto-mental system I visualize as one in which physical and psychological or mental are undifferentiated. It is a matrix from which spring the *phenomena which at first appear* – on a psychological level and in the light of psychological investigation – *to be discrete feelings* only loosely associated with one another. It is from this matrix that emotions proper to the basic assumption flow to reinforce, pervade, and, on occasion, to dominate the mental life of the group. Since it is a level in which physical and mental are undifferentiated, it stands to reason that, *when distress from this source manifests itself, it can manifest itself just as well in physical forms as in psychological.*
>
> (Bion, 1961, p. 102; italics added)

Bion's remark is especially significant in so far as it aims to account for the notion of an image (a psychic representation) 'translating' something which is somatic in itself. It also illuminates how such a reversibility between body and mind can operate not only within one individual, but also between two different persons. Furthermore, Bion explains how, due to the incessant and unconscious interplay between analyst and patient, the analyst's reveries can sometimes 'translate' traumatic experiences of the patient inscribed in the non-repressed unconscious – traumas which produce a hole in the sensorial floor of the Ego. In other words, he implicitly argues that, in the same way the reliability of the setting (and the physical and rhythmic elements that make it possible) can increase the patient's ability to think, the work of figurability carried out by the analyst can heal the wounds of the body-as-semiotic-device – i.e. a body understood as a language/way to generate experience which is certainly prevalent in early life, but will then always go hand in hand with symbolic language.

In this respect, one may even hypothesize that, precisely in those circumstances when the analyst deals with 'black holes' in the inaccessible unconscious of the patient (veritable open wounds that may lead the latter to the verge of the breakdown of non-representation), the restoration of a certain degree of figurability may constitute a crucial therapeutic element.

Casting

In the autistic and psychotic areas of the mind, it is difficult to translate the proto-sensory data (beta elements) of the experience into images. This becomes the main problem we should address. Grotstein (2007) has called this process 'mentalization': the passage from beta to alpha elements, in opposition to the stage (of 'thinking') in which alpha elements are ordered in a narrative sequence. In order to create meaning for and with the patient, we will find ourselves in a position of building it pictogram by pictogram and thereby developing a function of 'basic figurability', rather than making its more complex levels explicit. It is impossible to film reality – in favourable scenarios, after a long time shooting short films may become possible. Initially, pictures can only be taken one at a time; at first they will be out of focus and grey in tone, then clearer and more colourful.

This is what I tried to do with A. Using the notions of projective identification-reverie circuit and negative capability↔selected fact oscillation, I engaged with her, first by allowing my thinking to operate in a regressive mode; then by 'rebuilding' the fictional scene of the setting, restoring its rigorously inclusive nature. Thus, I slowly managed to progressively 'introduce characters' into the analytical field. It is crucial to stress that, in doing so, *I did not follow a pre-established or mechanical procedure*. I simply 'waited for them to show up for casting'. That is, in a state of negative capability, reverie and free-floating attention, I placed my faith in my analytic intuition and spontaneity, checking only that each 'character' was suitable – e.g. had enough talent – to play a certain role. This approach allowed me to access the 'traumatic tears' in the fabric of the patient's non-repressed, inaccessible unconscious.

In working this way, as in art, it is important to join skill and spontaneity. When an 'actor' shows up with a particular flair for a certain part, it creates a truth effect, which only certain dream images have, thanks to their character of presence and vividness, an epiphany-like quality which outside of dreams is only found at the best of times in the art that moves us. In that happy moment all the factors that are part of the aesthetic experience can be found: the effect of a pleasant surprise, the context of make-believe or play, a vibrant and almost immediate feeling of expansion of the experience and the creation of meaning.

In the beginning of analysis, the scene with A. was miserably empty. Except for the character 'miserable emptiness', which dominated the stage, other characters needed to tell the story of our relationship, the analysis and her life were missing. In such a scene, the analyst's ability to be a good casting director is needed to induce change in the field. But higher tensions would be intolerable, so minimum voltages can be introduced in the form of characters in the dialogue, unconsciously expressing the patient's or the analyst's point of view. Or perhaps they are dressed up as roles/emotions looking for an author, and given an audition, where they would have to read something from the script, act something out of their own repertoire, talk about themselves and so on. If the audition is successful and the patient takes up or makes use of the character that the analyst offers, then the actor is definitely cast.

However, the casting can also take place only in the analyst's mind, where the 'story' evolves even though no *explicitly* shared narratives are developed. Indeed, if the analyst is attentive and receptive, even his interiority represents a place within the analytic field. If something happens there, all the other elements of the field will also be transformed. Even if the analyst chooses to omit the interpretation, the new character nevertheless enters the analytic field and the game of crossed projective identifications that defines it. And if the decision to cast the character is a good one, then the field – the capacity of the analytic couple to dream or think – will expand.

My reveries can be seen as narrative turns of the emotional field in which we were both immersed: the result of the continuing, invisible unconscious communication between analyst and patient. The 'transformations in dreaming' (Ferro, 2006) from which the characters that may initially be perceived as intruders originate (sometimes these are material objects in the analyst's office) or seem to come exclusively from the patients, are in fact equally co-created. Godzilla, jellyfish, the sharks, 'the old patient', the coral reef, the pumas on the tennis shoes, the cartoon rabbits on the bag and so on are all functions of the intermediate space we generated together, a kind of in-between or halfway psychic region. All of them are 'characters' in a polyphonic novel constantly engaging with each other and voicing different points of view. Thinking of them as products of the (interpsychic) emotional field opens up the road to A.'s (intrapsychic) imagination. This road also leads to her emotions when the glass man, the maths devil, Amélie – 'characters' that SHE introduced verbally – all appear followed by the cat and Peter – a child beginning to dream! I also consider this polyphony as a self-representation not only as an emergent function of the field, but also as an index of the progress *she* made in analysis and as reflecting her potential to advance in her studies and live out a loving bond with a boyfriend.

These are the fairy-tale appearances that bear meaning – at last! – when faced with inaccessible states of mind. They eliminate boredom and arouse feelings of awe, interest and relief, because they make us think something can come to life in the relationship. They appear like a series of scattered elements that organize themselves into a meaningful configuration and reflect the patient's absorption of the analyst's capacity for reverie and of his analytic stance and method.

Observed from this standpoint, analysis appears as a field of ever-expanding transformations more concerned with the future than with the reconstruction of the past. Or, better still, it focuses on the past to the extent that it lives on in the present, even in the form of negativity. The successful psychic transformations from beta to alpha always mark the discovery of invariants in the patient's experience of reality, that is, constant and (subjectively) significant relationships between the different elements by which the patient's reality is formed.

The shifts from Godzilla to the puma and from the puma to the cat are all transformations (the former being my own reverie and the latter being an image from A.). However, all of them also originate from the 'primary indistinctness' between physical and psychic (as well as between subject and group) which, from different perspectives, Bion, Ogden and Ferro have termed proto-mental system, intersubjective analytic third, and analytic field respectively. Each shift from beta to alpha ($\beta \rightarrow \alpha$) marks a point where dispersed, confused, undefined and unlimited psychic data acquire definite boundaries, consistency and order; the mental space becomes tridimensional. The β/α ratio within the analytic field is slowly reduced. We can thus perceive an aspect of O (Bion, 1970) – 'the name of that which has no sound, smell and texture . . . of what there is before our senses tell us what it is' (Vitale, 2004, p. 73) – as a knowable, phenomenal reality. The bundle of unprocessed, non-representable proto-emotions from which mental pain originates is gradually disentangled. The patient's psyche is reinstated into the body and its wounds stop bleeding. The contact barrier is restored together with the binocular functioning (conscious/unconscious) of the psychoanalytic function of the personality – the shades protecting our retinas from the blinding glow of the Real.

2

POETRY OF DREAM AND DE-PERSONALIZATION

The commonest experience of depersonalization occurs when a physical trauma changes our habitual sense of psycho-somatic coherence and we painfully realize that we are living in a place that is no longer familiar and where we have no command of the language. It is of little consequence whether or not there is a wound that can be objectively measured, because the event is not limited to the body but instantly cracks the integrity of the self and calls all the available psychic defences into action.

An interrupted dream

> I was in the car with someone, on the passenger's side. Out of the sky enormous car tyres were raining down on us, maybe from trucks or buses. I was upset and scared that any moment I'd be hit. But it didn't happen the way I was afraid it would. Instead I was fascinated by the scene and started filming it with my iPhone. Then we were hit from the other side by endless dead or injured birds falling onto the roof of the car and making a red carpet of blood all around. At that point I woke up.

There is nothing in the imagery of the nightmare that directly recalls the trauma of which it is the consequence. Yet the case alters if we think of dreaming as a metaphor for the emotional experience. Ada's dream is trying to represent in a poetic manner the distress which was afflicting her at that time, concerning her fear that she had lost her hearing after a serious ear infection. Suddenly

Ada could no longer hear her own voice, and the voices of others sounded distant and metallic. Her body and the world abruptly ceased to be hospitable. The work undertaken by dreaming in order to transform such devastating emotions has failed. This is why she has the nightmare. And yet in part the dream succeeds in mastering Ada's turmoil, and gives her these images.

In the days that followed, Ada came back repeatedly with this thought, to try to grasp its secret, to nourish herself with it, to find a possible meaning for it. As she had been at the moment of having the dream, she was fascinated by the weirdness of the situation, which points ambiguously in various directions. The scene troubles and intrigues her as it did in the dream. It reassures her and almost makes her smile at the idea that she could recapture it with her phone's video camera. She thinks it means all is not lost; that perhaps it is simply a matter of regaining, a little at a time, her mind's capacity to reflect, and of finding some distance from what has happened to her.

In the dream Ada's act of filming the scene highlights how important it can be that we remain able to construct a continuous film of meaning which defends us against possible traumas. The psychic skin produced by the dream is the mask of self-deceit/fiction, in the etymological sense of the Latin *fingere* (to shape, to think), which allows one to become a person. Indeed, in Latin 'persona' means mask. We could call this capacity 'the mind's poetic function'. By this I mean that we can see dreaming, whether at night or when awake (according to Bion's concept of waking dream thought), as an unconscious and conscious[3] psychological work of digesting proto-emotions and proto-sensations. The adjective 'poetic' indicates that this is not a question of a merely logical or abstract necessity but also a physical and emotional necessity.[4]

Giving meaning to experience in such a way that what we live may be felt as true and real is a matter for the emotions. Hence I adopt the metaphor of poetry (and of art in general), because when it moves us, when it is not interrupted, as it would be by a nightmare, it satisfies us on both the affective and intellectual plane, and helps us to rediscover a harmony between body and mind, to give body back to mind or vice versa, and to reinstate the psyche in the body.

The ability to dream, which we all have to a greater or lesser degree, makes us all poets. This ability to compose the 'poetry' of the real, which Bion calls maternal reverie and Winnicott 'primary maternal preoccupation', helps psychological birth, and once introjected gives savour to our whole existence. It sets up the 'psycho-somatic collusion' on which we base the naturalness of our bodily experiences, the alliance which suffers or is broken when we are prey to experiences of depersonalization or de-realization (which are simply two sides of the same coin).

In fact the unconscious, repressed or not repressed, cannot be thought about if not in relation to the other; it is always rooted in the symbolic. The subject is constitutionally trans-individual: for Bion the mind can only exist in a group, for Winnicott there is no such thing as a baby. For Laplanche the unconscious is formed by the translation of the enigmatic sexual messages sent by the mother to her baby. In other words, no subject can exist except on the understanding that it is part of a field of relationships. The ego is not master in its own house; its dwelling place is sociality. For the same reason we can say that the unconscious is also not master in its own house. The decentring of the ego is a re-centring on the Other and on the relationship with it. In Seminar VII Lacan (1986), using the neologism *extimité* (foreign intimacy/internal exteriority), puts together exteriority and intimacy to indicate what a problematic distinction there may be between subject/object or external/internal. Interiority is external, intersubjective or social to the same degree that the external, as the real, is also that to which the subject belongs. For Derrida (2008) the temporality of the signature (the subject) is already produced by the future perfect tense of the social, political and collective counter-signature.

This is why, when the body or the world become alien, the crisis of meaning never actually refers to the subject as being isolated, but to the subject in its fantasied relationship with the other (the group).

Thus the natural propensity to transference which Freud attributes to dream can be found again in Ada's impulse to tell her trauma and its connected dream, not only to me, but repeatedly to herself and potentially to everyone. In this way she tries to repair the alliance with the other out of which she was born as a subject, and which now feels ruined. As Ogden (2005) splendidly suggests, the model for all treatment lies in this search. Depending on the gravity of their suffering, patients ask us only to help them to dream the dream that they have never succeeded in dreaming, or to resume the dreaming of their interrupted dreams. After all, this is a matter of regaining contact with the primary object, if it is true that, as Pontalis (1972) maintains, to dream is to be reunited with the mother in a space before time.

The blood that covers all the surrounding land in Ada's dream is a terrifying image. Rationally, being 'awake', we could say it is certainly out of proportion to the event; but the dream amplifies the smallest emotional signal thanks to its characteristic 'hypochondria' (Freud, 1917a; Fedida, 1972; Aisenstein and Gibeault, 1991). In reality, that which *seems* an amplification to our conscious thought is the *exact* representation – even if only for the fraction of a second – of how the event felt in the inner world with its *real* emotional impact. This is why, when we listen to patients, if we want to shed light on psychic reality, as after all Freud said he did (Botella, 2012), we must listen to the (derivatives of) our unconscious thoughts, and put material reality in parenthesis. The analyst must enter into a state of hallucinosis which is the inverse of, and symmetrical to, that of the patient (Bion, 1970). Only in this way can he see what the patient sees, including his hallucinations.

Naturally we could put a lot of effort into decoding the dream in order to give it a symbolic reading: the blood, the birds, the wounded narcissism, the presence of the mysterious driver, the phone as a technological prosthesis in the service of a fantasy of immortality (Civitarese, 2010), etc. But in reality, this work of deciphering, which would have meaning if undertaken from the point of view of a study of the other as a subject in isolation, would not help her in her effort to give a poetic (integrative, emotional) meaning to the trauma she has experienced. It is true that Freud links the recovery of the repressed to its reconnection with the corresponding affect, but he nevertheless neglects the role of the object, or as he himself explains, he constructs a model based on a fiction of the object in isolation.

In terms of intersubjectivity, what should be done is *not understand* the dream so as to let it try to be dreamed again. In reality this is obviously a question of making oneself open to a different kind of understanding, not abstract or intellectual but un/conscious; and this is so precisely because the poetry of the dream dreamed by the unconscious reintegrates psyche and soma. As Ogden writes, the unconscious speaks with an accent of truth that our conscious experience lacks.

From the analytic point of view, it matters more to focus not on the nexus between the trauma and the dream, but on the telling of the dream as a derivative of the here and now of dream thought, and we will then be able to think of it – for example – as marking a feeling of fragility in the analysis and the start, in the present moment and with ambivalent aspects, of an intense persecutory distress.

The voices of the world

Dream thought, which in everyday life allows us to 'digest' emotions, can also be used as a technical resource in analysis. I shall give an example. Thinking about Ada's dream, which strikes me forcibly as I hear it, and connecting it to her distress and her feeling of bodily change which, I repeat, goes well beyond its concrete and objectively appreciable character – and clearly I am concerned here with the real distress of a depersonalization unleashed by the trauma – at a certain point in the session there comes into my mind a book by Robert Schneider (1992) called *Brother of Sleep*, that I had read some years before. The protagonist of the novel, Elias, suffers not from hearing loss but from an equally painful over-acuteness of hearing. Just like Ada, but in the opposite way – precisely because it is not the nature of the wound in itself that matters, but what it means practically in terms of identity – he is not screened off from the voices and noises of the world which penetrate him, leaving him defenceless against them.

Ada's dream and Schneider's novel show that psychic equilibrium is founded on a harmonious dialectic between identity and difference, between being open and closed to the stimuli of internal and external reality; in Bion's jargon, between alpha and beta. Any excessive closure implies an automatically heightened opening and vice versa. It is an alternating game which can only oscillate within parameters limited by transformation in hallucinosis and transformation in dream. Elias suffers an experience of depersonalization during which he develops a truly extraordinary power of hearing, and meanwhile his body is transformed into that of a monster, before returning to what it was before, apart from the colour of his eyes. He falls, and while falling his hearing increases hyperbolically. The body is transformed. The eyes push themselves out as if they want to get out of their sockets. The pupils dilate. The iris changes colour. The backbone bends and stiffens. The abdomen swells. The face takes on an expression of terror.[5]

So there are very striking descriptions: of how the heightened faculty of perception extends step by step into a 'hypochondriac' hearing by the body; the perception of a situation of disharmony with the object (in this case, the father, but which can also be understood more in abstract terms as the paternal function); and lastly the evocation of a primordial world which we can imagine as the chaos of signs with which the baby is bombarded from birth.[6]

Elias begins to hear noises, voices and sounds never heard before with incredible sensory vividness. He almost sees them: the running of his own blood, the rustle of the hair, the rush of breath, the creaking of bones, the rustling of veins and arteries, the roar of the shots of cough. Sounds from infinite distance, of humans and animals, mingled with those rising from the body. Whirlpool sounds hurt the eardrums. In this chaos he distinctly hears in his heart the heartbeat of his father. But it is a disharmonious, arrhythmic beat, and he is taken to a dark despair.

In these extraordinary pages we can clearly see how necessary it is to have a filtering/modulating function for the sensory stimuli and raw emotions which assail us: for Bion (1992) the alpha function transforms beta elements into alpha elements, stripping them of their excessive emotional charge. In a 'hypochondriac' explosion, Elias suffers a tearing open of the film of meaning which protects us from the sleep of waking, from the naive realism with which we look at the things of the world. The wound feeds an artistic vocation. He becomes a prodigious musician but remains alone, never finds love and ends his life tragically.

We can ask ourselves, what does this reverie of mine add to Ada's dream? I think that above all it adds the colours of the troubling emotions I had felt when reading the novel. So it adds the traces of an understanding that is not merely intellectual but also physical, bodily, non-verbal. Above all then, but on a different, more informative level, it is clear to me that this is not so much about the fear of losing a physical capacity, but a terror of being abandoned by everyone – even by me! – of going mad, of becoming a pariah, as happens to Elias. It is that the voice and body which feel changed are not only her voice and body, but the maternal tongue and body. This intuition allows me to make her observe her emotional problem against the backcloth of Elias's, about which

I have no need to tell her anything (even if I could have), and thereby see the anguish expressed in the dream from a perspective which greatly enhances its meaning. From this memory/reverie I feel I have succeeded in speaking to Ada with an accent of truth which perhaps I would not have been able to if I had limited myself to *understanding* the dream and not given myself the possibility (the time) to re-dream it, or to *assimilate* it, not only rationally but also emotionally. The other thing that I find extraordinary in Schneider's novel is the turning of a disability into a superpower – but that is the story of all the superheroes in the comics and films. This too puts us in contact not only with Ada's hearing loss and her narcissistic wound but also with the hyperaesthesia that is typical of the paranoia which derives from it and is at the core of depression (the Freudian 'shadow of the object' stretches over the ego like that of Murnau's *Nosferatu* over the defenceless victim) and of depersonalization.

Lastly, the vignette is also an example of how we can be cast as characters in the analytic dialogue in order to develop the narratives in the field and to broaden the range of meaning.

Out of life

To take another step in the theoretical understanding of depersonalization, I now propose to examine a poem by Camillo Sbarbaro entitled 'I come out from lust' (1914, pp. 45–46). In this poem there is a striking link between lust and mourning on the one hand and the derealization/depersonalization symmetry on the other. The poet is no longer able to weep, nor to feel anything else. Everything is deserted. He feels like 'a machine', a robot. He is 'outside life'. He is deaf, but so is the city. The city is a city 'of stone', uninhabited, but he himself has also been turned to stone. The cause of this unhappy state is 'sin like an immovable boulder'. But what does this mean and why the phrase 'I come out from lust'? Literally this would mean he is coming out of a brothel; psychologically what he is moving away from is the image of the lustful woman as a Medusa figure, a castrating, divine enchantress. She is the seductive but ambiguous mother of Meltzer's aesthetic conflict. This could be translated in terms of a maternal in which there is no inherent Oedipal/paternal function, as we have already seen in Schneider's novel. Could this be the 'distance' from the sister (mother) and father to which the poem alludes? A sudden, astronomical psychological distance? Incestuous seduction? The anti-Oedipus that Racamier speaks of? Could this be the origin of depersonalization – the impossible mourning, the tears that can no longer be wept?

However, the most relevant aspect of Sbarbaro's poem and the reason I am quoting it is the description of how an internal event may be instantly projected onto the space of the city, creating a stunning correspondence of object-body-world. These lines echo a striking passage from *L'Afrique fantôme* by Michel Leiris (1934) – it is precisely my 'performative' choice in a work on the 'poetry' of the mind to call on poets and novelists to give their testimony – where the distance from a woman is described as a living and a moving in her body, but a body now become absent, dissolved, no longer separate, a pure ghostly space.

Elsewhere (Civitarese, 2011b) I have analysed Verlaine's extremely beautiful poem *O triste était mon âme* in relation to hypochondria and to the triad of exile, sadness and paranoia.

Simultaneity

The same feeling of being outside life afflicts the heroine of a very beautiful 1972 story by Ingeborg Bachmann, entitled 'Simultan', translated into English as 'Word for word' and published by Holmes and Meier in a collection with the title *Three Paths to the Lake* (1989). I suggest that we can see in this story the psychological significance not only of spatiality, as in the other examples, but also of temporality in relation to the feeling of depersonalization.

The protagonist of the story is Nadja (a girl's name of Russian derivation meaning 'hope', but which in Spanish is close to 'nothing' or 'no one': multilingualism is one of the text's predominant stylistic features). Nadja, having just missed out on an opportunity to marry, has left her city, Vienna, and her country. She lives on the move around the world, passing between luxury hotels which host the important meetings which she attends as a simultaneous interpreter. The story describes a journey through Italy from her point of view, from Paestum to Maratea, in the company of a man who is also of Viennese origin and is employed by the FAO in Rome. During the week in which they run into each other the man restores her language to her. Something moves inside her, and Nadja is compelled to think about the deep meaning of her flight as a state of *Heimatlosigkeit*. The man reminded her of accents, gestures, details that she missed; he gave her the feeling of being at home, a home that now no longer existed anywhere. Words had lost their meaning. Nadja had been nullified as a subject. The world had been reduced to a babel of languages. But the reintegration of the self is not pain-less. A crisis of panic confronts her with the void from which she has always tried to distance herself.

Nadja realizes that she has deceived herself into thinking she could do without an identity, or that she could make do with a fictitious one. At the same time, Nadja realizes that she has done this because she has an identity which has been torn apart and that she has used her job as a defence against the pain of loss. And yet it was an enormous effort – there is evidently a price to be paid.

In the story, which is told in a stream of consciousness, the use of different languages conveys Nadja's partitioned experience of reality. Simultaneous translation as perfect translation which does not betray,[7] which allows us to live with 'pas une seule pensée dans la tête', without differences, gaps or misunderstandings, is the metaphor for the kind of temporality in which Nadja has immersed herself and by which she has ordered her experience of things. At the level of fantasy she is thus held in a condition of fusion with the object. *The desire used to correspond to its satisfaction*. It was a way of erasing the body in so far as it was separate from the mother's body. The body which then becomes significant is the body of language as signifier, which is why it cannot be reduced simply to meaning, to that which is signified. And emotions are erased along with the body.

However, Nadja begins to feel the symptoms of a profound unease. The man makes her intuit that she can live, not simply look as if she were living. So the crisis becomes an opportunity, a 'catastrophic change' (Bion, 1965) through which she arrives at a different conception of 'translation' – that is, of her life – as no longer an automatic and depersonalized activity, but effectively as the recreation of meaning out of her own subjectivity and in a new context: from simultaneity as a way to short-circuit time, waiting and absence, to simultaneity as a capacity to see things from more points of view, all active in the present moment according to the ideas of modern physical sciences. In the end Nadja resumes her own existence. The positive outcome of her experience naturally introduces us to the topic of the reparative possibilities in analysis, but first I would like to summarize the theoretical significance we can give to the terms personalization and depersonalization.

Personalization

The infant's mind develops through being reflected in the mother's face – a face that in reality is more an indistinct field of experience in which, little by little, primitive and still crude sensory rhythms are set up. At the start of life the initial nucleus of identity is produced (and thereafter continues to be produced) by sensory, bodily, tactile, musical means – in a word, pre-representative or semiotic: following Ogden, we could say from a zone of sensations with a calming quality to a state that does not differentiate between subject and object; or following Merleau-Ponty, from a state of intercorporeality.

From the mother the infant internalizes the capacity to form visual images out of proto-sensations and proto-emotions, and thus succeeds in personalizing reality, making it subjective and assigning it a personal meaning. Like the cells of the body, those of the psyche also need to be constantly regenerated. The function which governs this activity is the alpha function, the ability to transform sensations in order to create emotionally significant images, not pure perceptions (and it is clear that no perception can be split off from an associated affect). Bion repeatedly uses the verb 'assimilate' to differentiate *having* a consciousness from *becoming* a consciousness: that is, the innate capacity to perceive stimuli and an understanding based on culture (and these elements are not dissociated). The Self is not achieved once and for all. Dreaming repairs/constructs the psychic skin, the film of meaning which protects us from the impacts of reality, a concept outlined by Freud and later endorsed by other writers.

But why dreaming, and not logic or rational thought? Because in my opinion every dream, as 'poetry of the mind' (I derive the metaphor from the splendid one in Freud's paper *On Aphasia*, 1891), gives the body back to the mind, or rather vice versa reinstates the psyche in the body, constantly seeking to rediscover harmony between body and mind. I picture every successful dream (and what is dreamlike in the session, reverie) exactly as a poem, as something that extends our knowledge of reality, helps us to make it more ambiguous/richer and speaks both to the body through the play of the body of the word, the signifier, and to the mind.

The mind (thought) is not born from the absence of the object, but from the *bearable* absence of the object, from the happy rhythm of absence/presence, on/off, *Fort/Da*. Presence, which is also a matter of quality, is experienced every time we are able to log in to the Wi-Fi area of unconscious interpersonal communication and to live in an experience of emotional unison, the experience which Ada, Elias, Sbarbaro and Nadja feel is painfully missing.

If once again we want to use Bion's terminology, to be in unison could mean to effect a transformation of emotional experience for/with the patient, painting it in the colours of reverie as a painter would colour a landscape: that is, in a way that is *recognizable*. It might be that these colours are what Bion calls the *invariants*, the *quid* that is difficult to define but which allows us to ascribe a subject to the picture and vice versa. The same face can be described in words, or painted, or animated as a cartoon, etc., but should always be recognizable and if possible always hold our attention and move us. These would be transformations in different media, but they all obey the same psychological logic. What matters is to pass on a technique for making these transformations more than their contents: using Winnicott's ideas, to satisfy the needs of the ego and not only those of the id.

De-personalization

As we know, the ego is based on the bodily ego. Thought – as we have said – emerges from the body as poetry does from the mind. Depersonalization – in the title of this chapter and the heading of this section I have written the word with a hyphen to emphasize that it is the opposite of what Winnicott calls 'personalization' – is the symptom of a dissociation between mind and body. It is a break in the 'psycho-somatic cohesion' that is the basis for a healthy Self ('which is not the ego, is the person who is me, who is only me'; Winnicott, 1989, p. 271), a loss of '"psycho-somatic unity" in experience' (ibid., p. 113). The disturbance takes hold when the subject is bombarded by dissociated messages from the object(-world) which it is unable to decipher.

Then the emotions are evacuated straightaway before having been transformed into representations or, in more favourable cases, they dry up into the sophisticated defences of intellectualization. In both situations a psychic haemorrhage occurs. In the language of Bion (1992, p. 161):

> Evacuation of emotion, evidenced by the absence of all connections that *are* emotions, leads to disintegration of the patient because that which holds the objects together is no longer available. This differs from splitting in that it is a passive falling apart of the objects.

Think of the Hulk. When he gets angry he swells up and tears his clothes to shreds. This makes extraordinarily visible what happens in reality in the head and to the psychic skin. There is a reduction in the capacity to contain and transform emotions in such a way as to sustain oneself by the motivating pressure of their cognitive content. This ability to transform emotions is not inborn, but is acquired if another mind or minds is/are available. When something has gone wrong, the disharmony in relationships, reflected in the internalization of an impaired alpha function, can become body dysmorphic disorder, hypochondriac anxieties, the feeling of not living an authentic life, every kind of symptom from mild to serious, and even the sense of not being at ease in one's own skin.

From a certain point of view there is not one symptom that cannot be seen from the perspective of depersonalization and of exile from the land-mother, from the social matrix of subjectivity, even if it is yet to be understood why some people develop one symptom and others a different one. Hypotheses about fragilities, whether constitutional or generated by emotional or physical traumas, particular sequences of alpha elements (Ferro, 1992) or the variable distance to which it is necessary to throw beta elements (Bion, 1992) are perhaps risky but not wrong-headed. The fact is, we do not know; but if we view psychoanalysis as a domain of transformation, then enquiring into the psychopathological distinctiveness of a certain clinical scenario is a matter of only moderate importance, and one which fundamentally contradicts the requirement that we renounce the objectification of the other.

Things can go wrong for various, even opposite, reasons, as Bion writes (1965, p. 62–63) in a passage from *Transformations*:

> The mother's incapacity to accept the projective identifications of the infant and the association of such failure with disturbances in understanding is matched by complications arising through the existence of an extremely understanding mother, particularly understanding by virtue of the ability to accept projective identification. A reaction associated with this resembles character disorder, an unwillingness to face loss of an idyllic state for a new phase, and suppression of the new phase because it involves pain. It is against this background of hallucinosis, projective identification, splitting and persecution, accepted as if it were the ideally happy state, that I want to consider the domain of verbal communication. The sense of well-being engendered by a belief in the existence of a perfectly understanding mother (or analyst) adds force to the fear and hatred of thoughts which are closely associated with, and may therefore be felt to be indistinguishable from, the 'no-breast'. A painful state of mind is clung to, including depression, because the alternative is felt to be worse, namely that thought and thinking mean that a near perfect breast has been destroyed.

If Bion underlines the mother's inadequacy, Winnicott (1989, p. 271) makes us see things from the opposite direction, because the problems can also come from the child:

> The mother is continually introducing and re-introducing the baby's body and psyche to each other, and it can readily be seen that this easy but important task becomes difficult if the baby has an abnormality that makes the mother feel ashamed, guilty, frightened, excited, hopeless. Under such circumstances she can do her best, and no more.

I myself have given a lot of attention to these topics through, for example, the concept of aesthetic conflict or writing about hypochondria as the exile of the subject in the body-world, about how the depictions of beheadings in classical paintings may be an allegory of how one 'loses one's head' in affective relationships, of the kinds of internet dependency which we observe nowadays, in the forefront of which is the search for simultaneity – just like Nadja's – as a way of not thinking.

Language of achievement

If depersonalization opens a breach in being, if alpha function is impaired either because it has encountered a traumatic reality or because it is defective from birth, the problem is how to re-form this unity: how to tie affect and representation, emotion and thought together again? How to heal the wound? Various answers can be given, not least because we would need to speak of therapeutic actions in the plural. Nevertheless, I would like to privilege here the Bionian language of achievement. With this formula Bion shows how the analyst should speak to the patient and communicate 'aesthetically', putting himself on the same wavelength so as to transmit to him the re-composition of the psycho-somatic unity of experience which he has in the meantime succeeded (temporarily) in achieving.

In a paper devoted to this subject Bonaminio (2009) uses a pregnant image when he describes the game with the watch that the father of a little patient plays as a way of trying to help his son rediscover a feeling of security, of reinstating the temporality which is our only means of forming a mind. It is a beautiful metaphor to express what, in my opinion, is the main therapeutic factor in analysis (and child analysts know this better than anyone): walking in step; dancing, in fact; being in unison.

When we are not in step, the patient's depersonalization is reflected in the depersonalization of the analytic field. A 'depersonalized' field would function too concretely or too intellectually. But how do we treat a depersonalized field? What can we learn from Ada's dream, from the books by Schneider and Leiris, from the lines of Sbarbaro and Verlaine, and from Bachmann's story that will help us answer this question? I would say, that the poetry of dreaming – whether nocturnal or waking – allows us to rediscover the psycho-somatic unity of experience inside ourselves and between us and the other.

This transformation is the premise for gaining access to the 'Language of achievement'. We have seen the importance of the analyst's personality, his style. Style, writes Victor Hugo, is the depths of the subject incessantly called to the surface; it is like *émail sur le dent*, enamel on the tooth. For the analyst, as for the artist, style is no mere external adornment, but a way of thinking and knowing, and of expressing himself.

Interpretation should be immediate, communicative, alive, simple and free of jargon; it should go right to the heart of the matter. Style – that is, the persona, the signature, the subjectivity of the author – is the indicator of the analyst's profound engagement and at the same time of his ability to feel and observe, even while maintaining a certain distance. It is also true that interpretation is often silent and nevertheless transforms the analytic field.

The patient must be able to have an emotional experience. He must see and recognize himself reflected in the text of the interpretation, and if possible feel the same happiness in it, the same sense of well-being or feeling of fullness of life that we feel when we have an aesthetic experience, an event in which we make contact with something that we have inside us (without knowing it, or without knowing it enough) thanks to the mind and the artist's creative capacity (for reverie). Hearing an interpretation means letting oneself be heard by its text, letting this illuminate one's experience and understanding of things.

In his Paris seminar with Resnick, Bion invites analysts to make themselves artists in speaking to their patients, to use the colours they have and that they often do not know they have (Ferro and Civitarese, 2015). This is a way to underline the importance of trusting the unconscious work of the mind, and to use, albeit in a disciplined manner, the intuitions given us by dreams.

3

EMBODIED FIELD AND SOMATIC REVERIE

Dreaming in the body

With the passage of time, I become more and more convinced of the importance of inter-body communication in analysis. What I have elsewhere called the 'symbiotic bond' (Civitarese, 2004, 2008a) is the background of continuity that permits the acceptance of difference. This shared background is usually invisible. If it does not hurt, it is not felt. It is noticed in the event of the onset of powerful tensions that endanger the setting at the very moment when they reveal its texture. These may be due to breaches of the formal setting of the analysis in terms of space and time, as well as, however, to breaches of the internal setting. I see not a discontinuity between the two, but a continuity. There is never just a symbolic exchange. Words are always used also as signifiers. They participate in generating the concrete environment in which analysis takes place; but sometimes they exert a pressure that is so intense that it becomes almost *physical* – is distinctively felt as such – as if one were actually being touched, cuddled, repulsed or cradled. With one patient I have several times had to hold myself back from literally stopping up my ears, as if his words were piercing my flesh and making me bleed. On other occasions I have experienced symptoms of cardiac neurosis owing to the build-up of tension. In still other instances it is silence that makes one feel held captive in an unbearable straitjacket or trapped in a claustrophobic, timeless space.

These situations manifestly involve a serious difficulty of symbolizing due to the absence of foundations for more mature mental functioning – that is, a background of sufficient familiarity or continuity of being. To re-establish movement, the path to symbolization may pass by way of the analyst's capacity to maintain the faculty of imagination, but even before this, by way of the capacity for sensory reverie: 'not thinking or fantasizing, but the recollecting and experiencing of inner sensation' (Bernstein, 1975–1976, p. 540; Ogden, 1989).

The need is to dream in the body (or, better, in the 'somatic field') what is happening, so to get in touch with the crisis, and to provide an initial representation of it, this representation itself affording virtual salvation. In terms of Bion's model of the analytic field, sensory reveries (or rather, bodily reveries – i.e. ones without *immediate* representational content or perceptive quality) are a way of bringing about initial transformations in the direction of thought. In particular, like 'true' reveries and narrative derivatives in the case of emotions, they make it possible to apprehend the vicissitudes of the most fundamental, or subterranean, levels of identity at issue, and to construct a container, structure or a *semiotic* chora (Kristeva, 1974) in order to confer meaning on the formless, infinite and insensate. In my opinion only the Bionan field theory (BFT) can help us, by derealizing any text, including one written in the body – e.g. by referring a sensation to a shared unconscious procedural/implicit 'fantasy' – to recover an internal setting and allow us to think of what we are experiencing as an intersubjective phenomenon, a phenomenon bearing some relation to what the patient is feeling, or rather, to the unconscious emotional field established by analyst and patient together.

I shall now start by presenting three vignettes, all of which concern patients who have permanent difficulty in symbolizing or whose capacity for symbolization is temporarily impaired. In all three cases the setting takes a leading role as a protagonist, gradually standing out more clearly against an at first indistinct background. Normally silent, it here takes the stage as the fear, or conviction, that the analysis will be broken off (Vignette 1); as an involuntary breach on the part of the analyst (Vignette 2); or as the surprising emergence of the positive institutional dimension of identity (Vignette 3).

Politically correct

E. comes in and lies down on the couch. So far, the very frequency of her therapy – two sessions a week – has indicated that only half, or only two-thirds, of her was coming along. And substantial portions of her life were indeed completely split off – for instance, those connected with aggression and sexuality. Furthermore, we had been proceeding along the lines of an inquisitive little girl constantly plying her father with questions. I had noted a 'diabolical' ability to make me talk and explain, which sometimes occupied almost the entire session. I had accepted this game, marvelling yet again at how each therapy had its individual fingerprint that was unlike any other (and how I myself behaved and felt very different things with one person than with another). This seemed to me to be the only way to forge a link. One morning E. mentions how annoying she finds it to have to be politically correct. She doesn't see why she should avoid terms like 'negro' for black people or 'queer' for homosexuals. She uses them with her black and gay friends; she is OK with them and they certainly don't have a problem with that – no way! I find myself unable to contain my irritation. While speaking calmly, I point out to her that, sure, excess is always annoying and can extend to the point of fanaticism, but all the same words can be like stones, as they convey ideology, imply definitions of the other in relation to oneself and ultimately give rise to exclusion and violence; what is more, we should always question even our good intentions because we are not so much masters of ourselves as we'd like to think.

However, my arguments in what has become a kind of quarrel in effect bounce up against a rubber wall. I hear myself say aloud in exasperation that we seem to be speaking two different languages and that I am sorry. At this point it crosses my mind that E. might decide not to come back any more, which would mean *a catastrophic rupture of the setting*. I feel I would almost prefer it that way.

It is only when the session is over and I have had to force myself to be kind that I begin to realize what has happened. First of all, I had neither practised transformation in dreaming (Ferro, 2008) nor interpreted. There had no longer been any trace of an internal setting. Yet such violent emotions had never come out in this way before. Only now could I say that I knew E. better. Only now could I postulate that there were split-off areas of her personality, or non-negotiable places in the analytic field, perhaps because Ku Klux Klan contents (kkk ♂) had to be banished so that they could not do irreparable damage. After all, this might perhaps be E.'s chosen way of making me see how intolerant of her other people were – including myself now, and feeling myself to be in the right into the bargain. Had she not induced me to reject her? Had I forgotten that Philip Roth, one of my favourite novelists, had written a novel against political correctness? Wounds and scars in both parties had come to resonate explosively with each other, giving rise to something completely new.

My aim in presenting this vignette is to demonstrate the importance of not trying to be too clever with the patient. In that way one would be avoiding immersion in the more turbulent dynamics of the relationship. It would merely be a more subtle form of rejection. What matters, on the other hand, is to make oneself available within limits, even if one makes mistakes, and then to reflect and turn back. The 'negroes', 'queers' and 'lesbians' as characters stood for unthinkable lumps of emotions. The transformation that has subsequently taken place, in the re-establishment of a psychoanalytic vertex and a capacity to contain the rage that had developed in the session, is the necessary condition for understanding E. from the inside, for understanding how she must have felt and feels now, and for accepting her instead of repulsing her. However, one character that is a protagonist of the field is her deafness to the violence of words, a deafness which had also become mine, and was waiting to be transformed – and which, of course, in transference terms one would perceive as the deafness of others to her which she experienced. It was as if she had asked me: If I show you the dirtiest parts of myself, what will you do? Will you take them on board or will you show me the door? She was in effect asking me if it was all right for her to be 'politically incorrect' and hence to become more integrated.

Spacings[8]

As I listen to L. rather inattentively, I take a quick look at my table clock. The minute hand almost points to 9. It is time to stop, I think, and I do so. Only when she has already gone out do I realize that I have shortened her session by ten minutes: the scheduling of the session starting on the hour and ending at a quarter to is for the following patient. I had behaved *badly*. However, L. and I have been saying for some time now that she is 'too good'.

Perhaps, by overlapping her session with that of the other patient (Irene, an authentic 'bad girl') and thus making L. feel angry, I have unconsciously tried to draw out from L. too a split aspect of her self that I somehow perceive but which does not manage to come to the surface. My involuntary breach of the setting, a kind of Lacanian *ponctuation*, is also due to the fact that L.'s sessions are not scheduled at the time I usually start working in the morning. However, in this context, it also acquires one further meaning: a gap can be used to restore a whole. Indeed, the chiastic crossing of L. and Irene (actually, 'Irene', i.e. the other patient becoming a character of the analytic field in L.'s therapy) and their sessions allow me to see them both in a new light.

I repeat the same mistake two or three times, feeling increasingly embarrassed and disappointed. Of course, the 'bad girl' lurking within L. eventually wakes up and makes herself heard, thus becoming a subject of our conversations. All of a sudden L.'s analysis, previously boring and sterile, becomes engaging and productive. We somehow managed to get out of the sweetish, collusive atmosphere we were stuck in and build a representational space for her intense unconscious rage against a controlling and intrusive (or, alternatively, absent and indifferent) internal object. Significantly, however, only after the above-described developments in L.'s analysis were we able to acknowledge this feeling and its nature.

These accidental breaches of the setting seen as the place where the symbiotic bond establishes itself can be extremely useful, as they sometimes help to bring to the surface the psychotic/regressive/primitive aspects of the personality (of the meta-Ego) deposited in the setting and its repetitive rhythm (Bleger, 1967). Similarly, such breaches can enable even more primitive types of psychic *dys*rhythmias to achieve representability, therefore creating the necessary conditions for their transformation/evolution. What was once not representable can be finally seen or 'enacted'. In this respect, the 'extrasystole' produced in the rhythm of the setting by the shortened sessions can be understood as the sensorial manifestation of a traumatic event ingrained in the inaccessible unconscious.

On the one hand, the fact that such traumas are reproduced in the framework of analysis has a positive significance. In fact, to the extent that their repetition also suggests their thrust towards representability, they have a productive connotation. However, on the other hand, the 'silent' quality of these traumas highlights their negative effect, i.e. actually eluding all forms of representability. In any case, unless repetition encounters the analyst's capacity for reverie, it will not become a starting point for transformation. With L. such an encounter did take place when L.'s and Irene's faces overlapped in my almost hallucinatory 'vision' (like Elisabeth and Alma in Ingmar Bergman's *Persona*). This interchange has several simultaneous layers of significance. On a superficial, more developed (Oedipal) level, it reveals L.'s split or repressed feelings of rage. On a deeper, pre-Oedipal level – which, in my opinion, is where L.'s problem is mainly rooted – it constitutes the symbolic equivalent of how a mother may happen *not* to see her daughter as she is, but only as she would like her to be. For this reason, it can be argued that this interchange, undoubtedly *also* induced by L., provided her with an opportunity to represent what might have been her first, unbearable experience of the dysrhythmia/dissonance produced by a (relative) mental absence of the object. In turn, L.'s early traumatic experience may have left some areas in her mind unable to contain 'warmer' emotions such as those characterizing more developed stages of mental life and relationships.

Mirror drinking

S. always arrives on time. Indeed, hers being the first morning session, she is sometimes waiting for me in the street. Prior to starting work, this meeting has now become a part of our ritual. I take the lift and she goes up the stairs. In this way we have already mimed a meeting, a fleeting separation and a happy reunion. We go into the apartment and then into the consulting room. She sits down on the couch, takes a bottle of mineral water out of her bag, drinks and then lies down. For some time I too have had a bottle of sparkling mineral water within reach, but it is only with S. that I notice, to my profound astonishment after having done so several times automatically, that I too take a sip 'as if in a mirror' at the same time as herself. A banal action (or, if you will, an enactment) is suddenly charged with many other meanings. I instantly realize that something that has for some time made me despair, the element of empty small talk that characterizes our conversations, is for S. in fact essential – that is, part of a mirroring situation that precedes any possible step towards differentiation.

A kind of *sensory and physical unison* (like being one and the same body) is needed as the basis for a more emotional and conscious unison. Does my drinking a sip of San Pellegrino (and as I write

I am also putting on my saintly halo, like someone who has put up with prolonged, boring sessions) constitute also a kind of unconscious interpretative action (Ogden, 1994a)? Is it like – on a more evolved level – a preparation for confronting a certain emotional aridity that we are about to experience immediately afterwards? So is there a clear-cut boundary between the physical and symbolic levels and between subject and object? Are we not part of a 'proto-mental system' (Bion, 1961, pp. 101–103) in which all these barriers can be thought of as utterly permeable?

At the window[9]

Mario is an 11-year-old boy who was adopted at an early age. He knows that his parents are not his biological parents and he is obsessed by the idea of running into his 'real' mother on the street. To allay the anxiety that sometimes overwhelms him, at home he scratches his skin and makes real cuts on his arms. It was his idea to ask to speak to a doctor and almost immediately the therapy affords him some relief. He is always on time. Each time he comes, his parents leave him at the door. At the end of each session, when the hour is up, together with the therapist he looks out of the window to see if there is somebody waiting for him already. Mario says that his parents don't ring the bell because they don't want to be a nuisance.

This is another example of how a way of doing things, which has become a *habit*, acquires broader shades of meaning. Here, too, one cannot speak of true 'interpretive action' given the spontaneity and unpremeditated simplicity of the gesture. Observed more closely, however, it is a gesture which presents itself as a kind of understanding *in action* of an essential element in the emotional life of the analytic field. It is as if the analyst were accompanying Mario in spirit as he roams the streets hoping that one day his mother's gaze and his will meet and he will be able to read in her eyes a possible explanation for his illness. The act of leave-taking is a 'cut'. Each question is a matter of life and death: 'Will they come and pick me up? Will someone remember me?' As in a real reverie – which is what it in effect becomes when we examine its meaning in supervision – the action expresses a deep sense of welcoming and acceptance; it contains and testifies to the analyst's investment in his patient.

Vis-à-vis

Close on a year after beginning analysis, out of the blue A. asks to continue the sessions from then on face to face, explaining that he likes it better that way. The analyst realizes immediately that something essential has changed, but is unable to say exactly what it is. A. appears to her in a new light. Now he is not only a person in difficulty who obsessively describes almost disjointed and surreal thoughts; he also talks about how he manages to attend to his own practical affairs and to make decisions.

For the first time the analyst specifically notices his blue eyes: 'They're just like Charlton Heston's!' she thinks.

Curiously, given the more concrete nature of the conversations they have been having, the analyst is surprised to find herself paying much more attention than before to the current situation, and almost forgetting certain aspects of the past that used to repeat themselves with unbearable monotony.

We can now ask ourselves whether the jointly staged action of changing an aspect of the material setting might not reflect a kind of unconscious self-understanding in the embodied field of the analysis that important aspects of the relationship had not been sufficiently 'seen' under the previous arrangement. Perhaps there had been too much focus on the patient's biographical and material reality, and it was for this reason that he did not feel sufficiently seen? Perhaps for A. it was important to be fully known by the analyst if he were to first achieve greater integration in her eyes? Perhaps he could finally 'seduce her' – in the sense of making her like him.

Touch[10]

Francesca, 18 years old, comes along to the first meeting accompanied by her mother. The analyst gets a rather confused impression. It is unclear which of them needs treatment. Francesca has been referred to her by a colleague who had already seen the mother, and it was the mother who made the telephone call.

Francesca feels different from her peers: she is very thin, has lots of hair and in the past has had episodes of bulimia and cutting, which cause her feelings of great guilt. She is afraid of losing her teeth and her hair. . .She has read that one of the consequences of stopping the pill may be hair loss. . .The analyst tells her that she does not look as though she doesn't have enough hair. . .(at that moment she thinks of Samson. . .While she speaks the analyst looks at her in fascination. . .She thinks she has a lovely round face, two small eyes, a soft chignon and falling curls. . .She looks like a lady from the nineteenth century).

During a session, at some point Francesca gets up from her chair and says: 'Have a feel. . .it's not that thick. . .', and lets the analyst touch her soft chignon. She then connects the fact of having little hair to genetics. Her mother too has little hair, and she sees a difference between before and after. . .'. . .I also have holes in my head where I have less hair!' she adds.

What I find remarkable here is Francesca's gesture of getting her analyst to touch her hair: in terms of the dream of the body, re-establishing physical continuity with the object for an instant is equivalent to an unconscious request for help in finding a basic somato-psychic unity – the unity that at birth can only be the result of a symbiotic bodily bond, from being the same body. This gesture too could be taken as a kind of understanding or, better, pre-understanding, as something pre-categorical, an acting-out that comes this time from the patient, from her thinking body. Or more precisely, from the *embodied field*, in other words, from the area of intercorporeal communication that establishes *a two-person thinking body*, a single body – because the body is never only material and, in that it has always been immersed in human sociality and always affected by language, it is also the locus of the production of meaning.[11]

But what I find even more striking is the form of expression chosen by my colleague when writing up the case she has brought to supervision: she makes extensive use of ellipses, which I have reproduced when transposing her notes in indirect speech.

It is as if she were trying to introduce intervals or 'spacings' that might allow Francesca to gain some distance but without exposing her to the fear of feeling torn from the mother's body, now identified with the body of the analyst or the field. In the text she gave out there is in fact no space after the punctuation marks (in this case the three dots), as if to show (more than simply talk about) not only a movement towards breaking away but also the need to remain firmly anchored to the object. At the same time the dots stand for Francesca's 'holes in the head': patches of alopecia, but in reality holes in her thinking. The pimples she torments and from which she squeezes out the pus have a similar meaning. The image that comes immediately to mind is the poster advertising the film starring Nicolas Cage entitled *Lord of War*. If one looks closely at it, Cage's face turns out to be made up of shells and bullets (but they may also look like mines (in Italian: 'mine')).

Indeed, running through her rather confused story are a series of vicissitudes that have to do with relationships from which she was excluded, or from which she deliberately cut herself off, girlfriends being stolen or boyfriends being stolen by girlfriends. Perhaps one should try to figure out why in the 'dream' of the supervision we arrived at mines (curiously, in French 'mine', cognate with 'mien', means 'face').

The symbiotic bond exists on two levels – corporeal and mental. Physical unison is needed to establish emotional unison. This physical unison comes out of the sense of belonging to a steady flow of actions, habits and feelings. Art reveals how knowledge comes about through movement and how we are at one with our surroundings. Walking inside Richard Serra's installation at the Bilbao Guggenheim, we feel contained by the space, our experience is affected by the forms we move through. We wear the architecture as if it were a second skin in which we can feel at ease, under pressure or anxious. Likewise, 'we put on' the setting as if it were an item of clothing.

In general, then, communication between bodies is understood as a dialogue between postures, which is later brought back to the visual level, to visual perception – though in reality it is also olfactory, tactile, auditory and proprioceptive. If we inhabit a space, can it be said that we are reading it with our body? Or that we're interpreting it? Is it not the same thing as skimming over a page with our eyes? Don't traces of the experience of movement perhaps remain in the body? And is movement not a mode of knowledge? If dreaming is a psychic function whereby we constantly try to digest experience, can we say that the initial digestion/comprehension/transformation is essentially physical?

The body thinks

> Her pure and eloquent blood/spoke in her cheeks, and so distinctly wrought,/that one might almost say, her body thought.
>
> John Donne

Bion tells us that, in order to perceive the patient's 'hallucinations', we must trust our own and apply active and total denial to material reality. But building a model of how the task of symbolization takes place in analysis requires a conceptualization both of non-verbal and verbal communication, including the non-verbal part contained in the verbal, and which genetically precedes the establishment of an ego and self-reflective capacities.

Now, the analyst's body is a place in the sensory/somatic/semiotic/embodied intersubjective field of an analysis, and as such registers its crises mostly as breaches of the setting. Can these breaches be seen as transformations in hallucinosis in the body, or first as hallucinations in the body, and then, if an awakening (an interpretation, even implicit) follows, as 'somatic' reveries?

The potential advantage of regarding them as such is greater ease in achieving an integrated, non-split-off somato-psychic understanding. To paraphrase Ogden (2003), one could also contend that the non-repressed unconscious most often speaks with a quality of truthfulness that conscious experience usually lacks. (As it has been noted, there is an unconscious understanding-work which goes in a parallel but opposite direction to the dream-work described by Freud.)

Indeed reveries emanate from the unconscious seen as the psychoanalytic function of personality that constantly seeks to re-attain basic psycho-somatic integration, not because abstractions (etymologically the maximum simplification/depletion obtainable from sense experience without complete loss of meaning) are not useful, but because it is emotions *and* concepts that impart meaning to existence, and not just concepts. That is why I use here the expression 'somatic reverie' and not 'enactment', which derives from a different model of the unconscious than that of Bionian field theory.

As these vignettes show, we 'interpret' the patient (the turbulences of the field) with our procedural, implicit knowledge too, which is not directly reducible to words, concepts or representations. These are lived interpretations, which are at first totally unreflected but may later perhaps become conscious. True awakening, however, is accomplished with reflective interpretation: *it is precisely this quality that justifies the description of this kind of semiotic knowledge as admittedly bodily, but also as reverie.* Of course in order to interpret it as a reverie we require an appropriate conceptual framework to confer order and discipline on our intuitions, which in our case is given by the theory of the analytic field. Even unintentional actions or behaviour that is an expression of a habit change in the session if the theory of the unconscious changes.

These bodily metaphors – which is another way we could refer to them – are real symbolizations and not symbolic equations. Why? Because we are not working *within* the 'dream' but after waking from the dream. The definition of dreaming should include awakening. It is only then that the dream gives us the insight that we live simultaneously in multiple worlds, and that we have an inner reality which is completely virtual but in its own way just as concrete as material reality. True symbolic equations, on the other hand, are the characters of material reality in the analytic text when they are taken only as such, and not de-concretized or transformed in dreaming.

Since human beings have acquired the ability to think their own thoughts – or in other words, a mind, in the sense in which we ordinarily understand the mind as a product of culture – there is no point in splitting it off from the body. There is one simple reason for this: the relationship between the two is one of mutual and recursive generativity. It is not enough to say that our cognitive structures represent projections of how we are made biologically and how we move (in other words, to say that the body creates meaning). We also need to say that the mind creates the body by entering as a powerful adaptation factor in human development. Thus, the way in which we give meaning to both procedural and semantic experience is always the result of the indissoluble interweaving of biology and sociality. For us biology can never be merely biological nor can culture ever be completely detached from the body. As has been pointed out, the body is in fact a metaphor incarnate. If metaphor is how thoughts are created, even the most abstract thoughts, then the body is thought. The body thinks with 'musical' ideas, with forms of intelligence that cannot be separated from their tangible manifestation, '*negative ideas . . .* knowable by virtue of difference', which we do not possess but by which we are possessed (Carbone, 2011, p. 27).

But what does the body think? In its whole being and at every moment it thinks or transforms the primary emotion that is born out of friction with reality. What is the point then of excluding the action of analysis by relegating it to the category of enactment?

Strictly speaking, this would not make sense, but it does follow the economic principle or the idea of simplifying observation and the experience of the field. The metaphors through which the body knows reality are far more opaque than linguistic metaphors, at least semantically speaking. They are not devoid of meaning, but they are more complex. So it is as if we had decided to do without them as far as possible. Sometimes, however, we have to deal with both the patient's actions and our own. Hitherto we have seen these as the result of discharges of impulses and looked at them in the same way as we do lapses, dreams, symptoms; namely, within the concept of the repressed unconscious. However, if our idea of the unconscious changes and we regard it more and more as a psychoanalytic function of personality, then action too is seen in a different light. If the dream thought of the unconscious becomes the poetry of the mind, then the action is equivalent to the performance of the artist.

Would this then be enough to make us all analysts/performers? No, because – I repeat – analysis needs to carve out a field of observation that is as limited as possible. We focus on the word because language is much closer to the pole of abstraction and is less ambiguous than body language. By doing so, however, we pay the price of sacrificing, at least in part, the emotions and the body.

Other psychotherapeutic practices do not make this sacrifice, but we can make do with the body that is in the words and with the dimension of intercorporeality where even the most abstract exchange takes place. The fact is that when an action enters the scene in some way unconsciously, we do not see it automatically as a break in the setting, but rather as an attempt to reinstate/heal the setting. Indeed, precisely the unconscious quality of the action expresses its potential usefulness. This is why we can speak of reverie, because the action appears without being invited; it comes as an unexpected guest whose arrival never fails to surprise us.

4

TRANSFORMATIONS IN HALLUCINOSIS AND THE RECEPTIVITY OF THE ANALYST

Then I explained my magic sophisms with hallucinations of words! I ended up believing my spiritual disorder sacred.

(Arthur Rimbaud, *A Season in Hell and Illuminations,* 1873)

How to be permeable to the patient's communications is a key problem in psychoanalysis. Freud (1912) resolves it with the concept of free-floating or evenly suspended attention. Nevertheless, the tools we use in clinical work need to be maintained at the necessary level of efficiency and to be constantly updated in relation to the most current epistemological settings. To this end I am here drawing on the concept of 'transformation in hallucinosis' (henceforth, TH) with which Bion addresses the subject of the analyst's receptivity; however, the concept is little known – with only two references in English in the PEP archive: Riolo, 2011; Emanuel, 2012 – outside the tight circle of Bion scholars: Meltzer (1978), López-Corvo (2002), Grotstein (2007).

Bion brings the term 'transformation' into psychoanalysis from geometry, using it to stand principally for psychic transformation (for example, an emotion which gives rise to visual images and thought), because it is abstract enough to describe phenomena which are identical but conceptualized in a different way in the various psychoanalytic models. He aims in this way to obtain a more scientific theory, one on a higher formal level, which will permit more accurate clinical observation and will above all lend itself to overcoming the theoretical divisions between analysts, such as those created in London by the Controversial Discussions.

So he describes three kinds of transformation which entail differing degrees of distortion in the emotional element of departure: in rigid motion (RMT), projective (PT) and in hallucinosis. The first two correspond respectively to the transference and to projective identifications. To describe the third type of transformation, however, which is an original construction of his own, Bion borrows from psychiatry the term 'hallucinosis'. Hallucinosis is defined as a hallucination experienced by a person in a lucid state of consciousness: the subject critiques what is happening and recognizes the unreality of the hallucinated object, as can be observed in certain partial epileptic seizures, in brain stem disturbances, ophthalmopathy, organic poisoning, etc.

But the use which Bion makes of it is predominantly analogical. If he speaks of hallucinosis it is because he wants to describe some scenarios touched by psychosis, in which there is no significant loss of contact with reality, and so no 'real' hallucination. Subsequently, as has happened with many psychoanalytic terms (from repression to transference to projective identification, etc.), that of TH, already in the work of Bion, has come to indicate not only situations which are clearly pathological, but also those which are physiological. Surprisingly, in the end, as I have suggested, Bion indicates that the best way for the analyst to intuit the facts of the analysis is for him also to approach a state of hallucinosis.

In order to try to bring a little clarity to what appears to be one of the most enigmatic but also most promising concepts in the theoretical and technical development of psychoanalysis, I shall examine the concept of TH from these two points of view: first, that of pathology – from psychosis, above all in the area of paranoid disturbances, and manifestations which are veiled but dysfunctional in neurotic patients – and then from that of the physiology of the mind, so as to describe Bion's final proposal regarding psychoanalytic technique. In this way I shall follow the trail which he himself delineated at various points in his work.

Transformation in hallucinosis and psychosis

To begin with, Bion linked TH to specific psychopathological settings and described it as a dynamic process which entails an impoverishment of the capacity to be in contact with reality; that is, to have a full cognitive and emotional awareness of it. Regression can also produce situations of psychotic imbalance resulting in evident hallucinosis. The less the subject is in contact with himself, the more he unconsciously paints the world in the colours of his own psychic reality. However, the most interesting clinical scenarios, and those in which the concept of TH is at its most illuminating, are the intermediate ones. Genuinely suffering, but in a manner which it can be difficult to grasp, the individual maintains a superficial adaptation to reality. Indeed he can even seem too adapted.

This is why Bion uses the term which in psychopathology indicates the presence in an individual of hallucinations experienced in a state of lucid consciousness. In pathological TH of a less than extreme degree there are no real hallucinations. His emphasis is not on hallucinations in general, but on hallucinations which take away meaning, those which are invisible or negative (Green, 1998).

In analysis the TH are typical of situations in which an excess of concreteness generates a climate of melancholy indifference: a mixture of boredom, the sense of being blocked and of being powerless to re-cathect the world. These patients give the impression of being lost in a sea of objectivity, of factual reality, of things.

The analyst can allow himself to be sucked back into this world dominated by the 'forced rationality of wakefulness' (Bion, 1992, p. 173). In the session he expresses himself in a rational manner and pigeon-holes everything into the well-known models of psychoanalysis. He explains everything, or nearly everything, to perfection. He attributes to everything the solidity of the objects which furnish the room.

Simply as a reflex the patient assumes a pedagogical, moralizing or authoritarian attitude. That is, he tends to adopt the superior position of one who 'knows'. He makes use of hallucinosis to deny his dependency and maintain a position of false self-sufficiency. Fantasies of superiority are the rules of transformation in hallucinosis. Connections to emotionally pregnant facts are dispersed across an enormous arc of time and their meaning is diluted almost to the point of dissolution.

It is as if one were looking from very close up at a letter of the alphabet which had been enlarged almost to infinity (see Figure 4.1).

Figure 4.1 This is how an 'E' would look if enlarged more than a thousand times in the 'container' of an A4 page

Some elements are clear-cut but the general atmosphere is troubling, though in a subtle manner. Things stand out brightly but as if suspended in a kind of vacuum, as if they were living in a story by Kafka. We do not see the part of the 'E' which ends off the page, and the part we do see no longer has any meaning even though we can perceive it correctly. We catch a few details but lose sight of the figure as a whole. If this is a story, we have lost both its plot and its meaning.

In these situations real emotions rarely appear to give coherence and vitality to the conversation. It is as if analyst and patient are imprisoned in an effect of reality (Barthes, 1984), not in 'real' reality but in a flat reality with no depth, like that of the phoney scenarios of certain films coming out of the studios. Those which 'appear to the observer as thoughts, visual images and verbalizations' are nothing but 'scraps of imitated speech and histrionic synthetic emotion' (Bion, 1970, p. 13).

Paradoxically, the patient thus reports having suffered from 'too much' reality, internal or external; from having been struck repeatedly by surges of emotion so violent that he finds himself with a damaged capacity for symbolizing the real (that reality 'without categories' which Bion calls 'O' (Grotstein, 2000, p. 316)). In so far as they are defences, the TH reveal the excess with which existence has been traumatically marked by them, overturning its sign and converting it into a vacuum. This means, Bion writes, that upstream from all of that 'an intense catastrophic emotional explosion O' (Bion, 1970, p. 14) has occurred. The crazed splinters of β elements, that is proto-emotions and proto-sensations, which are thus produced have found no one to receive them, to give them a form and transform them into psychic elements which can be dreamed and thought. In other words, the patient has suffered a traumatic experience of failed psychic containment, one of those states of anguish which, if not calmed, grow in intensity until they become 'nameless dread' (Bion, 1962).

After the catastrophe he inhabits a deserted world, devoid of life and prey to hatred. It is intolerable to think about his pain because it would be felt as an annihilation. This is why, in order to defend himself from his emotions, he projects them into the void (perhaps it would be better to say he is unable to hold them back) as undigested facts or β elements. But he does not find a container outside himself to receive them. In reality he no longer seeks one, and acts as if he had no need of it. In exploding, the container has become infinite, like the gigantic face of the mother which the child tries in vain to touch in Ingmar Bergman's *Persona*. Emotions are scattered in an astronomically vast emptiness. They are certainly felt, but no longer suffered since they no longer have meaning (Bion, 1970).

But without emotions, without the truth of the subject about itself – for Bion, emotion always has something to do with a relationship, and so is always an expression in various combinations of the ties of love (L), hate (H) or knowledge (K) of the object – one is impoverished and can become ill. Losing one's emotions is like internal bleeding after a surgical shock (ibid.). It means forgoing vital preconceptions and the realizations to which they could correspond; having to resort to 'hallucination' for its ability to offer an immediate solution, but above all to be a lifeboat indispensable for maintaining a minimum of representational activity, for giving a minimal meaning to things. We understand why the patient reacts badly when we want to deprive him of his delusions. However, even if the hallucinatory gratification works in the short term, frustration grows over time and he interprets it projectively as the effect of the analyst's rivalry and envy, which he experiences as coming from someone who wants to rob him of his capacity to satisfy himself in an omnipotent manner.

He now perceives reality as still more persecutory, and as a result can barely keep his hatred in check. The more the space of the original three-dimensional container (of the object) becomes limitless, and in fact annihilates itself, the more the mental space of the subject becomes restricted and flattened out.

The patient, who is both object and subject of abandonment, has a great fear of finding himself in this situation once again and so resorts to pathological defences, entering into an endless loop. He makes the object magically disappear. In leaving it behind, he unconsciously avoids making it the container of his emotional states. Unlike ('Freudian') transformations in which the subject projects onto an object, or ('Kleinian') projective transformations in which he projects into the object, here he seems to project into a void. As we see, he repeats the initial crisis ad infinitum, but does so by scaling down its violence and deluding himself that he is controlling the game.

But how does one make the object disappear? To explain this point, Bion imagines that the senses can function like muscles which evacuate perceptions into an astronomical space. The dispersal through space also implies a dispersal through time: an infinite amount of time is needed to set up a relationship between two points which are now separated by an insurmountable distance. In this way we can understand the Bionian notion of an 'attack on linking'. The expelled β elements are different from those β elements which have not been expelled in that the latter are still emotional proto-impressions and raw fragments of sensation. They are saturated, carrying within themselves traces of Ego and Superego, and they constitute the so-called 'bizarre objects' (just as fragments of food vomited up carry traces of gastric juices).

While transformations in rigid motion (RMT) and projective transformations (PT) produce less distorting transformations and conserve a link with the object, TH tend to lose this link because envy and frustration reciprocally reinforce each other in a vicious circle which Bion calls 'hyperbole'. Once the limit of tolerability has been crossed, instead of 'digesting' the real, the mind rejects it: that which is expelled is a mixture of β elements not transformed, of partially digested β elements, of fragments of α function and α elements as recollections removed from their work of re-signifying memory and used as hallucinations to staunch the emotional haemorrhage (the fading away of contact with reality that only emotions can ensure).

On the clinical level, states of hallucinosis and genuine hallucinations create, respectively, forms of hyper- or neo-reality.

Hallucination puts up a protective screen against the potentially traumatic nature of the real; a real which from the start of life is identified concretely and forever thereafter identified with the object in unconscious fantasy. This screen also functions as a canvas for the pictures which perception pours back onto it. From this point of view the hallucination is a minimal representation. In hallucination, according to Cesar and Sara Botella (2001, p. 44), a process of 'primordial abstraction' is achieved which precedes the secondary abstraction of reflective thought. Hallucination and memory are intimately connected. Hallucination is a memory which physiologically acts as a background to perception and thereby safeguards identity. If, however, reality becomes too violent, the hallucinatory screen grows denser, and normal 'invisible' hallucination can turn into full-blown hallucination.

What is most dazzling about the inspired Bionian model of the 'attack on linking', of 'bizarre objects' and TH is that, despite the 'absence' of the object, these processes are understood to be occurring within a wholly intersubjective framework. Unlike RMT and PT, in which the object is, so to speak, interchangeable, in essence inert, since on the theoretical plane these two types of transformation are still attributable to a unipersonal psychology, in the TH model the role of the object is both contemplated and at the same time held to be decisive. If something happens, it happens 'between' A and B, not only in A or only in B. In the consulting room this implies a precise conception of what may be the key therapeutic factor: to make a mind, another mind is needed. If one mind is struggling to grow, the other is failing in the task of nourishing it.

So the void is a fullness because the object participates in the process; it plays its part in the formation or destruction of a joint mind, 'the something between' with which the analyst is concerned, as Bion says. It does not function only as a mere support for the projections, as it does in the other two types of transformation. In fact, the object seems to have vanished into nothingness because it is hidden by the hallucinatory veil, but in reality it is all the more burdensome by virtue of its absence. In the TH model the subject hides the object from view because it meets reality not with preconceptions but with predeterminations: that is, with already saturated preconceptions. But this is the 'reversal of thinking': failing to assimilate anything new means being inhibited in one's capacity to know reality.

We cannot really understand the meaning of hallucinosis and hallucination except within the frame of relations with the object. Hallucination invokes the object, and resorts to memory to rediscover it, not to do without it. It reveals its thirst for the object, precisely because it grows when the object is not there. It does not distance itself from reality, but is the first step towards rediscovering the object, the symptom which is the reason why it is urgent to return to reality. Thought is not born because, having discovered from experience that hallucinatory satisfaction is illusory, the infant would automatically address its attention towards reality. It is born instead from the prompt enough response of the mother and from her ability to bring down the fever of hallucination.

At the same time the Bionian concept of no-thing already shows in the body of words the structure of an essential rhythm. It is like a no-thing-nothing-no . . . i.e. presence/absence, Fort/Da, on/off, and so on. I repeat, thought is not born from the mere absence of the object but from the happy rhythm of absence/presence with which the object modulates and renders tolerable the frustration which it has repeatedly aroused by its disappearances. The 'no' is the canvas placed at the disposal of memory; the 'thing' is the perceptual contribution from outside.

Thinking, giving a personal meaning to reality – which, in terms of the Bionian conceptions of the unconscious and of dream, means dreaming reality, doing psychological work, both conscious and unconscious, to create new emotional links and to construct a meaning – is no trivial matter. It is the measure of how far we are able to bear the absence of the object (nothing). If there is sufficient tolerance of frustration, a word ceases simply to have a merely indicative meaning as a name that joins several elements in a constant conjunction, but takes on a significant meaning and thereby certifies the very non-existence of the thing being represented. The symbol testifies to the absence of the breast, and imposes the need to deal with the emotions stirred up by the intrinsically negative nature of any definition.

If all this is not tolerated, deep down it feels like being killed by a cruel object while, seized by a homicidal rage, perpetrating in one's own turn a vengeful 'real murder' of the object. Thinking involves this kind of vertigo. The price of meaning is a struggle against ghosts. Someone who is too afraid of ghosts gives up meaning. He feels the absence which the name recovers (Bion, 1970, p. 9) and sees what is not there, 'and the thing that is not there, like the thing that is there, is indistinguishable from an hallucination', or rather, according to Bion's own definition of hallucination, from a β element.

For this reason, restricting the range of emotions which one is permitted to experience goes hand in hand with losing the meaning of things. We cannot have one without the other. That is what makes the TH. In hallucinosis the senses work in the opposite direction. Instead of digesting the psychic tension – that is, the β elements – they vomit it out. They use words as things and not as symbols. In this way one achieves a fictitious and omnipotent independence. A 'background of hallucinosis' pervades reality, keeping it apparently intact (Bion, 1965, p. 63). With transformations in hallucinosis one creates perfect illusory worlds set apart from all 'rivalry, envy, greed, threat, love and hate' (López-Corvo, 2002, p. 293). Since the pain is not tolerable, hallucinosis denies the absence of the breast (of satisfaction) and the consequent frustration. The absent breast (zero-breast or no-thing), the pre-conception of which is indispensable for symbolization, is reduced to a 'noughtness' and is 'hostile, envious and greedy and does not even exist as it is denuded of its existence' (Bion, 1965, p. 134). The void of representation becomes the analytic scene without characters and without emotions. 'The emotion is replaced by a no-emotion' (Bion, 1970, pp. 19–20).

As we see, the concept of TH has a powerful descriptive (and, I would say, mythopoeic) value in relation to a great many scenarios which are as difficult as they are evanescent, but not only in relation to these: do not all patients to some degree bear signs of this disequilibrium between hallucinosis and dream?

Transformation in hallucinosis as 'psychosis of everyday life'

The Bionian theory of TH was born in the wonderful 1958 article on hallucination, reprinted in *Second Thoughts* (1967) and developed in subsequent books. Faithful to his method of transcending the caesura and to his Cartesian principle of systematic doubt (Civitarese, 2008a, 2011a), Bion wipes out all distinction between perception and action. As we have said, the sense organs can function as if they were muscles, getting rid of aspects of themselves which have been identified as dangerous. They expel the images

> into the external world. These hallucinated images are then 'perceived', seen, heard, smelt, felt, as if real, and provide instant satisfaction to the omnipotent self. The emotional experience, the reality of the session, is transformed into sense impressions which are then evacuated as hallucinations, yielding pleasure or pain but not meaning.
>
> (Symington and Symington, 1996, pp. 115–116)

The choice of sensory apparatus involved in the process could depend, from one occasion to another, on 'how far' it is necessary to hurl the fragmented objects (Bion, 1992). The hypothesis very interestingly addresses the enigmatic subject of why, as the result of a certain deficiency 'upstream', a given symptom develops rather than another. As we have seen, the aim of the operation is to reconstruct a world after the catastrophe and to avoid this happening again. Naturally, it will be an illusory world populated by automata and 'reasoning and working' men, and almost bereft of life (of emotions) but not entirely deprived of sense relations. It is important not to conceive of the psychotic part of the personality as a malign and perverse entity, as Bion's combative emphasis sometimes portrays it. We would lose sight of the sense of emergency surgery which characterizes the operations which it undertakes.

Nevertheless, as I have previously suggested, understood initially as a substitutive mechanism of denial (the classical psychoanalytic notion to which it comes closest), the TH becomes steadily more 'physiological'. If it is true that the TH are governed by the psychotic part of the personality which is in everyone, this means that each one of us has suffered inevitable (physiological) micro-traumas from an 'explosion' of the container ('disappearance' of the object), and that the TH are not only the prerogative of individuals who present genuine and obvious psychological disturbances, since they would ensure the endurance of the psyche in this kind of predicament, and indeed would confer the necessary background of familiarity and predictability on our perceptions. As is evidently the case with any psychic defence, it is a question of degree: only a principle of consensuality can lead us to an idea of how far this or that individual has trespassed into the pathological. The final goal of this process, which removes the connotation of abnormality from TH, can be considered the 1977 paper in which Bion (1977a) includes hallucination in row C of the Grid along with dream thought, myth and dream.

The same 'sleep' which guarantees us a certain stability in analysis obviously accompanies us in everyday life. Indeed, taking our cue from Bion, we could emphasize the non-pathological aspect of TH. The concept lends itself to describing with extraordinary efficacy both the 'psychosis of everyday life' and, beyond a certain threshold, the false reality which can worm its way into analysis. It is worth asking oneself if the spasmodic need for the new, so evident in fashion and art, is not born of a deep drive to break free from the stagnation of habit; in other words, to clear away the patina of psychosis which becomes deposited on all of us in everyday life and suffocates our vitality.

It can definitely be said that Bion identifies a type of ubiquitous psychic transformation which accounts for how we construct reality: from physiology to pathology what varies is the degree of distortion involved in the transformation, which in turn depends on the greater or lesser capacity of the subject to give meaning to an experience. But what is distinctive about this third type of transformation compared to the other two? In my opinion this is the most noteworthy aspect of his proposition: while the first two can be viewed from a theoretical framework in which the subject is isolated (they are seen as functions inherent in the psyche of a subject who 'transfers', 'projects', etc., onto another object), TH is an 'authentically' Bionian transformation because it is set within a model of psychic functioning in which what is relevant and indispensable is the interpsychic dimension.

Transformation in hallucinosis as an instrument of analytic technique

That the interpsychic may be the essential dimension for the analyst is demonstrated by this passage from Bion:

> The relationship between the two people is an activity in two directions, and since one is concerned with showing that

> relationship, it is not a question of speaking about analyst and analysand; it is a matter of speaking about something between those two.
>
> (Bion, 1978–1980, p. 28)

On how he believes one can grasp the 'something between', let us read this other extract which introduces us to the third meaning which TH assumes in his work:

> Thus an analyst may feel, to take a common example, that his married patient is unmarried; if so, it means that psychoanalytically his patient is unmarried: the emotional reality and the reality based on the supposition of the marriage contract are discrepant. If this seems to suggest that the analyst must preserve his capacity for memory, I maintain that he always does (as does the patient, however regressed), but error is more likely to arise through inability to divest oneself of memory than through forgetfulness . . . But in psychoanalysis such matters as the patient's marriage have to be considered deeply.
>
> (Bion, 1970, pp. 49–50)

The two quotations give the x and y axes of analytic work: (a) the analysis takes place in the space between the analyst and the patient; (b) the reality that counts is emotional reality (what Bion elsewhere calls the 'O' of the session, 'one of the few things that analysts have the privilege of seeing as a "fact"' (1976, p. 317). The area identified by the two coordinates of an ideal graph is the field of the unconscious communication which is ceaselessly generated between analyst and patient and of the emotional turbulence which strikes it. The sentence: 'But in psychoanalysis such matters as the patient's marriage have to be considered deeply' (Bion, 1970, p. 50) means that the analyst must look at the 'facts' from a psychoanalytic vertex: that is, one must 'divest oneself of memory' (ibid., p. 49).

But why does Bion state a principle which goes so precisely against logic? What sense does it make to invite the analyst, even if he is proved wrong by the facts, to refuse to believe his own eyes and ears? Why should he take seriously an impression or perception which has clearly shown itself to be erroneous? Lastly, why does he refer to a type of experience which 'may appear to differ from what would be expected in the light of accepted analytic theory' (ibid., p. 49)?

I shall try to answer: because he knows that common sense, what seems evident from the point of view of the senses or of a certain theoretical system, can easily obstruct the analyst's ability to perceive something new, and hence to be receptive to the facts of the analysis. But, for Bion, it is of the greatest importance to be receptive; literally, as we understand from his brief text 'Evidence' (Bion, 1976), a matter of life and death (Civitarese, 2013a).

To make possible a coordinated functioning of the senses that allow us to know external reality – which may seem to be a matter we can take for granted, but, as misperceptions show us, it is nothing of the kind – or to use psychoanalytic models to intuit the reality of a session, requires a notable effort of learning. When this effort has been successful, it is not easy afterwards, I do not say to forget – which would be both impossible and disadvantageous – but even simply to keep in the background all that we have learned and recorded in our memory. In order to be in contact with reality, we are compelled to re-clothe it unconsciously with the more or less translucent film of things we already know. A molecular activity of transference constantly filters perception and thereby maintains our naive realism and our need for identity. As the philosophers say, to perceive is to imagine and to imagine is to perceive (de Saint Aubert, 2012).

Now, to come into contact with the immaterial facts of the analysis – with the patient's hallucinations – Bion confronts us with another of his many paradoxes: he asks the analyst to make use of his 'negative capability'; to listen 'without memory, desire and comprehension', intentionally to reduce to the minimum possible level the act of 'perceiving', the activity of grasping new elements of reality, in order to elevate 'imagining' (hallucinosis, which is in itself unconscious), the activity of re-clothing the reality of elements already noted. At this point he will find himself in an emotional situation – a kind of experimental sensory deprivation – conducive to a state of hallucinosis.

So Bion asks that we wipe out external reality as far as possible in order to enhance the perception of that which is internal; in other words, to increase indirectly the hallucinosis of external reality: that is, unconsciously to see external reality with the greatest possible subjectivity, so as to give oneself a way of intuiting more easily the current emotional reality of the relationship, as the following quotation shows:

> The ideal state for intuiting psychoanalytic realizations may be compared to situations which have arisen in the moment in which one is about to have a hallucination. The hallucinator is one who has sensory experiences with no context in sensory reality: in the same way the analyst must be capable of intuiting a psychic reality bereft of any prior sensory realization.
>
> (Bion, 1967, p. 248)

Given that when we encountered it in *Analisi degli schizofrenici e metodo psicoanalitico* [Analysis of Schizophrenics and Psychoanalytic Method] (Bion, 1967)[12] hallucinosis was a concept which explained an aspect of psychotic functioning, it comes as a surprise to find Bion, in *Attention and Interpretation* (1970), employing the concept of transformation in hallucinosis (TH) in order to describe an 'ideal state' of analytic receptivity.

Thus a state of hallucinosis may be always present, although unnoticed, even in a normal person, corresponding to the inevitable activity of projection of whatever belongs to the subject, an activity which permits us to live in a sufficiently familiar and stable world: but this turns out not to be the last time Bion will wrong-foot us! His final book, if we exclude the trilogy, *Memoir of the Future*, has as its subtitle 'A Scientific Approach to Insight in Psycho-analysis and Groups' (in other words, how to appeal to scientific intuitions!), and focuses on clinical phenomenology and psychoanalytic technique. In the general context of this volume – which is entirely dedicated to determining what the most favourable mental state may be for grasping the facts of the analysis, 'facts' which can be intuited but not perceived with the senses – hallucinosis surprisingly takes on the meaning, beyond its original sense of pathological defence and then of a component present even in the 'normal' state of the psyche, of emotional vertex which the analyst must adopt in order to apprehend the psychic reality of the patient, in order to take hold of something that is true even if proved false by the reality of the senses.

It is as if he were saying that to make contact with a patient who finds himself in a pathological state of hallucinosis, one must give oneself the freedom to function in the same way. How? Bion writes that one must intentionally (note this) put external reality in parentheses with an intensity that matches that of the patient who is genuinely hallucinating – and are hallucination and delusion not the most extreme resources for disregarding material reality and for expressing psychic reality instead? And this would actively make oneself ready for a kind of pre-delusional mood or state of mind: a situation of such openness and doubt, we might say a paranoid-schizoid emotional position, as to turn out inevitably to be persecutory and so to favour the irruption of hallucinosis or of delusional constructions. The analyst, writes Bion, 'knows phenomena by virtue of his senses but, since his concern is with "O", events must be regarded as possessing either the defects of irrelevancies obstructing, or the merits of pointers initiating, the process of "becoming" O' (1970, p. 27), and are therefore interpreted as if they were dream events and seen as indicators of the unconscious transpersonal communication. Bion struggles to find the expression which best conveys the meaning of this astonishing and paradoxical technical guideline: 'Faith', 'ability to forget', 'disciplined denial', 'denial of reality'.

Naturally it would be a contradiction in terms to maintain that one can discipline something which, like TH, happens unconsciously. So what can he mean by it? He means us to try, as we do when we are feeling ready to go to sleep, to reduce the psyche's introjective activity mediated by the senses so that we can enhance the work of the negative which nestles in perception. But isn't this a way of dreaming while awake? – just as we say psychotic people dream when awake; that is, when they hallucinate (which is not a waking dream in the sense of reverie, for that always involves a dimension of awareness). In what way is it different from true hallucination? In that the analyst is able to wake up! That is, to grasp the contradiction between his 'delusional' or 'hallucinated' idea and reality, at the very moment in which he becomes aware of it. However, at this point he sends down a probe to plumb the emotional depths of the analytic field and – how shall we put this? – to take a 'pure' sample, rediscovered in his own experience, of the patient's (the field's) psychic reality. In fact, the hallucinoses of the analyst are only of significance if we accept the second postulate, which is that they reflect an aspect of the 'something between' which is unconsciously produced between him and the patient.

So it is as if Bion were telling us that we need literally to dream in the session – as happens when we are travelling and become sleep-deprived over a long period, and enter into immensely rapid cycles of micro-dreams – and not only dream metaphorically while awake, as we do in reverie and, as we shall see, in transformation in dream (Ferro, 2009). In this way, hallucinosis becomes the deepest probe for exploring transpersonal or interpsychic unconscious emotional reality . . . as long as one can get out of it again! What the patient cannot do, and which the analyst must succeed in doing, is to wake from the hallucinosis. It is here that we can demonstrate its usefulness. On waking, the analyst transforms into dream the nightmare in which he has lived for a time with the patient, and thereby frees him from the state of excessive hallucinosis by the very fact of living through an experience of emotional unison and transmitting to him in various other ways the understanding he has acquired.

For this reason we can say that to liberate the patient from hallucinosis (the mental state with the lowest possible tolerance of ambiguity and difference) or, rather, to bring him back within physiological bounds, we need to enter into a state analogous to hallucinosis: I repeat, an active and conscious denial of material reality which allows us to live the unconscious denial which the patient brings to the same material reality, and to do so at the very moment in which he is seeing it entirely in his own most subjective terms.

The aim is enter into a profound resonance with his psychic reality (with that of the intermediate area of the analysis, in which analyst and patient are places). The patient unconsciously wipes out psychic reality, building himself a hyper-concrete world, while the analyst in his own turn consciously wipes out this world in order to come back up to the terrain of psychic reality of which it represents the transformation. The next stage is decisive, and is achieved when the hallucinosis is replaced by a critique of the hallucinosis: what we call waking from the dream.

In other words, if Big Jim in *The Gold Rush* hallucinates the tramp (Chaplin) as a chicken in order to forget that he has nothing to eat – but also to remind himself that this is what he urgently needs! – the analyst must ignore the reality on which he focuses with his senses, so that he too can see the chicken that Big Jim is chasing around the room and in this way can understand his hunger.

Like the hallucination of the chicken, the hyper-reality which is the outcome of excessive TH is a heartrending siren sounding the alarm about an imperative need to rediscover a true contact with reality: that is, one based on emotions and on the value system which they embody. Essentially, hallucinosis does what it can to redress the deficit in the capacity for representation, but if we are able to listen to it, it never fails to represent with great vividness the patient's very inability to represent.

So the active denial which, in an almost military tone, Bion prescribes for the analyst does not concern itself (nor could it) with normal hallucinosis, which infiltrates his own perception of things (as part of the mind's need to affirm its identity), but instead aims to enhance his hallucinosis at the expense of his mind's capacity to differentiate between external and psychic reality: that is, to dream reality.

Attention and Interpretation is a long and extraordinary reflection on how easily analyst and patient can collude in erroneously judging reality and explaining the facts rationally to themselves so as to 'prevent emergence of an unknown, incoherent, formless void and an associated sense of persecution by the elements of an evolving O' (1970, p. 52), and on what to do in order to free oneself from this situation. To illustrate this type of unconscious collusion, Bion gives the paradoxical example of the analyst opening the door to a patient who is already in therapy and thinking he is the same person that he met before. What could be more obvious than a thought of this kind? Isn't it a good example of normal hallucinosis? But are we sure that this really is the same person?

If we were to scrape off the patina of hallucinosis in analysis we would see the patient as if for the first time, hear his words as if they were always the retelling of a dream, and keep reinventing psychoanalysis for each patient. If we think it is the same patient as yesterday, says Bion, we are treating the wrong patient. In analysis, even outside borderline cases and psychosis, the patient is by definition defending himself against a traumatic reality and thus against those feelings which could reconnect him to that experience. He has a vision of reality, or of some aspects of it, which is flattened, monocular. So as not to collude with this defence and in order to be at one with his O (his emotional reality), Bion suggests that the analyst should also enter consciously into a parallel state of hallucinosis, which enhances the expression of emotional reality at the expense of material reality, brackets off the hyper-reality which the patient constructs for himself by evacuating the feelings with which he is not in contact and which for this reason is (pathologically) false. The analyst's hallucinosis helps him in fact 'to see what the patient sees' (Bion, 1970, p. 40), to intuit his 'hallucinations'. Only in this way can he then 'effect transformations O→K' (ibid., p. 36): that is, derive knowledge (represented by K) from experience, when he makes waking follow dreaming so that dreaming becomes an authentic dreaming.

In other words, the analyst deliberately obscures present (and past) external reality as not pertinent, irrelevant – in the example quoted the fact that the patient really is married. In the same way as the patient – who is anchored to reality, but a fake reality because it is interwoven with so many fantasies – he must come to see everything in the terms of his own psychic reality, of the unconscious, in order to recover a critical perspective later on. Temporarily suspending material reality helps him to be receptive to the patient's projective identifications (β elements), and so to 'see' his invisible hallucinations. This is how I understand Bion's observation, equating hallucinosis with 'an act of faith', that:

> to appreciate hallucination the analyst must participate in the state of hallucinosis . . . By eschewing memories, desires, and the operations of memory he can approach the domain of hallucinosis and of the 'acts of faith' by which alone he can become at one with his patient's hallucinations and so effect transformations O→K.
>
> (Bion, 1970, p. 36)

I repeat that, viewed in this way, hallucinosis marries up in metapsychological terms with the Freudian concept of denial (or, according to Riolo (2011), of 'rejection' (*Verwerfung*)) and, as a principle of technique, with the concept of free-floating attention, of which it finally becomes the most extreme version. Re-christened 'Faith', it becomes fostered in the analyst as the mental attitude known as 'negative capability'. As we can see, to make hallucinosis not only a type of unconscious psychic transformation which may be found in pathology and normality, but also a mental state of the analyst in the session is another way of de-pathologizing the concept of TH.

So the analyst will no longer consider his own possible 'hallucinoses' as something of which to rid himself, the product of a mistake, but as a derivative which 'fishes' in the 'something between' that constitutes analysis, in the intermediate area produced by the communication from unconscious to unconscious. In this way, hallucinosis comes to enrich the dream spectrum in the session, along with reverie, dream flashes and transformations in dream.

With this bold theoretical development, it is as if Bion wanted to push himself yet further in radicalizing his principle of listening without memory and desire, with 'negative capability' (a negativity which, it should be noted, is positive since it is the fruit of experience and knowledge: a capability, from the Latin, *capere*, to contain or understand). After such a *coup de théâtre* it is not enough to say that what counts is the capacity for reverie of the mother with her child or of the analyst with the patient. No, what we need is the capacity for 'delusion' and 'hallucination' (and besides, didn't Winnicott (1956, p. 359) speak of primary maternal preoccupation as a 'psychiatric condition'?).

Transformation in hallucinosis, reverie and transformation in dream

Having described the three ways in which TH is present in Bion's theory, we can clarify some differences between TH and other phenomena on the dream spectrum in the session, such as reverie and Ferro's transformation in dream (TD).

Reverie is a dream with the eyes open. We are more or less aware of it: waking is presupposed from the outset. By means of a reverie I could also take account of the idea that the patient is thinking or behaving as if he were unmarried (even though he is), or arrive at it by association. But hallucinosis has another quality. It is equivalent to a micro-delusion or a hallucination which I can come out of after a second or after a year. Even if it were only for a fraction of a second, I am absolutely convinced that what I have thought or seen, and which later reveals itself to be erroneous, is true. Hallucinosis speaks with the accent of truth which is typical of the unconscious.

With the concept of transformation in dream Ferro (2009) proposes the technical guideline of listening to the whole conversation with the patient as if it were the recounting of a dream: in practice it is enough to introduce the patient's words (but also the analyst's) with the formula: 'I dreamed that . . .' (or, maybe better, 'I am dreaming that . . .'). In this way, the activity of waking dream thought comes to the fore, no longer obscured by the hallucinosis of everyday life. If Sara tells me that the cat scratched her, I hear it as if she were telling me that she had dreamed it. Then I can more easily bring myself to ask what the cat, as a character in the session, may be telling me about what is happening in the analytic field.

TD is an extraordinarily valuable principle of technique in clinical work because it helps the analyst to take responsibility for the unconscious communication which is happening with the patient, and for his own ineradicable subjectivity. As we see, the emphasis here is on intentionality (the analyst does something with a deliberate purpose). TH, on the other hand, is experienced unconsciously, and it is factual reality which has the task of waking the analyst.

I said that TD is a valuable tool, but it is also delicate. We should not resort to it in too active a manner: TD could lead one to illuminate the analytic field too brightly, and to read it mechanically. In such a case it would amount to a real hallucinosis, and could even be dangerous. That is, it would give the analyst the illusion of understanding everything in real time, but without a real hold on the unconscious, and not in the temporal dimension afforded by *Nachträglichkeit*. In my opinion, it is only by looking back that we can be sure of comprehending anything.

To ensure that it does not become hallucinosis – to use a psychoanalytic theory like screening with regard to the patient – TD, once assimilated, should likewise be forgotten and float freely in the analyst's preconscious. Ideally it too would re-emerge as if in a reverie. When the analyst wakes from the dream of reality and surprises himself by observing it from the perspective suggested by Ferro, the principle of TD returns as in a dream, as the mature fruit of the work of the unconscious. Ultimately, TD is at the opposite pole of the dream spectrum in the session, an unbroken sequence which starts with hallucinosis and continues through reverie, dream flashes, etc.

However, it clearly makes sense to use TD in a more systematic manner for heuristic or didactic purposes, and perhaps also in those situations in which we need to 'force' waking up from the nightmare of an analysis without real dreams. In that regard it has at its disposal a practicality which TH and reverie, for obvious reasons, do not.

I hope it is clear at this point that I am not proposing an alternative technique to TD but, drawing on Bion, systematizing the inclusion of the analyst's hallucinosis in the dream spectrum of the session and clarifying its unique character as a technical resource. TH, TD and reverie are therefore quite diverse conceptual instruments and not alternatives to one another. All three are of great value for becoming the O of the session, for deep immersion in the emotional reality of the analytic field and for activating an unconscious work of understanding (Civitarese, 2013b). If this immersive quality decreases in passing from TH to TD, then all the experiences to which these concepts apply have in common the important 'aesthetic' factor of surprise which we feel every time we make the passage through the border control (in French *rêve* was used to mean customs (Quignard, 1995)) which leads from dream to waking. I shall now try to show in three clinical vignettes – one more extensive and two very brief ones – how these different moments play out in the session.

V for Vendetta

As in Bion's passage about the married/unmarried patient, the most striking examples of the analyst's hallucinosis are those episodes in which a perception or a belief asserts itself, only to be proved wrong by the facts – a fragment of 'psychotic' hallucinosis. I myself have described elsewhere how, working with patient L., it often happened that I ended the session ahead of time, confusing it with that of another patient, I. In doing so, I was unconsciously forcing the reintegration of emotional aspects up until then separated off as being L.'s, and now instead evident in I. Instead of seeing the confusion as an error or an enactment, I interpreted it as the accurate 'perception' of something fundamental related to the psychic reality of the patient, or in terms of the field, of the couple.

A similar example can be found in a vignette recounted by Ferro in which he tells how he used to hear the heels of a young patient, Anna, as she came up the stairs, only to realize that it was in fact . . . Antonio! But he had hallucinated 'Anna' – who immediately became a character in the analytic field – who did indeed tell him something essential about Antonio which he had never noticed until then.

The analyst finds himself in a state of hallucinosis both when he is obviously mistaken about factual reality but has not yet awoken, and when he confines himself to considering only common sense reality: this would be a state of normal hallucinosis, but nevertheless unsuitable for the purposes of analysis because it obstructs the attunement with emotional reality. For this reason it is good if he wakes from this realistic viewpoint. At the same time he must leave himself free to live in both these dimensions because only in this way can he become the O of the session, of the patient and the field.

I shall now report a fragment of a session from the third year of S.'s analysis, a young woman in her late twenties:

PATIENT: I asked my mother to come with me to the doctor. She can't because she has to go to the hairdresser. Same as always. She isn't available. But when I came home my dog really made a celebration of it![13]

ANALYST: He's always available!

P: Even though I'd left him behind all weekend. If he could speak he'd have said: 'You went away, and I should be sulking about it!' And instead of that he runs up to me and wags his tail.

A: Of course, one understands why Snoopy can do all sorts of things and he's saner than all the rest of them in *Peanuts*! [and I mean that he is indulgent and affectionate towards her. Then I add:] It seems like Monday was a real celebration!

P: Well, I was so glad that I could come home to my dog! . . . Did you see that *V for Vendetta* was on TV on Monday evening?! . . . I managed to make Mum watch it. [Now you must see how angry I am?!] She was great. She watched the whole film. Usually she does crosswords and stuff. But she saw all of *V for Vendetta*, from beginning to end. I was really pleased. It made me happy that she was interested in a film I like so much. She followed it all, which I never expected, because it's quite a dark film where most of the characters die at the end [as a session ends, I reflect]. And the dog was asleep on my tummy . . . But this evening I'm going to the theatre on my own . . . They've given me a box . . . There'll be a fight over the seats.

A: *Orson Welles' Roast*? [I ask]

P: Yes! Have you seen it?!

A: No.

P: You're a magician today, you know in advance what I'm going to see. Let's hope it'll be really good . . . My boyfriend gave me a French game for the Wii [Nintendo (non-intendo?)], about two little rabbits who have to go back to the Moon and they build a heap of things they've stolen from here and there, all kinds of things you'd never expect . . . cactuses . . . piles of tin cans . . .

A: Like Cirque du Soleil . . . And . . . did they get to the Moon?

Listening to S., I think to myself that she is expressing her anger at my having imposed an unexpected separation. I had in fact decided to take a day off at Carnival time, not even on a national holiday. So I speculate that she is rebuking me for not being available for her, and at the same time is showing me how she reacts to these situations: by taking all the responsibility herself. If people leave her, it's her fault (she was the one who left her dog for the weekend . . . that is, she was left alone like a dog by a dog of an analyst . . .).

What is happening in these few snatches of dialogue? If I had listened in the usual way, using my main theoretical model, the theory of the analytic field and the concept of dream in the session (Ferro and Civitarese, 2015), I would perhaps have sharpened the focus on the prevalent emotion of that moment: the disappointment felt at seeing that the other is absorbed in his own affairs (seeing 'Mum going to the hairdresser' as a character in the analytic field) and has no time for her. Maybe I would have said something to enrich this account, in the attempt to know more, or to identify more exactly the emotion in play, or to sign the receipt for the return of the 'letter' which had been sent back to me.

Instead I find myself listening from the perspective of the transference neurosis, and so in the setting of a unipersonal model, bringing everything back to an actual event in our recent past – the session missed for the Carnival – without thinking that something was being missed now, in not being in contact with S. in the present moment of the session. Here, I think, is the 'perceptual' error: that of using a theory ('theorein' means 'to see') which – for my method of reading the facts of the session in an intersubjective tone – I consider an error, a micro-delusion or a hallucinosis. The error is not the banal one of placing everything in a context of pure reality, in which the mother would be the real mother, the dog the real dog, etc., but instead placing it in the context of a theoretical actuality, i.e. a concretized theory: how often it is this which, inter alia, leads us to make routine interpretations of the effects of the weekend break. Obviously I am not speaking here of hallucinosis in general, but as it relates to me and my usual mode of understanding (the one that, in my opinion, makes me see things correctly and which I feel as most 'true'). I am referring to the meaning which it has for me, and which it may not have for someone else: the use of a certain psychoanalytic concept in a particular way and in a certain situation.

But if that is how things are, what would be the truth in the error? What use can we make of it by thinking of it as a TH?

One possible angle could be to consider that this happens in order to keep things more 'at a distance'; that listening sceptically helps me to protect myself from positive or negative feelings which are aroused in this encounter and in actuality; to shelter myself in the idea, contained in the concept of transference, that it is always the patient who misunderstands. But we can only use TH when we come out of it and the hallucinosis transforms itself into a real dream: that is, when – perhaps alerted by S.'s insistence on the way the dog celebrated her return home – I realize that in fact I was not listening from the point of view of the session as a dream, and that perhaps S. is speaking not only from disappointment but also from the joy of our seeing each other again.

According to this hypothetical reconstruction of events, I would first have 'hallucinated' and then, on waking, 'dreamed' a negative transference in which even the celebration of the dog had become 'celebrate someone' in the sense of 'gun them down'. But then, if dreaming is the *via regia* to understanding unconscious communication, I have to think – just like Bion thinking that his definitely married patient is unmarried – that in the analytic relationship there may be a feeling of anger circulating, and that I (we) could not have made contact with it except in TH, and that the sense of frustration which comes with feeling unjustly accused (because 'of course', according to classical theory, it is somehow always the patient who misunderstands, distorts, etc.) in fact makes us grasp it all the better.

In the example I give here, reawakening does not lead to the rectification of a simple perceptual error. The negativity in the transference which I interpret to her, and which I would have also seen according to a reading of the analytic field, is confirmed at another level and speaks of an anger which I had not suspected was present, at least not to that extent. Here TH guards me from taking refuge in a kind of delusion of clarity in interpreting the clinical facts from the perspective of the field. It makes me understand that what I would be ready to admit on an intellectual level, I was denying privately and unconsciously.

The benefit which I take from using the technical resource of TH is that it enables me almost literally to dream what happens: 'literally' means at a deep level (and with a corresponding quantity of unconscious work of understanding) certainly not attainable by reverie and TD.

The reawakening which transforms hallucinosis into dream can occur in various ways: it can be the patient who corrects the analyst's hallucinosis, or the analyst himself may notice the error; in a supervision, it can happen that you are called back from it by the colleague, or the 'internal' supervisor we go back to consulting from time to time. It is certainly the case that, from the moment of reawakening, I try to consider the hallucinosis as an unconscious symbolic creation by the couple which has the potential to render me receptive towards a dimension of the relationship (or rather, of the analytic field) which up until then had gone unrecognized; or, if it had been recognized, not in that form or intensity, or else located in the wrong place.

Somebody might wonder what is the difference in the vignette presented here between the negativity concealed by an interpretation of the transference and that reached by considering it a TH? The answer could be exactly the difference which Bion makes between 'knowing O' and 'becoming O', between understanding something with the head or with the head and the body – that is, emotionally as well. Paradoxically, to hallucinate that I am attributing everything to S. is the symptom of a situation in the analytic field which sees me flooded with strong feelings and on the defensive. From my point of view, the hallucinosis is not a matter of thinking that there is anger but of thinking that the anger is only hers (that it is all part and parcel of her neurosis) and so suspending my ability to see the facts of the analysis intersubjectively.

If I interpret the error as a symbolic form, a micro-dream which clarifies for me what is happening, what I glean from it is the regaining of a greater degree of receptivity. What I say to S. immediately afterwards about Snoopy does not occur by chance: it still seems to be happening along the lines of TH (recalling her attention to the celebratory event = missed session), but it is in substance a true reverie. Why can it be considered in that light?

When I mention Snoopy, apparently in a very open and unsaturated intervention ('in the analytic field'), I am to some extent still really inside an interpretive perspective of transference; underlining how Snoopy is indulgent and affectionate with her, I go on to tell her that 'I am Snoopy' and for all that she may feel like, and indeed actually desire to 'celebrate' me (in the negative sense of 'do away with me'), I take it in a festive spirit and don't in my own turn become angry at her anger, and what is more I reassure myself about my psychic health.

However, there is more to the comment about Snoopy, because on another level it also testifies to a genuine joy at our meeting again. That under the appearance of staying on the same interpretative line, something like reverie had seeped in is demonstrated by the fact that Snoopy is not mentioned by S.: and yet it had been she who in the past had told me that the dog was the sanest member of the family. Here the dialogue takes on an almost dreamlike character. I find myself speaking to her in a way that has little to do with 'making interventions' or 'giving interpretations' (Ogden, 2009): in this way we develop a shared unconscious, preconscious and conscious psychological narrative weaving back and forth from the images of one to the other, in which we can think/dream and solve the emotional problem of the moment. What has happened is that I have allowed myself to wake up and speak as if I were dreaming (ibid.).

What 'woke' me was S., making herself perform as if she were an actress, giving a voice to her dog and making him speak directly ('I should be sulking at you!') which transported everything to the present. All at once it was clear that neither she nor I nursed the slightest doubt about the humanity of this animal (and of this analyst).

So, reconstructing how things went, first of all Snoopy came into my mind doing his dance of welcome. Then up came the memory of the poster on my bedroom door when I was a child, a picture of Snoopy with his goggles and aviator's scarf. A few days before the session I had taken down from the bookcase the precious Charlie Brown albums that I have kept for years. I wanted to give them to my children, who had recently started to read them and were becoming very fond of them. This moment had felt like a kind of ritual and very gratifying to me in my role as father. It was a precious gift. It suggested some special intimacy. These are not any old comic strips, however poetic; they contain a certain idea about life. For me they also hold the memory of when I was a child like them and spent hours reading on endless summer afternoons in the country. My gesture contained a feeling of tenderness and slight melancholy about the passing of time and the succession of the generations, but above all a doubt about how long, and if, I will be available for them when they need help with their lives, as my father was for me at some critical moments even when I had become an adult. It is as if I had made the same gesture for S.

That is to say, we simply live through an extraordinary moment of shared emotion, starting with the reverie provoked in me by the dog-speaking-as-a-person. We tell each other in this way and in the voice of this character that faithfulness and emotional warmth nourish the mind and create well-being. This is not a mere figure of speech, but my putting into action what I say through the way in which I say it. Then I surprise myself by speaking apparently without thinking or, it could be said, with a spontaneity that is not outside technique, but which perhaps one can only attain when one forgets it (enough).

So for a moment, thanks to the way TH has rebalanced my functioning in favour of dreaming, an emotional experience has been achieved (T→O, in Bion's idiosyncratic language) which has brought about the transformation of anger into intimacy and melancholy, bringing to life a situation of emotional unison and recognition, and also a lived understanding of the core unease which grips S.

S. replies positively to my comment about Snoopy, and I wonder if on that Monday evening I hadn't also watched *V for Vendetta.*

The film obviously symbolizes her thirst for revenge for external offences, past and present, both in the minute immediacy of the dialogue, but also in the sense of well-being and happiness which she experiences in feeling herself to be understood. The protagonist, V, always wears a mask because his face has been disfigured in a cruel experiment conducted by the regime(!). For this reason he is animated by an intense thirst for revenge. Detached from the plot, V is the portrayal of a person immersed in a paranoid environment which prevents him from being himself and condemns him to live prey to a constant feeling of anger, the consequence of a narcissistic wound that has never healed. However, V meets Evy, a girl who like him is fighting against the dictator. Evy succeeds in transforming him and containing his anger. Significantly, the name Evy contains the letter V and in English is very similar to envy. Needless to say, that same game is played in analysis.

The impression I have here is that S. (in reality, the little group-mind to which the pair of us have given life) is dreaming what happens between us: in other words, that in some ways I am allowing myself, even if perhaps unwillingly, to be cathected by her hatred because of what has happened and to try to bear it. I am there with her seeing the film of her life (of her waking dream thought). Moreover, I am aware how the violence of her emotions is heightened in the virtual scene of the unconscious and, being identified with the cruel character who persecutes V, I cannot stop myself experiencing a feeling of anxiety. But this is the bundle of β emotions which is to be transformed 'exorcistically' (Grotstein, 2007) once the demon of meaninglessness has been absorbed, and inside me first of all. It all seems to work out since the dog sleeps on her tummy, as S. tells me; and I think that maybe she dreams; dreams things inside her tummy, her most visceral emotions.

However, when we approach the end of the session, S. once again sadly mentions the evening and her feeling of loneliness. She will go to the theatre. Who knows if there will even be a seat for her?! I had also intended to go to that very same performance (which is why I knew it was on the playbill), but I also knew that I wouldn't be going because I had taken on another commitment. Added to the Carnival, this is another missed 'meeting' (but here we are about to say goodbye at the end of the session). I surprise myself by asking her rhetorically, as it were in an aside, if the play is about the famous American director, and so on. In some way I am making myself the bearer of her feeling of sadness about 'the missed meeting' which is the end of the session. In reality, the self-disclosure feels more like bringing a new character onto the stage to speak about what is happening. Asking her if the play was *Orson Welles' Roast*, I was asking her if she also felt she was on the grill.

After this came S.'s question, the reference to the magical mood (particularly communicative and intimate, perhaps because I was in tune with the rekindling of the inevitable persecutory mood at the moment of saying goodbye) which was created in the session, hence the image of the little rabbits in the Nintendo game, building a heap of stolen objects to get to the Moon.

To sum up then, in this vignette we pass from the painful theme of 'It's always been like this' to the dreamlike and magical spirit of the circus. In that moment we are engaged in a kind of dance. And I grant myself the freedom of talking-as-dreaming (Ogden, 2007), the freedom to be spontaneous and to trust the psychological work of the unconscious and the exchange of reveries in which I am engaged with S., to the point where I could not tell if what I say is more me or her. It is here that I make myself really available to her emotionally.

Daughter or wife?

I am never able to remember if G. is J.'s wife and R. his daughter, or the other way round, and so every time I have to name them, I hold back. For fear of getting it wrong, as has happened to me more than once, and very embarrassingly, I say, 'your wife' or 'your daughter'. This situation of 'chronic hallucinosis' has come up many times, and when I become aware of it I speculate that in fact for J. the two figures are not sufficiently differentiated. In analysis, analogously, my mistake could show that between the two of us there may also be a certain confusion of roles.

W(h)ell

In reading the record of a supervision, I happen to confuse 'well' with 'hell'. This menacing mistake, which I only discover on a second reading, is enough to prompt me to listen from an off-centre perspective to the apparently satisfied account which B. is giving of his married life: I glimpse hell behind the smiles over the morning cornflakes.

As we have seen, I regard such a lapse in reading less as a symptom of the return of the repressed than as the product of unconscious work of understanding. In other words, I privilege the expressive aspect of the dream, the creation of meaning, over its translational aspect, its destruction of the significance of latent thoughts (Pontalis, 1988).

Waking from reality, or dreaming

Viewed from within the oscillation hallucinosis↔dream, all the narrative developments of the session could be placed on a gradient running from hallucinosis – which, I repeat, stands for a dream really dreamed while awake (that is, the first part of the act of dreaming, the second part being the act of 'reawakening') – to dream, from the fiction of reality to the reality of fiction. In my opinion, the relevant thing is that one is the premise of the other and that only their integrated functioning allows us to have a correct view of reality, to digest it and be nourished by it. When someone suffers psychologically, this dialectical functioning is blocked in several ways. The task of treatment is to restore it both with TH and reverie (to which, according to Bion, we can predispose ourselves by 'Faith' or by negative capability), and with direct and intentional applications of transformation in dream (Ferro's TD), always with the provisos to which I have referred. In passing from hallucinosis to dream we gain new perspectives, we wake from the fiction of reality. The analyst becomes able to contain the emotion because, thanks to the waking from hallucinosis, he gives things a personal (integrated/somato-psychic) meaning.

The aim of treatment is to enable the patient to acquire knowledge that is useful for entering into contact with emotional experience, to learn from experience and so to give meaning to existence. By definition, if he comes to us it is because unconsciously he fears his feelings to a degree which cannot be considered physiological, and so he rids himself of them inadequately and thus hallucinates reality. Every time this happens, the expelled β elements carry behind them micro-fragments of α function (the capacity to transform crude emotions into visual images or pictograms or dream thoughts). So he needs to develop the psychic processes of dreaming/introjection and α function, which could never function at all – and this is the point – without the work of the negative which is undertaken by TH. Each time the cycle is repeated, the mind increases its capacity to dream O, the real unknowable in itself, the reality not yet symbolized. The success of the operation really depends on the fact that before reawakening not only the patient but also the analyst may be in TH in the sense of unconscious defence; that is, they may have passed through the experience of unconscious collusion which expresses itself in the hallucinosis of reality in analysis.

This is why the concept of TH is so valuable: because it gives us a way to conceptualize the dynamics and unconscious mechanisms which lead us to hallucinate reality and to live what can be defined as waking sleep. The amount of work it costs us to de-concretize reality is the exact measure of that species of gravitational force that is common sense, with which we normally cathect reality. But to a greater or lesser degree, the patients who come to us ask to be woken from this sleep which is, we could say, too deep and deprived of dreams, and also to be helped to dream their existence, to redress the imbalance between hallucinosis and dream which is caused by mental pain.

The concept of TH can legitimately be added to the other productions of the dream spectrum. To employ the concept from more points of view and according to different accepted senses, as I have tried to show in this study, means endowing oneself with a valuable security device against the risk of concretizing psychoanalytic theories in general, and TH in particular, by seeing it exclusively as an intrapsychic defence mechanism of the subject. Its versatility seems evident when we maintain its uniqueness as an exquisitely transpersonal/interpsychic concept.

It is only then that TH demonstrates its extraordinary theoretical, technical and clinical value – and its uniqueness compared to the other transformations (RMT and PT) – for bringing into clear focus some particularly evanescent clinical scenarios in which adherence to the concrete predominates; for illuminating in contrast the concept of α function and of dreaming/thinking; for further refining some technical tools such as Ferro's TD and Bion's reverie; and, finally, for feeling more sensitively the emotional waves which ripple across the surface of the analytic field and observing the facts of clinical work at a higher resolution.

5

THE UN/CONSCIOUS AS A PSYCHOANALYTIC FUNCTION OF PERSONALITY

> The patient awaking from a nightmare has reached the limits of his capacity for dreaming on his own. He needs the mind of another person – one 'acquainted with the night' – to help him dream the yet to be dreamt aspect of his nightmare.
>
> (Thomas H. Ogden, *The Art of Psychoanalysis: Dreaming Undreamt Dreams and Interrupted Cries*)

'"Unconscioused" = *unbewusst*. Oh, for a similar word for "projective identification"' (Bion, 1992, p. 353)! What might this mean? Why does Bion find the German term for 'unconscious' so felicitous? Is he fascinated by it because unlike the corresponding English term the German noun comes from a verb? Or is it because it already contains the idea that the unconscious is not a purely natural entity, but rather the product of a specific human 'action'? Or is it above all because his idea of the unconscious differs from Freud's, since for him it is not a 'place' but a psychic process?

The Freudian unconscious is formed by repression. The mind police apprehend all the criminals and dissidents that the current regime cannot afford to have running around when the authorities (of the superego) come to visit, and so they fill the prisons of the unconscious. Being confined to prison does not stop them from continuing their subversive activities (just like Mafiosi who conduct their business from inside prison through third parties), and in fact occasionally they even manage to escape. For Bion, too, the unconscious is the product of social 'pressure'. The agent behind this action, however, is not (only) the double censorship that blindly obeys the superego, as in Freud, but the alpha function, a set of mental operations whose task it is to digest reality in order to transform it into elements that can feed the mind and make it grow.

Before becoming autonomous intrapsychic activities, both censorship and the alpha function act from the outside – in the mother or whichever member of the social group (or in general, of sociality) may take her place – even though they rely on innate structures. However, unlike repression, which primarily performs control functions, the alpha function has a broader significance. It does not exclude conflict or even censorship, but subsumes both into the more general activity of symbolizing reality.

Freud sees culture as the repression and subjugation of drives, Bion as creativity and the development of the capacity for thought. Furthermore, from the theoretical point of view, for Freud in the earliest stages of life the direct mediating role of sociality comes to weigh almost entirely on the concept of primal repression, a concept which by his own admission is so obscure that it has difficulty bearing this responsibility. Bion's intersubjective model of the interaction between mother and child has broader shoulders and shows how from the beginning of life it is relationship that kindles the development of the mind. Freud is more interested in the subject; for Bion, one might say, a person does not exist if viewed independently from the group.

Curiously enough, the different formulation of a postulate that in essence they share, namely the idea of the unconscious as a product of sociality and language, gives rise to two visions that appear to be opposites. This is not, however, simply a question of the extent to which the various aspects of the same postulate are emphasized. This is true on a transverse but not on a longitudinal plane. Longitudinally, as we move from Freud to Bion there is a change in the epistemological frame within which their theories are situated. We pass from modernity to post-modernity (Civitarese and Boffito, 2012). It would be impossible to understand the differences in their conceptions of the unconscious if we did not take this essential fact into account. Bion can no longer subscribe to the positivist view taken by Freud, who despite everything is still guided by the search for ultimate truth. But like any rigid opposition even this is true and false at the same time. Let us take a closer look.

The gentleman in the havelock

> For the unconscious is . . . the gentleman in the havelock whose face I cannot see distinctly.
>
> (Groddeck, 1977, p. 58)

Freud subverts the classical concept of consciousness[14] and forces it into uneasy cohabitation with the new term, unconscious. The servant becomes the master in the house and the master becomes the servant. In fact, in Freud's second topography the Ego is in thrall to three masters: external reality, the Id and the Superego.[15] The primacy of the conscious is replaced by the primacy of the unconscious. After Freud the conscious can no longer be conceived of as the pure and pristine presence of the subject in itself, but only in relation to the framework of the preconscious and what is even more extraneous to it, the unconscious. By definition, the unconscious cannot be known directly but may be inferred from the effects it produces on the conscious. What we manage to see is only the shadow cast on things in the form of derivatives.

The problem with this theoretical operation is that purity, originarity, fullness and transparency – traditionally the attributes of the conscious ego – change sign and become the demonic, the originarity, the impure, the primitive of the unconscious; hence the representations of the unconscious as substance, system or psychic locality. They take various forms: a bilge where the most shameful and vicious impulses are collected, a 'maximum security prison' (de Azevedo, 2000, p. 76) or hell ('Acheronta movebo . . .'; Freud, 1900, p. 1). The positive sign (in that it is opposed to nature) of the traditional subject of philosophy and classical psychology is inverted into the negative sign of the decentered subject of the unconscious. The hierarchy between the two terms, however, is maintained, and with it the idea of being able to establish a plenitude of meaning. For example, quoting Theodor Lipps, Freud (1938a, p. 158) states that the unconscious is the 'truly psychical'; rather than deconstructing the traditional hierarchy C/Unc, he seems simply to reverse it. Derrida makes the comment that in Freud there still remains the 'horizon of the final *parousia* of a meaning at last deciphered, revealed, made present in the rich collection of its determinations' (Derrida, 1972, p. 384). Hence the apparently ungenerous criticism he levels at Freud when he accuses him of keeping within a logocentric or 'transcendental' logic.[16]

To avoid simplifications and once again to do right by the complexity of Freud's thought, we must say that we are indebted to Freud – after all, the title of one of Derrida's most brilliant books is *To Do Justice to Freud* (Derrida, 1992) – for laying the groundwork for overcoming this impasse. It was also Freud who 'discovered' the logic – as an 'alternative' to a naive conception of truth – of *Nachträglichkeit* (*après coup/afterwardsness*); a valuable discovery especially if we think of it in the light of subsequent extensions of the concept. Following Lacan, it was Derrida[17] who contributed more than anyone else to re-evaluating this concept and in fact can claim credit for having given it the greatest possible prominence, going so far as to make it the cornerstone of his philosophy. Introduced by Freud as a non-intuitive concept of psychic causality and memory function, with Derrida *Nachträglichkeit* became a general principle of how the meaning of the experience is structured through constant slippage and referral or 'dissemination': a psychic element (the trace of a sensory or emotional impression) is added to the text of memory and (potentially) changes it completely. It takes its meaning from what precedes it and at the same time confers meaning on it. The key implication of this dynamic mental state is to point out that at the dawn of the subject lies the non-origin of meaning, a constitutive lack, a void upstream; a void that can only be filled through the other, but which after an infinite regression we would find at the very origin of the species.

The logic of the supplement (*Nachtrag*), then, is always active. It coincides with the very possibility that there is such a thing as psychic life. It describes how a system of signs is set up and then how we give meaning to experience. No subject is possible outside the two-way logic of transference (also including *avant-coup*) which *Nachträglichkeit* establishes. The original structure is never (and can never be) enclosed within itself. *Nachträglichkeit* sees the very dialectic of Being and the dynamic and structural organization of the unconscious as a weave of differences.[18] On a practical level the relaunching or delay to which *Nachträglichkeit* constrains the understanding of things takes into account the fact that no one is immediately transparent to himself and that there are endless interpretations of the same event. Deeply influenced by Freud, Derrida's thought offers an appropriate philosophical framework for the theories of Bion and post-Freudism in general, acting as a bridge between the two. Basically one could say that, by adopting the methodological principle of hyperbolic Cartesian doubt, Bion completes the Freudian deconstruction of the ego or the subject, ridding psychoanalysis of the last remnants of the positivist dream. In this respect Bion's theory – a non-theory if we think of the lack of systematicity that characterizes it and the fact that each reader has to invent his own Bion – is in some ways close to that of Lacan, who takes inspiration from De Saussure's linguistics and the teachings of Lévi-Strauss.

This is because Lacan's theory of the unconscious, just like Bion's, is an intersubjective conception of the birth of the psyche. The subject is founded on primal alienation, on the model of paranoia. What is lacking in Lacan, however, is an adequate theory (and, consequently, technique) that would explain how this dimension is articulated in clinical practice; for example, what role the analyst's subjectivity (his unconscious life) plays. The Lacanian analyst is always *maître* of the situation, even, paradoxically, when he might wish to turn down the role of idealized repository of knowledge the patient assigns to him. For this reason, Derrida is very effective when he criticizes Lacan's concept of the primacy of the signifier[19] and when, in his comments during his seminar on Poe's *The Purloined Letter*, he also rebukes him for suggesting that he can grasp the 'letter' of the unconscious and arrive at a definitive truth about things. Bion, on the other hand, revolutionizes the classical theory of the unconscious by following the principle widely applied in his theoretical activity of 'transcending the caesura' (Civitarese, 2008b). Variously, as the case requires, he sheds light on one of the binary pairs of concepts that structure the traditional knowledge of psychoanalysis and gives it back its dialectical nature; by thus setting up a tension, he also puts the concept to work. The slash that separates the two terms can be conceptualized as a caesura that has the dual function of separating and uniting.

Among the oppositions that Bion renders *unstable*, transforming them from static into dynamic splits, although initially he may give the impression of simply turning them inside out, one can list: past/present (only the present is knowable), patient/analyst (where does the one end and the other begin?), outside/inside of the setting (what matters is what happens in the session), knowing/not-knowing (what one truly knows springs from doubt), memory/oblivion (negative capability or the absence of memory and desire is the premise of the Language of Achievement), body/psyche, foetal/post-foetal life, intuition/concept, psychotic/non-psychotic part of the personality, dream/waking (the very idea of waking dream thought brings unconscious experience close to conscious experience), emotion/thought, etc.

But the opposition that sums up all the others is the unconscious/conscious caesura. Rendering this caesura dynamic was what led him to formulate the concept of the unconscious as a psychoanalytic function of the personality. I use the ploy here of referring to this function as 'un/conscious', i.e. with the slash,[20] precisely to emphasize that the rigid separation between *Unc* and *C* breaks down, and that there is continuity between these psychic processes.

Let me first point out that in the 1923 revision of his metapsychology things started to change even for Freud himself. The systems of the *C* and the *Unc* were transformed into the equivalents of the ego and the id. The distances between the two in one sense become shorter, in another longer. To understand why, one need only look at the diagrams of the unconscious shown below.

In a series of figures in the seventh chapter of *The Interpretation of Dreams* (Freud, 1900) Freud draws a map of the psychic apparatus in three moves: a first figure (p. 537) shows a system in which the movement is from perception (P) to motion (M); a second (p. 538) introduces memory (Tmn, Tmn' and Tmn" indicate 'memory traces'); and finally, in a third (p. 541), conscious, preconscious and unconscious are separated out.

Let's consider now the diagram from the first topography by J. and A. Sandler (1983, p. 415). As can be seen, here the distinction between *Unc* and *Prec-C* is much more pronounced than in the last figure from *The Interpretation of Dreams* at p. 541. Now the three systems look like hermetically sealed compartments.

The second topography (see the figure in *The Ego and the Id*, Freud, 1923, p. 24) introduces further changes: now the ego falls seamlessly into the id and on the deepest levels they merge.

Instead of the continuous lines that separate the three systems we find a double dotted line with the ego behind it. The ego is nothing more than a surface offshoot of the id. This is precisely where Freud uses the famous image of the ego-rider who must go along with the impulses of the id-horse so as not to be thrown off.

Freud goes on to affirm the essential continuity between *Unc* and *C* in various other ways. Not only does the preconscious make its contribution to intellectual work of the most 'subtle and difficult' kind but also high morality is fostered in the id – because, as far as its greater influence on the individual is concerned, the moral conscience is unconscious.

Again, it is Freud who sets up the dialectical opposition between pleasure principle and reality principle when in the second topography he sees both sexual object drives (uninhibited and half-inhibited or sublimated) and the self-preservation of the ego in terms of Eros.

However, simultaneously, in the same section Freud detaches the ego from the id because he makes a sharp distinction between reason and the 'worst passions'. Moreover, while the unconscious of the first topography – by definition, I repeat, the locus of the repressed – is inextricably linked to culture and its norms, the id – the battlefield of the life and death instincts – in its most intimate essence appears much more blind, primitive and mysterious. It is as if Freud wanted to shift forwards the threshold of the psychic so as to encompass the drives that in the first topography could never cross that threshold, but only where their delegates could enter (see below).

In/C = Ψ (ξ) (M) or the equation of Un/conscious

Having discussed some of the principles of the Freudian models of the unconscious, let us now turn to look in more detail at Bion's models. First of all, a premise: Bion is not interested in personality as composed of structures, for example, those described by Freud in the second topography, but 'as a series of functions, of variables in relationship to other variables' (Symington and Symington, 1996, p. 97). He tries in this way to develop a meta-psychoanalytic theory of personality. In other words, he attempts to replicate Propp's brilliant idea (1928) of looking at the 'fixed' functions of the fairy tale and not the infinite individual characters that appear in them; this was the move that founded narratology. Leaving aside the structures in order to examine the functions (one might say, the relationships) greatly simplifies the field of study, because the structures can take countless forms, while the functions they have to explicate are limited in number. For example, we can have a thousand psychoanalytic theories, but all must explain the transition from feeling to thinking.

On this view, personality is made up of a set of stable 'functions', and these in turn are composed of a number of factors that operate in harmony.[21] Individual factors can be expressed by functions on a lower hierarchical level.

Bion chose the letter Ψ (psi: the first letter of *psyche*, but also the letter that he uses in the Grid for column 2, the column of lies – *pseudos* – or of dreams) to indicate the overall function of the personality, and ξ (ksi) to refer to the variable (or the unknown). Both Ψ and ξ also depend on the individual's inborn traits (M). The point is that, depending on the value that the variable takes in each individual case, the function determines the final result of the operation.

For example, Ψ (ξ) could be the function that corresponds to the preconception of the breast. Only when Ψ takes on the value of the actual experience of contact with the breast ('realization') is the function truly satisfied (Bion, 1962, p. 126ff.). It is then considered either positive or negative depending on whether the personality is growing or in crisis ($\pm$ Y). Hence the following summarizing formula: '($\pm$ Y) Ψ (ξ) (M)' (Fornaro, 1990, p. 141).[22] A personality grows or regresses, depending on how its inborn traits (biological inheritance, M) interact with experiential realizations (Ψ).

The equation of the unconscious as a psychoanalytic function of the personality would be: Un/C = Ψ (ξ) (M); where Ψ is the *preconception-functor.* Ambiguously, therefore, it is both the constant or formal scheme that operates the transformation and the potentiality that can be made actual only by an appropriate emotional experience (in each case a mental state of expectation ready to receive only a narrow range of phenomena). And ξ is the unknown that each time is saturated by a concrete experience.

Compared to the equation of the upper hierarchical level of the personality as a whole, that of the unconscious is a function of a function, namely the function on which the functor Ψ depends. Other examples are the alpha function and all categories on the horizontal axis of the Grid (psi, notation, investigation, etc.).[23]

The unconscious as a function of personality expresses the deepest psychological capacity that human beings possess for making sense of experience: the ability to compose the 'poetry' of reality, that is, to see it from different angles, as something rich and positively ambiguous. Dreaming, one of the forms of the alpha function, is its central component (the 'factor', thus the function of the function).[24]

The unconscious is a *psychoanalytic* function, because it was discovered/invented by psychoanalysis. It could be written as un/conscious, that is both conscious (in waking and dream) and unconscious, because consciousness is continuous with the unconscious, just as the tip of the iceberg is continuous with the submerged part. The way in which we make sense of experience comes from the dialectical function of what we call conscious experience and unconscious experience. This function is effective when it is able to produce two different but integrated perspectives on things – binocular vision. This means that every thing, every psychic event, every psychoanalytic object can be seen/is seen simultaneously both from the conscious and from the unconscious point of view. As a matter of fact, the two perspectives are not even contradictory, which is how they are often understood because they are not homologous as to level. In anatomy, for example, the level of histological observation does not *contradict* the anatomical or molecular level.

When in *Transformations*, Bion (1965) renames unconscious and conscious, as infinite and finite, respectively, all he is doing is retracing the path that by the constant subtraction of primitive emotionality leads from the infinite-as-O, or as-real of the chaotic perceptions of the newborn child, to the concept and thus the possibility of communicating and being aware. Thinking means passing from the infinite to the finite, for example, from all existing trees to the idea of tree, and being able to learn from experience by means of concepts.

If the un/conscious is a function, it should have a corresponding verb: 'to unconscious' (*inconsciare* or *inconscientizzare* in Italian). Thus we would use un/conscious to talk about the undivided set of processes that lead from the beta elements to the concept. Unlike Freud, Bion, who of course also took on board the Kleinian view of the unconscious based on the concepts of unconscious phantasy and projective identification, concepts that already potentially contain an intersubjective theory of the psyche, postulated an essential *continuity* between conscious and unconscious experience. He saw them as two dimensions of the psyche separated by a contact barrier, a semi-permeable film which allows a fluid osmotic exchange, a continuous mutual 'visual accommodation', and which is made up of alpha elements, that is, of memory traces of experiences with meaning. *Inc* and *C* are joined by a bond of antagonistic solidarity, by a secret cooperative agreement, the intuition of a common destiny marked by the stimuli of internal and external reality. They are no longer separated from the double censorship of unconscious-preconscious and preconscious-conscious but only by a caesura, that is to say, by a boundary understood as an area of functional articulation and not as an impenetrable frontier.

This can be regarded as Bion's answer to Kant's transcendental subject. Dreaming, as we have said, is the central component of the psychoanalytic function of the personality. Dreaming not only serves to preserve sleep. Dreaming is not only the most reliable Baedeker to the unconscious; it is not born out of the existential differential between conscious and unconscious. Rather it creates it itself; indeed, if for Freud the unconscious creates the dream, we can say that for Bion the dream creates the unconscious.

Accordingly, Bion argues that the psychotic is unable to dream and hence to differentiate between conscious and unconscious. At the origin of his diseased condition are in fact more or less serious deficiencies in the α function due to distortions in early interrelational experiences. In order to dream while awake (to daydream), a whole range of information which after being perceived would otherwise clutter the mind and prevent it from thinking must be constantly made unconscious ('inconsciate' in Italian). In actual fact, however, the process is simultaneous, although it depends on different neuroanatomical systems.

A clear illustration of how this function performs is to be found in two fragments from *Cogitations*. In the first Bion describes how the alpha function makes learning and psychological growth possible:

> A child learning to walk is engaged in attempting to make conscious material unconscious; only when this is done will it be able to walk. The same is true of any piece of learning ever done – its success depends on the central operations by which dream-work-α is able to transform conscious material into unconscious material suitable for unconscious waking thinking.
>
> (Bion, 1992, p. 71)

In the second fragment Bion imagines he is conversing with a friend about holidays and examines in detail the thought processes that produce the essential continuity between conscious and unconscious experience – which is what happens when one is capable of dreaming.

> [S]uppose I am talking to a friend who asks me where I propose to spend my holiday; as he does so, I visualize the church of a small town not far from the village in which I propose to stay. The small town is important because it possesses the railway station nearest to my village. Before he has finished speaking, a new image has formed, and so on.
>
> The image of the church has been established on a previous occasion – I cannot now tell when. Its evocation in the situation I am describing would surprise no one, but what I now wish to add may be more controversial. I suggest that the experience of this particular conversation with my friend, and this particular moment of the conversation – not simply his words but the totality of that moment of experience – is being perceived sensorially by me and converted into an image of that particular village church.
>
> I do not know what else may be going on, though *I am sure that much more takes place than I am aware of.* But the transformation of my sense impressions into this image is part of *a process of mental assimilation.* The impressions of the event are being re-shaped as a visual image of that particular church, and so are being made into a form suitable for storage in my mind.
>
> By contrast, the patient might have the same experience, the same sense impressions, and yet be unable to transform the experience so that he can store it mentally. But instead, *the experience (and his sense impressions of it), remains a foreign body; it is felt as a 'thing' lacking any of the quality we usually attribute to thought or its verbal expression.*
>
> To the first of these products, that of dream work-α, I propose to give the name, 'α-element'; to the second, the assimilated sense impression, β-element.
>
> (Bion, 1992, pp. 180–181, italics added)

The best examples of what happens when a person loses the ability to filter out sensory stimuli or consign them to oblivion can be found in literature. Robert Schneider (*Brother of Sleep*, 1992), Patrick Süskind (*Perfume: The Story of a Murderer*, 1985), Svevo (*Zeno's Conscience*, 1923) and Jorge Louis Borges ('Funes the Memorious', in *Fictions*, 1944) have created memorable characters, all unable to dream. One cannot live because he is forced to hear every single sound; the second because he cannot avoid smelling all smells; another, because when he walks he is forced to think obsessively about coordinating the functioning of his muscles, which makes him limp; and the last, because he cannot forget any of his perceptions. In all of them thinking is clogged up by an excess of stimuli that they fail to process and make unconscious. Significantly, some of these fictional characters had suffered from severe trauma in their past.

It is evident that according to Bion the unconscious is not limited to Freud's dynamic or repressed unconscious, but is much wider and also embraces an unrepressed unconscious.[25] But as in the fictional examples cited, not even an individual's purely cognitive functioning (implicit, procedural) could ever be isolated from the social, emotional and repressed unconscious. So how does the unconscious develop? How can we explain the paradox of an alpha function (dreaming) that is supposed to establish the unconscious (after all, the contact barrier may be a synonym) which lies at the very origin of its own activity?

The mother as the child's unconscious

For Bion, the unconscious is formed from the α function, the function that produces α elements – 'material suitable for dream thoughts (Freud's unconscious waking thoughts) or for a correlation with common sense' (Bion, 1992, p. 233), 'something between "visual image" and "thing-in-itself"' (ibid., p. 325) – starting from β elements. This means that each micro-experience of meaning enclosed in an alpha element participates in forming the contact barrier and in so doing broadens the unconscious; in other words, it enhances the individual's ability to do psychological work on stimuli that come from inside and outside the body. Forming the contact barrier is like learning to speak a foreign language word by word, sentence by sentence. Eventually one speaks automatically and without conscious effort, and one comes, as it were, to dream in the new language.

Constantly under construction, the contact barrier is the *semi-permeable* membrane that separates the conscious and unconscious and regulates the functioning of the apparatus for dreaming and thinking. To stay awake and be aware, a series of stimuli must first have been conscious (one might say 'conscioused') and, subject to the work of the α function, have become unconscious ('unconscioused'). In fact, the subject needs to make sense of the environment in which it finds itself *in real time*. Memory, which concerns the past or the future, is always and only a future or a '*remembered present*' (Edelman, 1989).

To put it another way, thought is the 'necessary dream' of O, the real. The neologism invented by Bion to translate *unbewusst* thus expresses the work which the α function performs when it transforms sense impressions into ideograms[26] that can be stored in memory, thus making possible the development of the ability to learn from experience and ultimately to distinguish the conscious from the unconscious. One can now perhaps better understand why the term 'unconscioused' (*unbewusst*) expresses the *active* work of constructing the unconscious that the infant must perform at birth in order to become a subject.

How then does the infant create an unconscious if it does not have a working alpha function? At birth all it has is a rudimentary alpha function (Grotstein, 2007) that needs to grow in order to establish a psychoanalytic function of the personality; in other words, the ability to learn, assimilate, digest the impersonal, formless, infinite real, the noumenon, '"O"[27] . . . the name of that which has no sound, smell or texture . . . that which *is* there – before sensibility comes along to tell us *what it is*' (Vitale, 2004, p. 73).

Bion says that before becoming unconscious stimuli must have been conscious. But since in reality most stimuli pass directly into the unconscious state, and because the conscious is the *effect* of this process and could not be its cause, perhaps it would be better to say that they must be perceived, thus leaving open the question of the type of 'consciousness' involved. In fact, Bion, speaking of consciousness in *Cogitations* (1992), distinguishes between *perceiving* and *understanding* and between consciousness and becoming conscious. These distinctions help us resolve this point of the theory of the α function:

> If the patient cannot have a conscious because of lack of α function, how comes he to have sufficient of one to perceive his emotions, to act as a sense organ for the perception of psychical qualities? He *can* have a conscious; he merely cannot *become* conscious.
>
> (Bion, 1992, p. 223)

The infant finds itself in the same state: it *has* a conscious but cannot *become* conscious (ibid.). It can receive sense impressions but has no self-awareness. It does not yet have a working alpha function, at best only a very primitive one. Bion explains what kind of 'consciousness' this is very clearly in *A Theory of Thinking*. It is the 'mechanical' consciousness present at birth, in other words the infant's ability to perceive external and internal stimuli but *in the absence of self-reflexivity*; it perceives without understanding.

The 'fully conscious' state of the infant is therefore very different from consciousness in the sense of self-awareness. Self-awareness begins to take shape only after the α function has formed ideograms represented by the α elements, which align to form the contact barrier and thus the system of the un/conscious. At the birth of the psyche, we can therefore, with regard to 'rudimentary consciousness' (Bion, 1967, p. 117), only speak about a consciousness understood in the narrow sense, a consciousness that only knows how to provide sensory data and raw emotions.

This consciousness, Bion writes, 'is not associated with an unconscious. All impressions of the self are of equal value; all are conscious. The mother's capacity for reverie is the receptor organ for the infant's harvest of self-sensation gained by its conscious' (ibid., p. 116). This is a wonderful image: the mother as the child's unconscious and thus a complement to the psychoanalytic function of the personality still in its nascent state!

This helps us resolve the problem, mentioned at the end of the preceding section, of explaining how an infant can form an unconscious without having the alpha function necessary to produce precisely that unconscious. Bion tells us that the child gradually constructs its alpha function by internalizing that of the mother. The role he assigns to the mother appears very different from the role Freud gives to the mother of removing harmful stimuli and providing food and warmth. So at birth the alpha function is just a set of expectations ('preconceptions') waiting to meet concrete experiences ('realizations'). For it to develop it has to be absorbed from the mother in a kind of magical osmosis. For the infant the mother's alpha function is expressed primarily as a sensory reverie, as an auditory-tactile casing/mirror and rhythmicity.[28] Just as in analysis the unconscious 'is contacted and known along a multidimensional, somatic path before it can be described' (Cogliani, 2004, p. 160), it is clear that these sense components[29] (although not yet meaning components, since the latter is more related to the aspect of language or evolved symbols) will never cease to exist.

At this point it also becomes clear what it may mean to *have* a conscious but not be able to *become* conscious. *Becoming* conscious is only possible if in the meantime the unconscious has formed and thus the ability to be self-aware. In clinical practice these distinctions chime in with Bion's (1970) distinctions between 'feeling' and 'suffering' pain (or pleasure). Among other things, with this theory Bion not only confirmed the total identification Freud had already postulated between language, consciousness and (negatively speaking) the unconscious, *but he also shed light on the relationship that exists between language and the unrepressed unconscious*; both that of the child who has not yet had access to language and who is not yet a subject, and that of the adult.

Strictly speaking, for Bion the distinction between repressed and non-repressed unconscious does not make sense until the child becomes a subject, that is, until he is able to say 'I'. However, this means that all the child's experiences, whether representational or not, will be influenced by the repressed unconscious . . . of the mother! For the child that has become a subject or for the adult the distinction merely describes the different ways of experiencing reality and storing it in their various memory systems. However, it cannot imply that the so-called cognitive unconscious – knowing how to do something without being able to say *how* one does it – has not been influenced by repression, and is not produced within sociality and its set of rules. What is more, *it does not even imply that it is not potentially located within a dynamic and conflictual horizon.* In other words, *no type of unconscious, whether cognitive, emotional or dynamic, is completely isolated from symbolic determinations, from language, from culture and social norms – in short, it cannot remain untouched by the shadow of the repressed.* It would be like saying that pure perceptions may also exist that are completely devoid of an affective substrate, however weak.

If the alpha function is not an innate structure of the brain, but a socially acquired 'linguistic' ability, the product of the encounter between the very rudimentary awareness of the child (again a Ψ) and the reverie of the mother (ξ), this means that for humans what is involved is always a social unconscious – the specific subject matter of psychoanalysis – and never a purely biological or cognitive 'natural' unconscious.

Un/conscious

Ogden takes Bion's dream thought equation and gives it, if possible, even greater centrality. He sees dreaming as 'our profoundest form of thinking [which] constitutes the principal medium through which we achieve human consciousness, psychological growth and the capacity to create personal, symbolic meaning from our lived experience' (Ogden, 2009, p. 104). In essence, this definition of the activity of dreaming is a way of emphasizing the constructive-po(i)etic and aesthetic potential of the unconscious. It is also a way of making the most of Freud's discovery of dream work (*Traumarbeit*), although under a different sign, and at the same time of capitalizing on Bion's reversal of perspective on dreaming.

Dreaming, I repeat, is one of the forms of the alpha function, additional to the primary function of transforming the sense data related to emotional experience into alpha elements. When these are connected to each other, they produce night-time dream thoughts and waking thoughts or waking dream thoughts, both of which are conscious. The transformation occurs when emotions are 'contained', that is to say, 'symbolized'. The metaphor of the container has the advantage of illustrating Bion's conception of psychic conflict on a more abstract level than Freud's: at every moment, as Ogden writes (2009, p. 151), 'the muscular interplay of thoughts and the capacity to think one's thoughts' is in action.

From this vertex the unconscious is not 'behind' or 'beneath' but *inside* the conscious. It is not only close to it (and/or hidden), but *part of it*. The unconscious is not a place but a psychic container-as-process and stands in a dialectical relationship with the contents (which are also processes)[30] as part of an ever-changing figure-ground relationship of reversible perspectives. Conscious and unconscious appear as dimensions of the same awareness. They are, therefore, not two separated provinces but are *the same surface* which, as in a Möbius strip, turns continuously along internal-external, high-low axes. When one observes small isolated portions, it looks like a sheet of paper. These qualities, however, apply only 'locally' because if you look at the figure in its entirety, they appear to be the result of mutual relations. If you follow it by activating a process that highlights its functions, the antithesis is cancelled and you go from one side to the (apparent) opposite side without any interruption. A pencil – attention, perhaps? – might be able to draw a continuous line over its entire surface without ever having to be lifted from the sheet. This means, among other things, that trying out the properties of a Möbius strip, that is, the un/conscious processes, implies temporality.

To repeat, this is the reason I sometimes use the contrivance of writing un/conscious with a slash: namely, in order to indicate two aspects of the same system or even to point out that the unconscious experience is *contained* in the conscious. The unconscious is a symbolic structure (actually it extends along a gradient that goes from the semiotic to the symbolic in the full sense of the word) because it originates in the primary relationship with the object, and it must differentiate itself more in order to bring about the psychoanalytic function of the personality; namely, the specifically human capacity to perceive reality (in fact, to construct reality) according to a double register: un/conscious, that is, both conscious and unconscious, symmetric and asymmetric. It is only this integrated operation that makes it possible to see reality according to a multiplicity of emotionally significant points of view, either simultaneously or over time; and at that point what we call maturity or mental health is achieved.

Writing un/conscious instead of unconscious/conscious is a way of indicating that each term is contained within the other. It emphasizes even more how illusory the idea of uncontaminated consciousness is, but it also stresses the idea of the unconscious as a region completely isolated from the psyche. The fullness of the one continuously spills over into the emptiness of the other and this unceasing movement of mutual inclusion is itself a precondition for their manifestation. The unconscious is not only that which disorganizes the conscious with its special effects, but is in fact that which constitutes its fabric.

In the word 'un/conscious', then, the slash has a twofold reference: it refers to a key aspect of the method used by Bion as a theorist of psychoanalysis and to the fact that since the concept of psychic place ambiguously persists side by side with the more complex and dialectical vision of the structural model (at least compared to the topographical model), the closed and guarded frontier that separates the conscious from the unconscious in Freud's theory becomes permeable and now also performs the function not only of separating but also of uniting.

The slash also symbolizes the contact barrier. What makes it possible to distinguish conscious from unconscious aspects of the same awareness is a semi-permeable, dynamic membrane, continually subject to the processes of analysis and synthesis. As we have seen, this membrane is formed by the activity of the alpha function – the conventional term for the set of currently unknown psychic operations which make the passage from the senses to the mind – and prevents consciousness from being invaded by too many unconscious contents, while also allowing it to be enriched by some of them and thus enabling it to fully perform its function. In essence, the contact barrier is a spatial metaphor (in concrete terms, it is not a membrane, although it performs the functions of one) that indicates the distance thought interposes between words and things. Thus it represents the symbolic matrix that the child gradually acquires in its primary relationship, starting from the experience of its emotions being adequately contained.

With Bion, therefore, the unconscious stops being a reservation for a population of 'aboriginals' (*Urbevölkerung*, Le Guen, 2008, p. 684) or a Guantanamo of the mind. It is no longer (only) disorder that irrupts into the civilized world of rational discourse as a symptom, producing its classic effects, either through incompletion (slips of the tongue, parapraxes, dreams) or excess (actings out, the misunderstandings dictated by transference, or also the 'deviations' from drive goals that occur through sublimation, and so on). It becomes, indeed, a 'psychoanalytic function of the personality', a symbolizing device that is based on traits that are innate but must also be learned (Ogden, 2009).

The unconscious does not stand in direct opposition to the conscious. It does not *interfere*, but it is in continuity with it. It is always the other side of the coin of the discourse. Not only does it talk, it talks constantly. The processes that govern the operation of the *Unc* and *C* are the same; they are in fact the *same* process. It varies in degree, but not nature. From the formation of the α pictogram to algebra, it is always a question of abstraction, rationalization, integration, narration.[31] Continuity also lies in the fact that words are hybrids, chimeras. They are also 'things' and therefore subject to the laws of general semiosis. Intersubjective agreement is what elevates them to the second level of symbols.

Bion thus dissolves the antinomy between primary process and secondary process. Neuro-scientific evidence appears to bear him out. Westen (1999), for example, holds that consciousness is only the tip of the iceberg of the unconscious. It is an integral part. It follows that the distinction between primary process and secondary process needs to be revised.[32] I agree with Westen that it is preferable to refer to unconscious *processes* and to go beyond the romantic and ultimately derogatory view of the unconscious that Freud held especially in the first topography (in the second he already conceived of it more as a function). Unconscious processes, seen as a continuum that goes from night-time dreams to algebraic calculation, represent the mode selected by evolution whereby the subject differentiates from the real in which it is immersed and digests the elements it needs to feed itself. The unconscious is not the place of absolute irrationality, but an early form of rationality. It is how the mind categorizes, forgets differences and keeps the models ('dreams') of the relationships between things. This explains how we can look at the famous series of paintings by Monet – which are all different but all on the same subject – and recognize in them the profile and shape of the cathedral of Rouen, and then also in those by other painters.

For the subject, staying in touch with the real – investigating the emotional truth of one's existence, being *curious* or indulging the urge for knowledge – is like procuring food or oxygen. But what precisely do the unconscious processes that allow us to stay in touch with reality entail? In essence it is a question of the basic psychological mechanisms that Freud discovered in operation in the dream work (condensation, displacement, representability and secondary processing) and that Lacan reformulated in terms of rhetoric as metonymy and metaphor. These are mechanisms that simplify reality, order it and make it coherent. How do they achieve this? In practice by (actively) cancelling out differences and keeping the invariants understood as relations between objects, or rather, between thing and no-thing. Invariants are our symbols, that *something* that lies between our perception of the object and our realization of its absence. Bion's theory shows us this intense activity of the psyche at a level which is at the same time both more primitive and more abstract.

Our ordinary sense of reality has its place along the continuous line of the processes of categorization or abstraction that oscillate between Row A and Row H of Bion's Grid; in other words, from maximum indifferentiatation to maximum possible abstraction. It soon becomes clear that if the 'sieve' (Freud, 1895, p. 313) of the mind keeps back too many elements of the real the subject 'de-differentiates'; if too few, as in transformations in hallucinosis, it loses touch with reality. The common sense of reality is the cost-effective point of balance between *narcissism* and *socialism* (in Bion's sense of the polarization of the individual with respect to the group as opposed to oneself), between the dispersion of a state of mind where sensoriality dominates and the aridity of science (by definition devoid of emotions because they are cognitively too complex and therefore meaningless vis-à-vis the type of manipulation science seeks).

So unconscious processes are the same as the dream (by which I mean the whole gradient of the oneiric, including dream flashes, reveries, hallucinations, etc.), as metaphor, and ultimately even as the most abstract operations of the mind. To add one table to another I must abstract from the differences I may find in nature. After all, even a mathematical operation corresponds to making a metaphorical connection between one term and another. Relying on the objectivist and 3D vision that our senses provide us of reality is simply what is most convenient, *a useful illusion*. It is the price we pay for the invaluable benefits that come from the ability to categorize, to construct concepts of things. Dreaming does indeed serve to preserve sleep, but one can say that it serves primarily to preserve waking sleep (and the sleep of reality; Civitarese, 2013b). In the end, did not Bion repeatedly make the point that the fundamental ability possessed by the human mind for the purpose of self-preservation is self-deception?

A new paradigm

For Lacan (1966), the real scandal that Freud provoked is not so much his theory of the etiology of sexual neurosis as the fundamental alienation of the subject – the axiom of the ego's extraneousness to its own home. Even in its later developments, Bion's model accentuates this aspect and completes Freud's Copernican revolution by turning the Cartesian subject upside down. And in fact not even the unconscious can be regarded as a master in its own house, for, as we said, it is born out of intersubjectivity; it comes from a field that amply transcends the individual and that to a certain extent continues to produce its effects throughout a person's life.[33] In my view, it is difficult to grasp the import of this change in perspective unless we bear in mind what happened, for example, in philosophy with Heidegger's existential analysis, and later with Merleau-Ponty's concept of 'flesh'. Both are harsh and persuasive critics of the Cartesian idea of the subject and of consciousness seen in isolation.

In Bion, the echo of this new momentous turning point resonates in his concept of the proto-mental system,[34] something that, like the drives, stands between the body and the psyche, and that is part of a broader proto-mental group matrix. However, there is a narcissistic resistance to accepting the idea of the social nature of the unconscious and its pervasiveness in conscious life – its effectiveness in the session and the radically anti-realist perspective that this effectiveness forces us to take towards the facts of the analysis – as there was a resistance to accepting the idea of an unconscious psychism. The subversive aspect of the unconscious becomes its continuity with the conscious, that is, the systematic way it intervenes in our consciousness and in our lives and the 'continuity' between the individual's proto-mental system and that of the group.

For Freud, too, the unconscious presses on the conscious but it is not 'close' in the way it is for Bion. The conscious does not only see the temporary irruptions of what comes out of the unconscious but is also *always* an expression of unconscious thought; not only, of course, in the depths of the psyche, *but also on the surface.*[35]

At the root of the Bionian revolution stands the notion of the essentially social nature of the subject. For Bion it makes no sense to separate the subject from the broader network in which it is constituted dialectically within a symbolic order that exists from birth – unless by employing a fiction.[36]

This means that as a concept the unconscious has nothing to do with the automatic mechanisms such as the stimulus-response of instinct but only with what has entered the interpersonal order of the symbolic. The human unconscious is by definition formed only by the mother's alpha function also with regard to the 'procedural' part or the so-called cognitive unconscious.

It is essential to understand how the psychic growth of the patient can be helped in the dual situation of analysis (a group of two individuals, or perhaps we should we say three if we include the reference to a third, paternal, entity – the Law). It is no accident that Bion uses the concept of the unconscious as a noun relatively infrequently (no more than a hundred times in five books), because for him this term refers primarily to a set of transformation processes.

It is human co-feeling that generates language and thus the un/conscious. It is not a substance but a process of categorization, abstraction, simplification, falsification;[37] it is a never-ending game of identity and difference, transference-metaphorization. Moreover, this meaning is present in the Freudian definition of the unconscious as the *other scene* (Palmier, 1972) and in the metaphor of the theatrical device (which, as a device, involves a process of subjectivation; Agamben, 2006). 'Unconsciousing' ('In/consciare') is a way of faking the real; seeing-as,[38] that is, through form. For this reason, as a place the unconscious is at most empty, because it is psychic work that is carried out on memory traces, or rather, the set of laws that govern their relationship. At the highest possible level of resolution un/conscious activity coincides with the essential psychological mechanism of metonymy, primary translation or exchange through contact or imprint.

When a paradigm shift occurs in the world of science, new questions are posed. Shared norms, beliefs, assumptions, methods and problems mutate in non-linear fashion. More than refining previous perspectives, new ones are adopted. New metaphors inform scientific research and play the same role as DNA mutations in biological evolution. For this reason we speak of incommensurability between paradigms.[39] Perhaps for the same reason Bion does not repudiate many of Freud's concepts. He does not mention them, or hardly ever, except when he ambiguously takes them for granted, in a way that ultimately removes them tacitly from the stage, and we instead find ourselves speaking a completely different language. Although preserved in theory, they shatter into a kaleidoscope of new concepts that demand from the analyst the exercise of doubt and the constant adoption of new points of view, as well as a wariness towards any scholastic dogmatism. It also leaves us a bit confused and unsettled.

As we have seen, Bion uses the word 'unconscious' very infrequently and hardly ever uses the word 'drive' (Fornaro, 1990, p. 26), even less so in the sense of death drive. He openly dismisses the distinction between primary and secondary process (Bion, 1962, p. 101), he plays dialectically with the distinction between the reality principle and the pleasure principle, makes sexuality less central, calls into question the dichotomy between affection and representation, empties Freud's energy model and gives it a different set of dynamics – and strictly speaking he also breaks up the Kleinian concept of internal object (Fornaro, 1990, p. 116).

Thus, unlike the Freudian conception summarized in the extraordinary 'Schematic diagram of sexuality' (Freud, 1950 [1892–1899], p. 202), sexuality can continue to be seen on the one hand as one of the achievements of **Ψ**, but on the other, as discourse in the session, as the *metaphorical description* of the more or less creative coupling of the minds in the session (Ferro, 2002) or as a real-time account of the greater or lesser degree of emotional unison. This is because narrative derivatives of waking dream thought can be found in any discourse.

Ultimately, the unconscious coincides with the alpha function, and perhaps what Bion calls conscious with Freud's preconscious. To which is added the third state of mind, described as 'inaccessible', the unconscious that has never been conscious (Bion, 1997). The drives live in notions such as H, L, K bonds, proto-mental system, emotional experience, truth drive and beta element. In particular, the death drive could be the transgenerational and undigested accumulation of beta elements (Ferro, 2002), and so on.

For Bion, the essential characteristic of the human species is the fact of having a mind; to put it in Heidegger's terms, to be 'creators of the world'. Self-awareness transforms animal instincts into drives,[40] into something psychic that is part of the symbolic order. However, by acquiring reflective thought, by ceasing to be animals (in itself an obvious evolutionary advantage for human beings), we face the paradoxical problem of how to digest, metabolize, absorb, contain and think about the instinctual drives.

Not only instinctual drives, however, because the instincts are merely part of the broader context of the real – one might say, of sensoriality – that presses on the psyche and terrorizes it. The purpose of the analysis becomes how to help a mind that is struggling with this essential task to grow and (also) to 'think' of drives. As far as we can tell, the problem does not arise for animals. The unconscious is a product of language. The concept of drive would make no sense for animals – whereas instinct obviously would. Animals have an elementary cognitive unconscious that is not influenced by culture. From this point of view, Lacan was doubly right in saying that the unconscious is structured like a language, because this now famous formula of his encapsulates both the artificial nature of the symbolic system and its functioning based on the interplay between identity and differences, what Derrida (1967b) calls the 'archi-text'.

We dream, and it is good so

In developing his model of the unconscious, it is as if Bion were extending fully the Freudian concept, expressed in *Beyond the Pleasure Principle* (1920), of dreaming as a way of metabolizing childhood trauma. But here what is to be metabolized is the potential traumatic nature of the real. To our magical/anthropomorphic thinking, on the level of phantasy trauma always has something to do with the other, even when it involves natural events. Here Laplanche's theory of the unconscious in some respects links up again with Bion's. This traumaticity is registered by the seismograph of proto-sensations and proto-emotions (beta elements) that pound the subject in waves and sometimes threaten to sweep it away just like a river in flood. In this sense we can say that proto-emotions exert pressure on the subject to evolve when they become true emotions (when they are mentalized), that is to say, they take on meaning/thought (to be understood along a spectrum of possibilities that also includes semiotic meaning) and they feed the mind by bringing with them knowledge (of the mind but also of the body) and motivation (emotional truth). Psychic transformations are writings that capture what is invariable; they thirst for order, coherence, predictability. In the wonderful metaphor Freud uses in *On Aphasia*, they are the poems which put the letters of sensory impressions into neat order.

The truth of Monet's series of paintings depicting the same cathedral emerges only from transformation, from that which remains recognizable and meaningful in the subject across endless variations/differences. Ultimately, it springs from a system of relationships, from a model, not from the thing in itself. Thought is born in abstraction. As Bion writes (1962, pp. 59–60):

> From these sweet, bitter, sour objects sweetness, bitterness, sourness are abstracted. Once abstracted, they can be re-applied; the abstraction made can be used in situations where a realization, not the original realization from which it was abstracted, approximates to it.

Bion does not deny the role of the drives, but rather he sees them as secondary to the drive for knowledge and the attendant drive for truth[41] (naturally, both defined in his own idiosyncratic way), the drive namely to construct oneself as a mind/subject *in relation to* the other. This is the essential point. The only true motivational factor is the search for truth (the 'truth instinct or drive'; Grotstein, 2007). Inevitably it is an emotional and personal truth ('Who am I? What's going on in my life?' Or rather, 'Who are you? How do you see me?'), which stems, however, from emotional unison (whose primal form is *communication* (*Verständigung*) as described by Freud, 1895): an immediate way of recognizing the needs of others. However, it also becomes the basis for a consensual truth *and ultimately for the ability to forge an intimate settlement with reality*, with what exists, and the ability to function as a (now dialectalized) pair – pleasure principle/reality principle (Grotstein, 2007).

If Freud starts from drives, Bion starts from emotions; it must be borne in mind that for Bion it makes no sense to speak of emotion *in isolation from* a relationship and from the meaning it assumes within the relationship. Proto-emotional experience is equivalent to drive activation, somatic excitation that encounters the reverie of the object. Cure consists not in removing the veil of repression but in promoting transformations that lead to psychic growth. However, these are not achieved unless they are imbued with emotions. Container and contained develop if they are joined together or permeated with emotions; otherwise they become akin to inanimate objects. Emotions are the messengers that inform the individual about the otherwise desolately opaque truth of 'O'.

Clearly, the criterion of truth comes close to being an aesthetic criterion. It is neither purely emotional nor purely logical and rational, but contains elements of both (Grotstein, 2007: see also Chapter 6 below). So even if Bion takes the role of drives for granted, he is more interested in seeing how the mind is shaped and how people think, not what they think. If we conceptualize the development of the psyche starting from the drives it is easy to forget that another mind is needed to create a mind. In Hegelian terms, as summed up by Kojève: 'The human being can be formed only if at least two of these Desires confront one another' (1947, p. 7).

Freud focuses on the 'negative function' of the mother as the agent that removes the disturbing stimuli of reality, and this becomes the model of the dream as something that conceals meaning, and also the model of repression. Bion, on the other hand, emphasizes her positive function as the creator of a *bearable* reality or world for the child through her capacity for reverie. More importantly, this principle has a number of specific implications for recasting the hierarchy of therapeutic factors in the analysis and for the theory of technique. Bion sees neither the group nor the unconscious 'as primitive in the regressive and devaluing sense' (Fornaro, 1990, p. 203). If anything, the Freudian unconscious

> carries out . . . deformations (*Entstellungen*), such as those of the manifest content of the dream, whereas for Bion the dream itself is a gradual transformation, which gives initial form (alpha-elements) to afferents that are in themselves confusing (beta elements). If for Freud dreams can be regarded as thoughts expressed in another form, for Bion thoughts can be seen as dreams expressed in another form.
>
> (Fornaro, 1990, p. 210)

Freud's unconscious is repressed and sexual (but things already begin to change with the second topography where the unconscious no longer coincides entirely with the repressed; Opatow, 1997). Bion's unconscious is an unrepressed unconscious – unless one interprets it in the light of the mechanism of container-contained – and, in Lacan, it is social, non-substantive, a symbolic structure. At the risk of simplifying, one could say that for Freud, it is all a question of seeing what the individual makes of the sexual drive (impulse), how he manages to (re-)find the object and achieve enjoyment, etc.; for Bion the whole question is to see how to think of the emotions that register the impact on the psyche of drives as thoughts waiting to be thought, but – we must always bear in mind – also to think of them and manage them without necessarily transforming them into representations or emotions felt with the clarity of consciousness.

6

BENEATH, BEHIND OR INSIDE? THE UN/CONSCIOUS IN CLINICAL WORK

To illustrate the concept of un/conscious or the continuity between the conscious and unconscious, and the relationship of reciprocal inclusivity that binds them to each other, let us now turn to some vignettes. What I want to emphasize is how the points of view of the conscious and the unconscious, the subjective and inter-subjective, are bound to flow into each other constantly; and how the unconscious is on the surface of conscious experience, how it is inside it at more symbolic levels (if we think of waking dream thought) and at more semiotic levels (if we think of sensory or bodily reveries; 'in action'). As Ogden puts it, we must transform the therapist's unconscious emotional experience into a psychological problem he can talk about with the patient.

I know the traces of the ancient flame

F. describes coming out of a cinema and seeing a teenage sweetheart with whom she had had a very intense but platonic relationship. For a split second she only *believed* she recognized him, but then she realized it really was him. She started then to listen to her own body and she felt relieved that, as she says, 'fortunately I didn't feel anything, no tachycardia, no skipping a beat'. I remain silent, but after a few minutes I find myself going back in my own memory to a similar incident when I had seen an old girlfriend some years after we had been together, and had felt the truth of Dante's line (echoing Virgil): 'I know the traces of the ancient flame.' I was pleasantly surprised because I hadn't imagined I would still be able to feel anything like the palpitations I had felt as a teenager.

I then tell F. that I wonder what she was really afraid of, whether it was of *not* recognizing her old flame, which is actually what happened, and especially of not being recognized in turn, rather than the opposite. I suggest this in the light of my own reaction to a similar situation, but where the effect was the opposite. I urge her to consider whether the thought she used to reassure herself did not perhaps express the need to escape from the risk of trying to live a life that was more unpredictable and adventurous but at the same time also more vital and authentic. The extrasystoles that I had registered, but which F. had not felt, stand for a reverie or a concrete metaphor that allows me to contain an emotion that F. does not know how to name or accommodate, which, if recognized and accepted, would be a prelude, also for her, to the moment of suspension or emptiness before the delayed heart beat. What F. fears most of all is the precise critical moment following the anticipated skipping a beat, the moment of suspension when one peers into the eyes of the other to see whether one should expect love or rejection. Since the fear of being rejected dominates, F. prefers to cancel out the emotion that would testify to a living desire. By doing so, however, she goes without food for the mind, both in the cognitive and motivational sense. Each successful symbolization in fact adds a further building block to the edifice of the mind.

In F.'s discourse the event that *didn't* take place (or that *did*, but to which she closes the doors of consciousness when she denies it) stands here for a wave of β elements that F. feels unable to hold/transform (an overspill that she can only try to staunch), because it would expose her to the incompletely healed wound of non-recognition and the fear that it might happen again; but, at the same time, it stands for something she feels as a lack, a hurtful void, a debilitating deficiency of emotion, a mortifying flatness of life. Like any other symptom, then, repeated negation says and does not say. It resonates both as a 'no' to life and as the slogan of a silent rebellion. In its most primitive-sensory iteration, which my memory-reverie helps retrieve, it hypothetically calls into question the most corporeal and earliest levels of the generation of experience, those attributable to the inaccessible unconscious and even, perhaps, other ancient 'arrhythmias'.

If I took a more Freudian approach, I might regard this dialogue as the record of a meeting that informs me of an episode in F.'s emotional life which reflects her conflicts and her defences. I would pay attention to a series of negations and I would be slightly suspicious of this insistence (and the model used here would be the unconscious that enters consciousness). If necessary, I might point this out to her. Interpreting the unconscious meaning of her words, I would break through the narrative framework she proposes (how to exit from the cinema screen to demonstrate the 'unconscious' devices of projection) and so on. At most, by identifying with the character of F.'s ex-boyfriend, I would be asking if some transference distortion is at work in the way she perceives me.

From a Kleinian point of view, I could think of the characters of her story as actors which are internal objects engaged in performing the script of some unconscious fantasy. I could then show her how *her* inner theatre colours our relationship.

From a post-Bionian field vertex, which is primarily what I use in the way I conceptualize the unconscious processes of the mind, I listen to F. (and also look at myself) as if she were alphabetizing the stimuli, including those that reach her from the place in the field which are her memories, rekindled by what she is going through here and now with me; and as if she were trying now to find significant links between her memories and the feelings that affect her simultaneously. I assume then that the characters in F.'s story, now already transfigured in a dream – the dream of the session – are talking to me about emotional arousal in the present, in the here and now. I think that perhaps F. is afraid to experience the intimacy of the analysis and to get in touch with the emotions it arouses in her. I also ask myself whether I might have led her to prefer a certain reassuring indifference to a more free and passionate participation in the analysis. We are writing the basic story of the session or a chapter of the novel of analysis. It goes something like this: two lovers meet but do not seem to recognize each other. Perhaps out of fear of discovering they are still in love. But then they are moved. This is the core of the emotional experience at work in the two minds that meet each other. The elements upon which each draws are like the day's residues in dreams. From this point of view, they are secondary. On the unconscious level, asymmetry is the rule.

However, from yet another point of view, if on the unconscious level the character in the analytic dialogue is seen as radically constructed together, it becomes something that belongs to both, and it could also speak of a defence of the analyst or the pair, which, however, the analyst is then able to overcome by means of a memory-reverie. Ultimately what happens is that an emotion is experienced for which there was no place. The mind of both feeds on it and grows. On the other hand, if we admit that there might be a reversal of the flow of pathological projective identifications, that is, from analyst to patient, it means that there is no way to control the unconscious communication but, as usual, all one can do is try to grasp its derivatives.

Moving from the perspective of the isolated subject, passing along the way the notion of 'weakened' subjectivity, which involves me reading the unconscious 'dialogue' between two minds – the patient who 'responds' with a character to the quality of the analyst's intervention – here I place myself instead in the radically intersubjective perspective of the two-person group. The important thing is to grasp the unconscious fantasy of the group, the basic assumption that governs its functioning. In our daily work not only do we adopt several explicit and implicit models, we probably also oscillate rapidly from the paradigm of the isolated subject to that of the mind of the group, passing through all the intermediate stages.

In practice, from a Freudian perspective I wonder about the series of negations that litter her text, and I wonder what the opposition sensual/platonic love may refer to; an experience of splitting, a form of somato-psychic non-integration, frustration due to abstinence imposed by the requirements of the setting? I decide against an abstract intervention, however, such as confronting her with one of these aspects. The idea is that if something arises only in the mind of the analyst it is a falsehood. Even if it is true, it cannot be true if it is not bearable for the other.

Instead I wait for something new and surprising to come into being, what Bion implies when he says that we must allow the O of the session to evolve, or that the analyst must become O. What he means is simply being permeated by the daydreams of reverie. When this happens, though it can take a long time, I feel that we have been touched by *something true*, because it has emerged from dreaming memory, the material of which analysis[42] is made, and from the analytic field generated by both. The theoretical basis of this technique lies in the idea that the reverie is an expression of un/conscious psychological work that the analyst is able to carry out if he is not too shielded, that is, if he is sufficiently receptive to the patient's projective identifications, and which puts us in contact with the α elements and with the experienced emotional truth about the relationship at any given time. Of course, the analyst's greater skill as a 'storyteller' represents an element of asymmetry.

Finally, when I suggest my interpretation (or, as I would rather put it, my point of view), I keep to the narrative level that F. chose because I believe it would be unbearable if it were stated more explicitly and expressed in openly transferential terms (I keep account of all the 'no's' and 'nots'). In other words, I'm also talking to her unconscious – as if I were asking her if she were scared of having feelings towards me or afraid of being ashamed or mortified if she stopped controlling her emotions so rigidly and let herself go a bit more.

Obviously I am working within a theoretical model that stands on the shoulders of Freud and Klein and has been supplemented by the invaluable contributions of authors such as Ogden, Ferro, Grotstein, Bleger and the Barangers. At its core is the concept of the unconscious as a psychoanalytic function of the personality, a conscious/unconscious binocular vision of the real to be transformed into a coherent phenomenal reality, and the essential continuity of conscious and unconscious experience. It is not about deciphering the unconscious, which is what I would be doing if I interpreted the symptom of a series of negations as a symptomatic expression of the unconscious, but about transforming the conscious into the unconscious. It is about dreaming, 'ambiguating' (poetically) conscious experience in order to enrich it and to capitalize on this transformation as psychological growth. The symptom is not so much an epiphany of the unconscious but the failure of the unconscious work of symbolizing emotional experience. Thanks to the alpha function of the mind, a set of operations transform proto-sensoriality (raw feelings and emotions, β elements) into α elements, mostly images or pictograms used to store or to dream and think, pieces of narration that enable her to assign a personal meaning to experience. These images cannot be observed directly; they can only be inferred from the narrative derivatives of waking dream thought. The path of choice is reverie.

The emotions that are asking to be transformed come out of the emotional field that is created by our being together. The field, or the intersubjective analytic third, is formed by the encounter between mutual projective identifications, that is, by the communication from unconscious to unconscious already postulated by Freud and reiterated by Bion with his concept of proto-mental system. The analyst makes up his story starting from what he can understand of the unconscious communication taking place.

Also the interiority of the analyst is a place in the analytic field. What happens there is influenced by all the other places in the area, and it in turn influences them. Reverie is a measure of the analyst's readiness to receive projective identifications from the other, in this case from the analysand who, like the child with respect to the mother, is usually less able to process his emotional states. In this model the analysis is the place where the analyst must be prepared to dream the undreamt or interrupted dreams of the analysand (or the novels that were never written or were left in a drawer), which helps him to develop his ability to think/dream or to contain disturbing emotions through moments of recognition.

Of course this technique rests on a precise theory of the unconscious based on the twin pillars of waking dream thought (ultimately, an extreme version of the Freudian paradigm of the dream) and the fundamentally social nature of the subject (again, we are reminded of Freud making the point that individual psychology is social psychology from the very beginning). What helps the mind grow are the moments of emotional unison. Reverie is the compass that guides us towards emotional unison and that by establishing an inner reserve of positive mirroring experiences broadens the oscillation band between the different points of view that the patient is able to bear (Ferro, 2010).

Frozen food and adulterous/ated lovers

G. begins by talking about A., a friend who for some time now has been taking him to ethnic restaurants, recently mostly Middle Eastern. Then he found out why: A. has a restaurant guidebook called *Il Pappamondo* (World Food). But he's a bit suspicious. These Arabs, Chinese, Indians don't serve us the good things they eat in their own countries! The Arabs seem to him to be the smartest of them all. One of them told him that, bit by bit, he had bought the whole building that has his restaurant on the ground floor and that he is not afraid about his son's report card because all the teachers go there to eat. Then, there is the risk of globalization. Someone told him to be careful because he might like it. 'Well . . .' he adds, laughing:

– I prefer my beloved frozen food.
– . . . You mean . . . your frozen beloveds?
– . . . Anyway . . . better than adulterated food!

(Note: this play on words depends on the double use of '*amato*' as an adjective ('loved', 'beloved') and as a noun, each with the added choice of gender and number (*amato/amati/amata/amate*). As a noun referring to a person, it means 'love', 'lover', 'beloved'.)

Play, comedy and an intricate series of narrative levels are concentrated in this rapid-fire exchange of banter. G. tells me that he is self-sufficient, that he doesn't need a woman to prepare dinner for him. I venture a pun alluding to the emotional ties he experiences in such a coldly intellectual way, and to his ability to enter relationships which are maintained but put in the freezer, and possible girlfriends systematically discarded (or even latent or unconscious homosexuality), and he responds by saying that he prefers solitude to betrayal. The patient is also talking about how little he trusts the analysis and how he can only stand very low temperatures in relationships. In his distrust of his own unknown, foreign aspects, he is envious of the analyst whom he describes as greedy and scheming. But globalization (merging and lack of distinction) is an even greater danger he must watch out for. Talk of adulteresses refers of course to Oedipus and the phantasy of incest. What I am trying to highlight in this vignette, however, is the ability to play, the result of years of work, which emerges from the highly condensed remarks we exchange, and that make sense in our idiosyncratic dialect. This is a case where the game of interpretation becomes an opportunity for emotional sharing. The therapeutic factor lies above all in this experience and only secondarily in the information and knowledge value of the analyst's intervention. One could even disregard them entirely in the sense that one could imagine always talking to the unconscious or preconscious patient and yet help him to develop his thinking skills (from a certain point of view, a bit like conducting surgery under general anaesthesia).

The vignette shows that analyst and patient move together – continuously and sometimes rapidly – along the Möbius strip of the unconscious.

The door

For some time now, whenever I have to open or close the door, it has been making an excruciating creaking noise. It is too heavy for me to solve the problem alone, so I am forced to wait for a technician to come and fix it. But it does not always emit the same sound. It seems to be affected by the temperature, by the meteorological conditions and by the speed at which I move it. One day, I accompany a patient to the exit and to my surprise and embarrassment I hear the door behind whistling after her! I wonder if she had the same thought as me . . . if the door had not helped me to intuit a feature of our relationship that I had never thought of before, in other words, an unconscious experience of irresistible attraction.

Unconsciously and by surprise

The continuity between conscious and unconscious experience lies in the fact that 'everything can be transposed' (Proust).[43] Every conscious communication or event in the field has its unconscious counterpart; in other words, it can be seen as a derivative of waking dream thought. A polyphonic vision of the analytic dialogue goes beyond the traditional concept of transference and counter-transference where each is considered as a product of only one or the other of the two actors on stage and not as factors of the field or of the intersubjective third of the analysis. Rather, each point (event) in the field influences and is influenced by all the other points; it is thus created together by the analytic couple. This also means that the analyst assumes more responsibility towards the emotional events constantly recounted by the text of the analysis.

Getting lost in the narrative/dream of the session means allowing unconscious thought to do its work. Reveries vanish as quickly as dreams (we experience this in sessions much more often than it may seem), but they are not easy to grasp. Continuity means that any event in analysis is rendered in the processuality of constructing the contact barrier. Analytic field theory achieves the fullest version of the principle of continuity between unconscious and conscious. The meaning of Freud's remark that dreams are thoughts in another form could be reversed and we could say that thoughts are dreams in another form.

Bion places Freud's theory on the level of content, his own theory on the level of functions. He is interested more in the mental operations that enable thinking and less in the content of thought. In this way, he presents his theory as a meta-theory. This is consistent both with the functionalist approach of modern cognitive sciences and with the centrality recently acquired by the question of emotions both here and in neuroscience.[44]

One could go on for a long time trying to establish derivations, equivalences and correspondences between the various concepts in the models of the principal authors – and in some measure this is work that needs to done: for example, between the concept of dream work alpha/alpha function and Klein's concept of unconscious phantasy.[45] Or else, one could reformulate the Freudian concept of censorship[46] as the consequence of a failed relationship between container and contained, or as the irruption into the psyche of killer-contents etc. However, my impression is that we are facing a paradigm shift, in Kuhn's sense of the term (1962).

In the session, the polyphony of the unconscious expresses itself in the play of the characters and the narrativity of the analytic field. The only hierarchy that is admitted is the asymmetry of work based on the differential in the analytic device and in emotional (narrative) competence between patient and analyst. Just as our two eyes share in constructing a stereoscopic view of the object-reality, likewise Unc and C are always simultaneously at work. There is continuity between the two sectors or functions of the psyche. As we have seen, the Möbius strip is the topological figure that best describes this paradox of two surfaces that are one single surface and one surface that continually winds in on itself. This means that, strictly speaking, there is no element in the field of analysis that can elude the two vantage points, whether they are only external or internal, only past or present, belonging only to the patient or the analyst, etc.

Treatment means restoring as well as possible this stereoscopic vision of things when for some reason it is obstructed. In Ogden's terminology, it is a question of dreaming interrupted or undreamt dreams; giving space to dreaming memory; allowing the introjection of a maternal alpha function, and reclaiming areas in the grip of minus alpha functioning (-αf): areas where projective identifications come back as nameless dread – terror that is not only unspeakable but so intense as to impede the use of symbols (names) – in a bottomless downward spiral that leaves the subject with the impression (which Winnicott described so well) of falling endlessly.

In other words, it is a question of restoring the psychoanalytic function of personality. By this expression Bion means the way the subject gives personal meaning to his/her experience through the operation of the Unc/C pair. For Bion mental illness is the result of the failure of thought. The problem is not the drive itself, but *how* to think the drive. Bion removes the slash that separates thought from emotion; by thought what he always means is thought *and* feeling. Dialectic means that a meaning is neither alone in itself nor alone only with respect to the other but both at the same time, which is different from the separative logic of non-contradiction.

For Freud the 'between' of the drive is between body and psyche, Bion's 'between' of emotion is between body and psyche, but also between subject and object. When in a session, through images of a daydream or through the narrative derivatives in the text of the dialogue created between patient and analyst, we go back to the images that are generated by the alpha function and synthesized by the apparatus for dreaming-thinking in the construction of waking dream thought, we have the chance to sense the *emotions* (essential narrative functions) that are present in the patient (or, rather, in the field). It makes no sense to ask whether this is an 'exclusive' projection of the analyst, because this would return us to the unipersonal view of two isolated subjects interacting. So we can tune into these emotions and try to transform them into better narratives, narratives that lead to a better, that is to say, more liveable, ending. Sometimes they produce a real happy ending, and sometimes the ability to represent the malaise – which is itself no mean achievement.

7

GIVING BODY TO THE MIND: A COMPARISON BETWEEN FREUD'S AND BION'S METAPSYCHOLOGIES

We do not know how the passage from body to mind occurs. Nevertheless, to borrow Grotstein's expression (2007), we can try to shine a beam of intense darkness on this enigma. My proposal is simple, although not easy to put into practice: I shall try to draw a comparison between Freud's and Bion's metapsychologies. Not in their entirety, however; just some of the key concepts. This will perhaps give us a more accurate idea of how the mind comes into being than would be the case if we examined each separately.

Poetry of the mind

Rereading *On Aphasia: a Critical Study* is an excellent way of approaching some of the most intricate nodal points of Freud's metapsychology. There is good reason why some consider it his first book of psychoanalysis. In one of its most significant passages, Freud illustrates the concept of the *representative* function performed by the image in the cerebral cortex based on the data the senses receive at the body periphery:

> Only in the spinal cord, and in analogous grey areas, do the prerequisites for a complete *projection* [*Projektion*] of the body periphery exist. For each peripheral unit of innervation there exists a corresponding area of grey matter in the spinal cord, and in the extreme case one single nervous element. Owing to the reduction of the projection fibres through the grey matter of

> the spinal cord, a unit of grey matter belonging to a higher level can no longer correspond to *one* peripheral unit, but must be related to several such units. This also holds for the cerebral cortex, and it is therefore appropriate to use different terms for these two types of representation [*zentraler Abbildung*] in the central nervous system. If the way in which the periphery is reflected in the spinal cord is called a 'projection', its counterpart in the cerebral cortex might suitably be called a 'representation' [*Repräsentation*], which implies that *the periphery of the body is contained in the cerebral cortex not point to point, but through selected fibres, in a less detailed differentiation.*
>
> (Freud, 1891, p. 50, my italics)

A few pages later Freud coins the wonderful metaphor of the poetry of the mind to express the same idea:

> We can only presume that the fibre tracts, which reach the cerebral cortex after their passage through other grey masses, have maintained some relationship to the periphery of the body, but no longer reflect a topographically exact image of it. *They contain the body periphery in the same way as . . . a poem contains the alphabet, i.e., in a complete different arrangement serving other purposes*, in manifold associations of the individual elements, whereby some may be represented several times, others not at all. If it were possible to follow in detail the rearrangement [*Umordnung*] which takes place between the spinal projection and the cerebral cortex, one would probably find that the underlying principle is purely functional, and that the topographic relations are maintained only as long as they fit in with the claims of function.
>
> (Freud, 1891, p. 53, my italics)

Clearly, what is at issue here is the problem of how the mysterious leap is made from body to mind; how it is possible for the mind to form images of reality based on its 'claims of function', that is to say, the requirements of the entire organism, and by mixing up 'topographic relations' with the same freedom as we arrange the letters of the alphabet to form meaningful sentences. Freud postulates two types of image: peripheral, which he calls *projection*, and *representation* (the German word here is *Repräsentation*), true representations. In the first excerpt above the 'leap' occurs when Freud suddenly stops talking about fibres and starts talking instead about images. In this way he builds an 'anatomic' model of the psyche, which we find again in drive theory and its psychic representatives: along the path from the periphery of the body to the mind there are components (fibres/projections) that take part in the process but are barred from entering the psyche. Other fibres (a handful of 'selected fibres'), however, take on the task, so to speak, of representing its demands. Three years earlier, in *Some Points for a Comparative Study of Organic and Hysterical Motor Paralyses*, Freud (1888, p. 161) also writes on the subject of the relationship – mediated, incomplete, not point to point – between the body periphery and the cerebral cortex; and here 'selected fibres' become 'representative fibres'.

The passages I have quoted from *On Aphasia* are extraordinary because they imply a complete theory of the movement from the somatic to the psychic, from instincts or emotions and raw sensations to ideas. They also illustrate the Freudian theory of 'indirect realism' (Napolitano, 2010): we do not know reality for what it is but because of the way we reconstruct it inside ourselves.

Rizzuto adds an illuminating perspective when she observes that the Freudian metaphor of the poem suggests the emotional aspect of the mind that we associate with the aesthetic experience in art and in analysis. Words have a body and rejoin the body. Ultimately, she writes,

> To speak, then, is to symbolize words in the representation of a body mind . . . the mind is the body in representation and its later elaboration . . . To be analysed is to rediscover one's body and its subjective and interpersonal meaning in the early [*primär*] representations of childhood experience. In the last resort, all personal words stem from our body.
>
> (Rizzuto, 1990, pp. 246–247)

In *On Aphasia*, then, we encounter a totally functionalist Freud, well in advance of the change of the second topography, which goes in the same direction. With each new emergence from grey matter, fibres change their functional meaning (*funktionelle Bedeutung*). The impressions that the fibres bring with them are associated with each other. Literally, they are 'knotted' together (the term Freud uses is *Verknüpfung*, which inevitably also suggests the weaving of letters into words and words into a text). The message they convey from the periphery of the body comes out each time enriched, because it has become more *abstract* and 'simplified' as it contains less information.

The formation, first of the image and later of the concept, involves a process of selection or loss of data that allows the passage from the particular to the general, from the chaos of infinite perceptions to categories of thought, from the infinite to the finite. The first application of this metapsychological scheme that arises in the neurological sphere lies in the theory of dreams. Transposed onto the psychic plane, the same type of relationship is found between the latent and the manifest content of the dream, in that it is an effect of the primary process of *condensation*. Freud expresses this concept clearly in the sixth chapter of *The Interpretation of Dreams*:

> Not only are the elements of a dream determined by the dream-thoughts many times over, but the individual dream-thoughts are represented in the dream by several elements. Associative paths lead from one element of the dream to several dream-thoughts, and from one dream-thought to several elements of the dream.
>
> (Freud, 1900, p. 284)

Free association thus appears as the centrifugal movement that deconstructs the text of the poetry of the mind and shows its most peripheral roots, like falling back from the centre of the representative images to the periphery of the images of *projection*. As De Lillo tellingly comments:

> Analogous are the processes of condensation, in the former case neurological, and in the latter psychological, *both in the primary and in the secondary process*. A neurological model which summarizes a process of synthesis-abstraction-categorization – this is the theoretical phantasy that on several occasions informs Freudian theory.
>
> (De Lillo, 2005, p. 58, my italics)

As we know, spectres (even theoretical spectres) always take their toll. Needless to say, we find them in disguise in the other professional mediators that are the psychic representatives of the drive. Let us take a look.

Psychic representatives of the drive[47]

Despite taking a monistic view of their relationship, not even Freud can avoid the conceptual opposition between mind and body. Even for him the leap from one to another is a leap across a gulf. To bridge this gap, Freud devises a kind of a walkway and invents the concept of drive. He speaks of drives in the plural as 'mythical entities, magnificent in their indefiniteness'[48] (Laplanche and Pontalis, 1967, p. 216). Their indefiniteness lies in the fact that, by definition, the concept of instinct lies 'on the frontier between the mental and the physical' (Freud, 1905, p. 168). At its origin, the drive is by nature organic and results from the excitations of the body that cause unpleasant increases in tension. To reduce the tension, it sends its psychic representatives (*psychische Repräsentanz* or *Repräsentant*) as delegates to the psyche, the place from which it is rigorously excluded.

The instinct thus has a *source*, it exerts a *pressure*, it searches for an *object* in order to achieve the goal of reducing tension, but in itself it is a force that is not, nor can it become, properly psychical. Once it reaches the threshold of the psyche, it stops and even if it participates in the decisions that are taken in that forum, it does so only by proxy. The word 'psychic' does not specify in which compartment the delegation of the drive is hosted, whether in the central offices of the ego, that is, in the *Prec-C* compartment or, already dismantled and rejected, in the prison of the *Inc.*

But why does Freud speak of drives and not simply of instincts? The only reason that suggests itself to explain what might have led him to talk not of instincts but of drives[49] is that he wanted to insert what might at first glance seem like an automatic reaction to a stimulus, such as we find in animals, into a pre-symbolic frame, that is, into a 'procedural' or semiotic symbolic order, which is then symbolic in the true sense of the word. This amounts to saying that the concept of drive has no meaning outside language, outside human sociality and its laws. The state of being between the somatic and the psychic, then, is not so much a question of something purely corporeal suddenly meeting a culturally mediated and non-automatic (instinctive) response – it would be difficult, and even logically impossible, to identify the exact threshold of the transition from nature to culture – but something/a push that stands between a pre-symbolic culture, in the sense described above, and a properly symbolic culture, because both are immersed in what Heidegger would call Existence (*Dasein*). If we did not concede that the body is already, and has always been, shaped by determinations of a social nature, we would fatally fall into a nefarious mind/body dualism. The drive then is an impulse that starts from the body, but from a body that cannot ever be thought of as pure materiality.

The delegation of the psychic representatives of the drive contains two different components, one an ideational representation (*Vorstellungsrepräsentanz* or, less frequently, *Vorstellungsrepräsentant*) and the other an affective representative or 'quota of affect' (*Affektbetrag*) (Herrera, 2010, p. 789). Elected in different constituencies, they can be seen as 'delegates' whose information comes either more from the inside (the affective part) or more from the outside (the ideational part), and who then transmit it to the psyche.

The drive and its delegates are therefore two separate things. This can be expressed using metaphors. For example, an engine propels a vehicle but it is the electronic systems that inform the driver about the state and functionality of the various other systems. Both are functional to the goal of moving around by car.

The metaphor Lyotard (2011) uses comes from the theatre: the drive is an impresario who sends his agent to the theatre to audition some actors (memory traces) for a part and to see who among them is best suited for the roles (thing representations) in a play he hopes will be a success.

Or again: the editorial staff of a newspaper, let's say the *New York Times*, are really excited because they have been informed that war has broken out in some faraway country. The region is inaccessible but they manage to get some reporters through. These reporters take some photographs and set out in search of news, avoiding military censorship and managing to get their stories back to the newspaper. At this point, an editor makes one last check and decides which text and which images to print. Finally, he publishes the article. The initial tension set off by giving news of the event fades and gives way to quiet satisfaction.

In all three examples then we have initial drive activation that originates from the body (somatic arousal, that is, an increase in tension), the emissaries sent to the psyche to invest the representations that can be used to carry out the work necessary to alleviate the unpleasant affect, the union with a verbal representation, the movement through the preconscious, the definitive access to consciousness and the possibility of tension release through some 'specific action'. Meanwhile, the play being staged, the news printed and the activity of the engine as made visible by the rev-counter have all had to undergo screening by two censors.

To reach definitive 'publication' in consciousness, the images must join the words, because there is no conscious thought without language, but not all images chosen (invested) can pass the test of the two censors. Some of them are separated by affect and then held back immediately (primary repression) or pushed back (secondary repression or post-repression) into the *Unc*, the Indian reservation of thing representations incompatible with the ego. At the same time, the affect is shifted onto another representation, and in this case remains identical to itself; or it is transformed into the opposite, repressed or left free to flow in the form of anxiety. If we want to better grasp the nature of the psychic representatives of the drive we cannot avoid entering into rather complex, albeit interesting, questions of terminology. We shall first examine the ideational part and then go on to the affective part.

Ideational representative

The German word coined by Freud to express the ideational element is a compound noun: *Vorstellungsrepräsentanz*. Linguists teach us that in these cases the basic term is the second (*Repräsentanz*), while the first (*Vorstellung*) has only attributive value (Cambon, 2008). It is therefore to be understood as something like *Repräsentanz* of the *Vorstellung* type, in other words, that comes in the form of *Vorstellung*. That said, it is worth considering the meaning of the two components of this expression separately, sometimes mistranslated as 'representative representation/representative', 'representation of the representation' and the like.

Vorstellung refers to the (predominantly visual) isomorphic, iconic or mimetic representation of a thing, such as, say, a map of a territory, and not a symbolic representation, such as a flag standing for a nation. The term, which comes from the verb *vorstellen*, has a long tradition in philosophical thought, and for this reason it is right to make reference to the German term. In particular, *vorstellen* means to represent, summoning up an image, an idea, a concept, and always implies a subjective dimension. For example, *sich vorstellen* means 'imagine'.

In Kant *Vorstellung* 'means the cognitive relationship with the world, and reproduces the semantic value of "idea" (which in Locke and Hume means a mental representation produced by sense impressions)' (Borutti, 2010, p. 78). In his *Critique of Pure Reason*, the term refers to a cognitive representation, 'the categorical synthesis of the manifold in decisive cognitive judgement, whose outcome is the construction of objects of experience' (ibid.). To put it briefly, a *Vorstellung* is a cognitive or anamnestic representation, more distant from the direct perceptual image of the thing, but still mimetic, its re-presentation before the mind's eye, and thus necessarily subjective; it is the investment of memory traces left by perception. It is nothing but the evocation of a memory, but always in the form of an image *similar* to the thing.

The 'cognitive representation or *Vorstellung*' (ibid., p. 79) could not occur without being preceded by a perceptual image. There can be no concept or category – for example, the image of a tree to think of all trees; the image and not yet the word – if the things had previously not been presented to the senses for intuition. Since in phylogenesis we enter into the field of the symbolic, the opposite is also true, however counter-intuitive this may seem. Inevitably determined by the social sphere, perhaps even at the level of implicit knowledge, in other words, before the establishment of the ego, it is impossible, unless a child is not brought up among men – and even here there would be the possible exception of the period of foetal life – for there to be perception that is not already also imagining.

So before having a representation in the sense of a *Vorstellung, perception* is already minimally categorical; it already implies a certain selection and reorganization of stimuli. The mind is never a *tabula rasa* upon which things impress themselves as they are. The apparent immediacy of perception is actually something derived. It is produced a posteriori. It is so in the first instance because of the form that the anatomy and physiology of the nervous system impress on it, because of the nature of the mechanisms of translation of stimuli[50] that belong to the material structure that supports it, but then also because in humans the mind is relational from the outset and by association it always takes on the values of the social group. It follows that neither the pure perceptual image nor the *Vorstellung* can aspire to being a 'true' copy of the thing; it cannot mirror it as it is.

The base term of the compound noun *Vorstellungsrepräsentanz*, i.e. *Repräsentanz*, is on the other hand one of the two nouns in German that refer to non-isomorphic representation, that is to say, symbolic representation (flame standing for passion, for example): *Repräsentanz* and *Vertretung*. These words derive from the verbs *repräsentieren* and *vertreten,* respectively. *Repräsentieren* is midway between *vorstellen* and *vertreten* (Cambon, 2008), which in itself does not suggest a connection with the image (Herrera, 2010). But, again, there can be no non-isomorphic or symbolic form or representation that is not preceded by an isomorphic representation or *Vorstellung*, just as, in turn, this cannot be preceded by a perception: '*Repräsentation* is a disquieting point of oscillation between "*form*", i.e. imaginary consistency, and *"representation"* [*Vertretung*] inasmuch as it is not isomorphic' (Cambon, 2008, p. 25).

That said, if we now go back to Freud's *Vorstellungsrepräsentanz*, we need to interpret it first of all as *Repräsentation* or *Repräsentanz* (a term which, I repeat, in itself stands between isomorphic representation *Vorstellung* and symbolic representation *Repräsentation*) in the form of *Vorstellung* (an isomorphic mental image that is the counterpart of the memory trace, which derives from the perception but is not identical to it, since it implies a higher degree of abstraction). We could literally translate it as follows: the delegates who represent (in the sense of stand for, take the place of, be an ambassador for, etc.) the drives in the guise of a representation understood as an act of imagining, that is, subjectively evoking memory traces already stored from a previous perception or the current presentation of an object.

But the expression 'representation in the form of mnemonic reactivation of an isomorphic image' is a kind of contradiction in terms. It is like saying a representation which is both isomorphic and symbolic. What does this mean? That there are isomorphic images of the object, stored as memory traces, which act as 'symbols' of the drives, but do not depict them; nor, given what they are, would they ever have the chance. One could therefore think of the psychic representatives of the drive more broadly as spokespersons in the form of (isomorphic) representations, in other words, something that comes from the innate imaginative faculty of the mind, which symbolizes the drive, meaning they are able to recall something other than what is offered by their perceptual and immediate appearance. To pick up the earlier image, it is as if a map, an isomorphic image of the territory of a nation, were taken as a symbol (not isomorphic image) of the character – not the territory! – of the people; say, for example, the hexagonal shape of France standing for the *esprit de geometrie* of its inhabitants. Summing up his linguistic analysis, to translate *Vorstellungsrepräsentanz des Triebes*, Cambon also proposes 'representative-representation-non-isomorphic-vicarious' in the manner of 'representation-*Vorstellung*' (2008, p. 33). We can see how the link between the two terms in *Vorstellungsrepräsentanz* – between the sensory-emotional-psychical representation and the image to which it is linked – is no longer a necessity, but rather non-intrinsic, aleatory, contingent. Different representations, in fact, could serve the same purpose. Cambon (2008, p. 31) points out that 'There is no link of connaturality between a drive and what "represents" it'. And further:

> Writing '(*Vorstellung-*)*Repräsentanz des Triebes*' in this way is a stroke of genius: *Repräsentanz* just slips in between *Vorstellung* and *Trieb*, just like the *slash* that always interposes itself between signifier and signified. It marks the relationship of *conjunction-disjunction* that governs the random and at the same time unchanging clash between representation and drive, which thus inevitably tips over into *Vorstellung*, and, regardless of its nature, on the side of the signifier has at least hieroglyphic status [. . .] It may be noted in passing the relative inadequacy of the words 'represent' and '*repräsentieren*' to express the 'vicariation' of a being that by its very essence can never be 'present', whereby I mean the *inadequacy* of the prefix 're-'. *Vertreten*, on the other hand, would be completely free from this drawback.
>
> (Cambon, 2008, p. 39)

Freud's expression is really quite brilliant because even in the simple choice of the term *Vorstellungsrepräsentanz des Triebes* he summarizes (invents, theorizes) a gradient that extends from body to mind, from thing to word, from image to idea; from the presentation to the senses (what is in front of the eyes) or current isomorphic representation towards the still isomorphic representation (but it is already less than the perceptual image, being a reproduction of it) of the memory trace (*Vorstellung*), going on to achieve a strictly symbolic representation (*Repräsentanz*). Although not directly part of it, the two extremes of *perception* and *vertreten* are notionally implicated in this progression. Under pressure from the drives, many images of similar things begin to be represented in the mind as ideograms and then these ideograms become letters of the alphabet, veritable symbols. Initially, however, they are sensory, semiotic, pre-reflexive ideograms.

The essential point is that in this progression the direct link with the thing becomes increasingly loose. But the distance gained allows for the substitution of thought. Thinking is nothing other than a process of abstraction or simplification that clearly traces the path along which the anatomy of the brain is organized according to the principle of 'neurological condensation' (Cambon, 2008, p. 71) that we saw in the first section. The *Vertretung*, observes the French linguist, gives up isomorphism in the same way as the projection of the medullary bundles makes it to the cortex, to be represented there, only after a process of reorganization and simplification.

Just as a small number of delegates in parliament represent all the people, so a small number of selected fibres represent the surface of the body at the level of higher grey matter and each time they re-emerge from a collection station they take on a different functional significance. In a dizzying synthesis, the expression *psychische (Vorstellungs-)Repräsentanz des Triebes* tells (and at the same time theorizes) the story of the transformations that move from sensory impressions and impulses to reach consciousness (symbols, language). It should be pointed out that in this expression Freud brings together and superimposes on each other two terms that define it differently, one being the ideational representative of the drive and the other its affective component.

The point is that if it is true that the real ability to use symbols comes into play only with the word and that this step requires the Other, even so it can be said that emotional or semiotic somatic 'categorization' (that is to say, the fact that certain emotional states end up 'procedurally', at a prereflective level, *standing* for a virtually infinite series of similar states, thus triggering more rapid responses to the stimuli that prompt them),[51] sensorial presentation, anamnestic recall and conceptual thinking are continuous with each other. However, saying 'semiotic' categorization – which strictly speaking means postulating a concept that is not a concept – implies, at least for humans, that the Other is already in play before a real subject is formed. By distinguishing instinct from drive, Freud was trying to take this into account. The former follows a logic of stimulus-response and is uniform in all animals, while the latter is virtually individual-specific and reflects culture and its laws. For this reason, Heidegger (1927) says that animals are *weltlos* ('worldless') or *weltarm* ('world poor' or 'poor in world').

The process that leads from the body to the mind unfolds in three stages: stimulus → instinct → representation (*Reiz* → *Trieb* → *Vorstellung*). Out of the 'friction' of the body with external and internal reality is born a proto-emotional reaction that selects from among the images of the object, that is to say, of the goal that might extinguish tension and provide pleasure. We see that, in its role as choir leader of the basic needs of the body, the drive is represented in its turn by the *Vorstellung*. The drive is *not* a representation, it has no form, it can only be replaced by a representation, but it would make no sense to think of it as an isomorphic, direct or mimetic perception or as a recall of such a perception, but rather as the investment of the memory traces of an image (*Vorstellung*) taken as a 'symbol' ('anchor', is how Freud puts it) of the drive. This means that the bond that joins it to the drive is both *necessary* and *contingent*, justified but also interchangeable. Many different images and ideas can symbolize the same thing to the mind and serve the mind to represent the need to eliminate a stimulus that occasions displeasure, such as, say, thirst or hunger. This is why Freud never says *Vorstellung des Triebes*, or *Triebvorstellung*.

The affect quota

Given the scientific evidence available to us today, there can be no doubt that unconscious affective evaluations precede cognitive processes. One can have an affective preference for stimuli that are not consciously perceived. It has been demonstrated that unconscious affective processes also exist in a dynamic sense, in the sense that we can defend ourselves unconsciously from a certain affect, and so on (Westen, 1999). Nevertheless, one of the theoretical problems of metapsychology has always been and remains the concept of unconscious affect. As Finelli writes (2005, p. 10): 'the drive affect, within Freud's work as a whole, lives essentially as hydraulic spread . . . It is the place of emotional energy, which Freud sees as free energy'. On the question of whether it is possible for unconscious affect to exist, Freud is clear:

> If the instinct did not attach itself to an idea or manifest itself as an affective state, we could know nothing about it. When we nevertheless speak of an unconscious instinctual impulse or of a repressed instinctual impulse, the looseness of phraseology is a harmless one. We can only mean an instinctual impulse the ideational representative of which is unconscious, for nothing else comes into consideration.
>
> (Freud, 1915, p. 177)

And further:

> in comparison with unconscious ideas there is the important difference [that] all that corresponds in that system [the system *Ucs.*] to unconscious affects is a potential beginning [*Ansatzmöglichkeit*][52] which is prevented from developing. Strictly speaking, then . . . there are no unconscious affects as there are unconscious ideas. The whole difference arises from the fact that ideas are cathexes – basically of memory-traces – whilst affects and feelings correspond to processes of discharge, the final manifestations of which are perceived as [internal] sensations.[53]
>
> (ibid., p. 178)

Semi comments as follows:

> The answer to this question can only be negative. In the unconscious feelings do not exist, but forces and energy charges do. However, if we look at psychic phenomena from a *dynamic* point of view, it should be noted that when a feeling is repressed, it is true that it does not exist in the unconscious, but it is also true that all the conditions persist in the unconscious for the energy charge of instinctual origin 'to try' as it were to work its way up to consciousness and then reappear in the form of feeling. So much so that, if one manages to overcome this repression, the affect reappears. This is why one can speak of 'unconscious affects'. Because we know that, under certain conditions, a repressed affect can come back to represent itself to

> consciousness. The difference lies in the fact that, as Freud points out, while a representation remains in the unconscious after repression, in the unconscious only potential corresponds to the repressed affect.
>
> (Semi, 2001, p. 142)

Affect, therefore, is present in the unconscious only as potential, as the ability, which can be awakened, to return to consciousness. The link between drive and image, which Herrera (2010) identifies with the goal of the drive, in other words with the object, is contingent, as we have said. What is, however, difficult to classify as contingent is the quota of affect that links up to the image-representation of the drive. One senses why Bion replaces the concept of drive with emotion (Green, 1995). It is as if he wanted to tighten the connection between the construction of the child's mind and the mother's mind, not so much and not only with the object, which is itself interchangeable, but with the specific quality of their relationship.

So we might think that the psychic representatives of the drive express more than anything else a *tendency* to link up to a representation – in practical terms, the emotional charge.[54]

The *Vorstellung,* then, only indicates an image of the goal, one among the many possible, to which is attached a quota of affect. We know two important things about the affect: that it can be found in the psyche and that unlike the representation it is not replaceable. The idea finds support in the interpretation Ricoeur gives of the psychic representatives of the drive. In *On Interpretation*, he writes:

> At a certain point the question of force and the question of meaning coincide; that point is where instincts are indicated, are made manifest, are given in a psychical representative, that is, in something psychical that 'stands for' them; all the derivatives in consciousness are merely transformations of this psychical representative, of this primal 'standing for'. To designate this point Freud coined the excellent expression *Repräsentanz*. Instincts, which are energy, are 'represented' by something psychical. But we must not speak of representation in the sense of *Vorstellung*, i.e. an 'idea' of something, for an idea is itself a derived form of this 'representative' which, before representing

> things – the world, one's own body, the unreal – stands for instincts as such, presents them purely and simply.
>
> (Ricoeur, 1965, pp. 134–135)

Could then the something that 'stands for' the instinct that Ricoeur refers to be identified with affect? Also according to Le Guen (2008), the author of an updated Freudian dictionary, *Repräsentanz* or *Repräsentant* refers to a *capacity* to represent, or the *origin* of a representation, and stands in opposition to *Vorstellung*, which is no longer a potential representation but the actual representation of a thing, object or word, created by the organization imprinted on the memory traces by the drive (by its representative!). The representatives of the drives thus enter the psyche as stimuli that arise in the body (*Reize*) already oriented to attach themselves (or as the potential to attach themselves) to certain images.

Taking the same line as Le Guen we find Racalbuto, Conrotto, Mangini and several others. Picking up the position expressed by Racalbuto (1994, 1997, 2003), Mangini interprets the psychical representative of the drive as a first transformation of somatic arousal in the direction of thought, but still as 'an indefinite and burning sensation, before any eventual signification, which is therefore still immersed in the primitive affective-sensorial pre-representative matrix' (2009, p. 56). The psychic representatives of the drive are affect-sensations and not yet proper representations. For this reason, he criticizes the recent translation of *Vorstellungsrepräsentanz* suggested by Ranchetti (Freud, 2005): 'psychic replacement (in the form of representation)'. He believes that the word '"ideational" . . . must be understood that there is a representation of the instinct in the representative, while with "psychical" (*psychische Repräsentanz*) an affective complex still in search of representation should be understood' (Conrotto, 1995, p. 586).

Mangini explains that a thing representation, in other words the image of the object that serves to discharge drive tension, is formed only when the psychic representative of the drive encounters a representation. Moreover, if, as he writes, we are to see the psychical representative of the drive as having 'a pre-representative sensorial nature' (Mangini, 2009, p. 59), as being a 'indefinite corporeal sensations . . . *in search* of signification or, alternatively, primary anxiety' (ibid., p. 60) – an idea that clashes with the current interpretation of the expression 'ideational representation' –

I wonder then whether it might be possible to borrow from Bion's language and identify the psychic representatives of the drive with beta elements. The expression *psychische (Vorstellungs-)Repräsentanz des Triebes* could then be read by reversing the order of all the German terms so as to capture the various stages of a process whose progression could be summed up as follows: drive (*Trieb*) → affect-sensation (*Repräsentanz*) → image (*Vorstellung*) → thing-representation (image imbued with affect, and thus something definitely 'psychical'). We would translate Freud's ingenious linguistic construction not so much in terms of the identity between representation and image, but rather as the *tendency* of instinctual representation towards the image.

Freud returns to affect in *The Ego and the Id* (1923), where he traces it back, as internal perception, to the pleasure-displeasure series and highlights its more primal or elementary character as against perceptions that come from outside. He also emphasizes that the feeling of displeasure has a strong motivational character. He then goes on to clarify another distinctive aspect of affect; namely, that in order to become conscious, an internal perception does not need to be linked to a verbal representation. It makes its way directly to the conscious. When it is not conscious,

> this something behaves like a repressed impulse. It can exert driving force without the ego noticing the compulsion . . . We then come to speak, in a condensed and not entirely correct manner, of 'unconscious feelings', keeping up an analogy with unconscious ideas which is not altogether justifiable.
>
> (Freud, 1923, p. 22)

Obviously this explanation raises more questions than it answers and inevitably it reflects the usual ambiguities in the definitions of the terms we use. As on other occasions Freud did not bother to clarify the uncertainties he left behind but simply skirted around them by proposing a new way of seeing things.

Primal repression

Entry into the psyche by representatives of the drive and their connection to an image is only the first stage in the constitution of the unconscious. The Freudian unconscious is in fact better represented by the second stage of repression – primary (*Urverdrängung*) and especially secondary (*Verdrängung*) repression. In primal repression the psychic representation of the drive (a quota of affect that has become attached to a thing representation) has the door to the conscious of the repressing agent slammed in its face. The thing representations which are already restricted from the outset in the unconscious gradually form a repressed nucleus. This pole will then always exert a power of attraction on images that have already been admitted to consciousness, thus promoting secondary repression.

Mangini (2009) explains this sequence in more detail. In his opinion the psychical representative of the drive only becomes properly ideational (by taking on a representative nature, or in other words, attaching itself to a certain image) through primal repression, which is to say as a result of the encounter with the object, and then only at the end of an experiential process that generates preconceptions and hierarchies of value. For this reason, he proposes translating *Vorstellungsrepräsentanz* as 'psychical representative of the drive'. What he means is something that stands for the drives in the psyche but is still not a true representation. In this way, he re-captures a sense of relationship in the process and valorizes the affective component of drive representation. I think we can say, in short, that he sees proto-sensoriality and proto-emotions as the true psychic representatives of the drive. Before being represented, therefore, the quota of affect must be fixed in the process of primal repression. It is up to the object relationship to carry out this preliminary fixing of excitement, 'a constituent part of the process of primal repression' (ibid., p. 61), prior to any more sophisticated psychic transformation (secondary repression):

> fixation is a mode of transcription through which 'still not yet representative' elements, identifiable as instinctual excitement or affects/sensations (Racalbuto, 1994) stimulated in the relationship with the object, scale the hurdle between body and mind thanks to primal repression.
>
> (Mangini, 2009)

But if we think of the interplay of loving glances between mother and child, which can also be seen as a metaphor for the tactile, auditory, etc., exchanges to which Mangini assigns this task of fixing/attaching an affect to an image, and of the transition from mental representation of the drive representative to thing representation, is this not what Bion's alpha function tends towards? In this form, the concept of primal repression would take account of the fact that the child cannot yet say 'I' and is not capable of thinking thoughts. Nevertheless, as its containing capacity is rudimentary, the process of repressing excess excitation would occur through the mother and the semiotic communication that takes place between them. In primal repression the mother attaches an affect-sensation to an image (a psychical representative of the drive), aroused by the enigmatic sexual messages she sends to the child (Laplanche, 2005; Heenen-Wolff, 2013). At this point a thing representation is formed in the mind of the infant that is immediately stored away in the unconscious in order to free up sufficient psychic space. The maternal 'gaze' is therefore an external agent which mirrors the child's psyche and structure. In analysis, Mangini explains, this fixation point is the transference. Again, clearly, the psychical representative of the drive is identified primarily with the quota of affect.

Thus understood, primal repression would explain why there can be repression before the Ego and self-awareness are established, and that is because it comes from the Other. In Mangini's interpretation the concept of primal repression becomes invaluable because it helps us understand how (through the mother) the repressed unconscious casts its shadow not only on the nascent repressed unconscious of the child but also on the non-repressed (cognitive or structural) conscious. This then forms an original repressed nucleus that imprints its dynamism on the nascent psyche.

However, the problem with this concept is that it remains nebulous. In the same year, 1926, in *Inhibitions, Symptoms and Anxiety,* Freud admitted that he knew very little about this. This is why it is still to be decided whether it is preferable to use the enigmatic concept of primal repression when describing the birth of the psyche. The point is that Mangini's interpretation – at least, in my understanding of it – is a highly relational interpretation of a concept that in Freud remains enclosed within a rather solipsistic view that sees psychic functioning in terms of an energetic-hydraulic model, making it very different from Bion's concept, the clinical application of which seems much clearer.

Continuity or discontinuity?

The idea of proto-sensoriality as something that first becomes an image and later a symbol is what Bion expresses through the concept of transformation from beta to alpha. It is as if with the theory of alpha function he were taking Freud's metaphor of the poetry of the mind literally. Maybe inverting the alphabetical order of the letters in the transition from beta to alpha reflects his intention to indicate, in the upward movement towards the 'top' of the alphabet, something that was gradually transformed in a similar way from the periphery back to the summit of the nervous system. Bion's metapsychology, however, shows a dramatic shift in emphasis from Freud's: the transformation of beta → alpha is the same as that embodied in the expression *Vorstellungsrepräsentanz*, and perhaps even better in *psychische* (*Vorstellungs-*)*Repräsentanz des Triebes*, but Bion replaces the Freudian mechanics of representations with an X and emphasizes the role of society, of the object, the environment as an agent of transformation. He shifts the focus from the mind of the child to the mind of the mother or rather to the relationship between the two. This aspect is already anticipated in Freud's theory, in the idea of 'communication' (*Verständigung*) in *The Project* (1895), and in the concept of drive, which, unlike instinct, already points towards culture.

We have seen that the concept of drive is ambiguous. At times identified with somatic excitation, at times with the representative of the drive (or *Triebrepräsentanz Triebrepräsentant*), which in its turn is considered at times as an ideational representative (or *Vorstellungsrepräsentanz-Repräsentant*) and at times as the 'aspect of the quantum of affect concerning which Freud said on occasion that it was more important in the representative of the drive than the representational aspect (intellectual or ideational)' (Derrida, 1997, p. 124). At times the affect itself is a metapsychological entity, while at other times it is seen as a conscious experience. The fact is that, whatever its level of importance, affect is the Cinderella of Freud's drive theory, which centres mostly on the 'empire' of the visual and the representative (Barale, 2008, p. 131).

Bion tries to overcome the ambiguities of Freud's drive theory and puts emotion at the centre as the non-contingent but necessary element that acts as an intermediary between the body and the mind. The emotion asks to be symbolized. It pushes towards thought. It seeks to lose the nature of urgency; it wants to be transformed from something non-contingent into something contingent. Cannot we consider this as a kind of thought? Managing to elude the pressing demands made by the present and by instinct? Affect is non-contingent, I would say, precisely because it can only be suppressed, inverted or reined in by another representation, but it is not (or only very relatively) interchangeable with another affect in the same way as the ideational component of the mental representation of the drive can be. In fact, as long as it can, the mind endeavours to deceive the affect with a kaleidoscope of representations.

The role of the object and the environment

In line with the interesting ideas put forward by Le Guen and other authors already mentioned, from the point of view of a Bionian model of the unconscious we could see the somatic excitations produced by exogenous and endogenous stimuli on the body, which give rise to the drive and the drive representation, as the tendency to invest an image, as proto-sensations and proto-emotions (β elements)[55] in search of a container. Thing representations would correspond to the first pictograms (α elements), i.e. β elements transformed (alphabetized) by the alpha function; and conscious representations and the affect that accompanies them as dream thoughts or thoughts plain and simple. Thing representations have been called 'the appearance of a "thing"' (Freud, 1891, p. 101); the β element 'the soul of a thought', in other words a proto-sensation, something that has not yet become thought. Freud's *Affekt*, on the other hand, could be equated with proto-emotion. Later, in the narrative sequences of the dream or waking dream thought the various pieces can be arranged using language, which enables us to give a name to the image content. So then we are in the presence of conscious images that also contain affect. It is also possible to think of pictograms that gradually become more and more permeated by language.

Unlike untransformed β elements, which can only settle as procedural memory, dream thoughts can be stored in semantic memory. But the word does not connect magically to the thing like a rabbit emerging from the magician's hat. One has to think of it as being already there in the form of prosody, rhythm, sensoriality, as one of the elements of the semiotic *chora* the mother makes available to the child. As always, it is difficult to establish a precise correspondence between terms that belong to different models. What remains, however, is the idea of progression from thing to word, from the wordless object to the objectless word. Green helps us out here (1998, p. 655): the hallucinatory satisfaction[56] with which the infant responds to frustration – the drive is a measure of the psychic work required from the psyche in response to frustration – 'can be related to a thing-presentation of the breast – in fact, a re-presentation. I think that this can be considered as the first achievement of an alpha function'. And further: 'The first registration is pictographic (an embryonic thing presentation). If this fails, the beta elements in the form of sensuous experiences are not transformed into visual images (primitive representations), but are felt as "things in themselves"' (ibid., p. 657). One could rephrase this in Bionian terms: the drive is a measure of the psychic work the child imposes on the mother's psyche in response to frustration!

In the transition then from somatic excitement, which collects in the 'tendency' of the drive, to the state of psychical representative of the drive to form a thing representation, we already have a series of transformations. The most significant difference between Freud and Bion regards *how* the transition from the drive to the psychical representative of the drive and from the thing representation to the word representation occurs. Depending on one's point of view, the differences can be emphasized or played down. Bion conceptualized this transformation in a highly intersubjective manner, which Green sees as 'one of the rarest examples showing the articulation of an intrapsychic perspective with an intersubjective one' (Green, 1998, p. 651):

> Freud's theory of representation is a spectrum that includes the drive, the psychic representative of the drive, the thing presentation or ideational representative or object presentation, the word presentation, and the representation of reality through thinking. If we consider the elements that take part in all these processes, the more we progress towards thinking, the less we refer directly to the object or to the senses, and the more we have to achieve a work of abstraction . . . As Bion suggests, emotional experience – another expression for drive activation

– is at the beginning. Emotional experience is the first step towards a thought. At the end of the road, we find thinking.

(Green, 1998, p. 655)

Green here establishes an equivalence between emotional experience and drive activation. One must remember that for Bion the emotional experience is always linked to a relationship; in the end it is always about social emotions. Even 'primary' emotions are always influenced by the symbolic network; they are always bordered by language.

It is true that a posteriori we could also discover an 'intersubjective' Freud. The concept of drive immediately inserts the newborn child into sociality; otherwise we would speak only of instinct. The dualism of life instinct/death instinct subordinates the existence of the individual to that of the species. Freud himself refers to his one-person model as a 'fiction'; and, as we have seen, he locates the basis of subjectivity in the understanding the child has with the mother and the basis of ethics in the child's helplessness (*Hilflosigkeit*); he then equates consciousness totally with language (Finelli, 2005), and in the end also the *Unc,* but in this case by 'subtraction' or negatively. The Freudian unconscious is in fact a place of bewildering paradox, because it too is the product of language – what Bion means when he says that it is dreaming or the dream-work-alpha which creates the unconscious – but by means of variance, subtraction, rejection, remains. The unconscious can be conceived of only in a dialectical relationship with the conscious and the dream. One is the negative of the other. The unconscious is peopled by things that still bear the imprint of the words that have been torn from it or which it has never been given. As a result the effects of language, in the sense of a symbolic order, exclude incompatible representations from consciousness both indirectly (via primal repression) and directly (via secondary repression).

Finally, in one of his last notes Freud (1938b, p. 151) wrote, 'I am the breast' (*Ich bin die Brust*). We know what he meant: he was talking about a way children like to express an object-relation by an identification, but this extraordinarily condensed phrase seems to reaffirm on the one hand that the ego is a body ego, and on the other that the ego is the other as object and the Other as culture, sociality; that the primitive ego is a sensory ego where sexuality rests on nurturing, 'an area of sensation of a soothing sort' (Ogden, 1994b, p. 174). A breast-ego even before it becomes an ego.

However, even Green, who in *Propaedeutics: Metapsychology Revisited* (1995) warns against falsehood and simplifications regarding drive theory, says on this point that Freud starts from the assumption that the child will autonomously find its own way to move beyond hallucinatory satisfaction. Bion takes a different view: he argues that without the help of the object, that is, without its capacity for reverie and a mature and intact alpha function, the transformation from β into α is by no means guaranteed. The mother not only gives milk, 'she daydreams feelings and "mental" states about the child. And so she enables the child to reintroject his own projections that are now changed through her' (Green, 1998, p. 656).

In his description of the nature of the drive, in his depiction of the representatives it sends to the psyche and in the distinction he makes between thing presentation and word representation, Freud elaborated a theory of thought, or rather of the passage from body to mind. But the type of conceptualization he chose is based on the assumption of a primarily one-person vertex. Freud is aware of this; he knows he is adopting a useful convention, a 'fiction'. Nonetheless, metaphors in scientific theories are not spurious or non-essential; they form an integral part of the theory. Freud's choice has consequences. What predominates in him is the idea of an endogenous thrust that produces certain transformations through investments of energy/neuronal excitation, and so on.

Bion takes on the same task but does so from a point of view that emphasizes the mother-child pair and the transformation of emotions. The transition does not take place without the α function or the mother's capacity for reverie. The functional rearrangements to be found at certain key hubs of traffic passing along nerve pathways are necessary but not sufficient. They extend along the psychic paths of the mind of the Other, or rather, of the members of the relevant group. To repeat, there is a rough equivalence between psychical drive representative and thing representation, on the one hand, and β element and α element, on the other; between word-representations and dream thoughts and waking thoughts. The alpha element can be thought of as the first product of meaning on the semiotic level of the encounter with the object, and the sequences of alpha elements, on the other hand, as well as dream images and thought as the product of the encounter with meanings conveyed by words.

Repressed unconscious vs. unrepressed unconscious

Although, as we have seen, Freud was the first to speak of an unrepressed *Unc*, for a long time for psychoanalysis the unconscious was by definition only the repressed unconscious. And, again, by definition, the repressed was something that had already been in consciousness – if primal repression, in that of the mother; if secondary repression, in that of the subject. Later it lost this quality.

The important question has now become how to take the unrepressed *Unc* into account not only theoretically but also clinically. If we want to understand the semiotic level of the organization of meaning that precedes the advent of language, the concept of repressed unconscious is of little help, except with regard to the object; the concept of primal repression is useful, however, because it forces us to take account of preverbal communication, and thus shows us what happens with the child.

What happens before the word? Is there already a level of meaning, and where does it come from, or is it only the transition to the word that introduces meaning? Here I think Julia Kristeva's distinction between the semiotic and the symbolic is essential. The child's semiotic experience of care – which parts of the body, say, are manipulated more and which less, to which sounds it is exposed and which not, or even *in utero* to which medicines or substances it is exposed and which not – conveys a culture, a society and its laws even before the child is constituted as a subject; the mother transmits them to the child. It follows that procedural memories also fall under the shadow of the repressed. Unlike what happens with animals, maternal care and the forms it imprints on the unrepressed *Unc* of the infant also always express normative values and convey codes of interpretation. It is true that the concept of secondary repression presupposes a subjectivity that is already up and running. Now, could it be that if primal repression continues to play, as Mangini puts, the whole of life as if it were the first half of secondary repression (although, in fact, parallel to it), primary repression is to be understood as that which 'distracts' the subject from certain forms of completely implicit knowledge and learning, but which nevertheless form the ground where secondary repressions take root?

One problem with Freud's model is that it does not make it easy to consider the semiotic ('poetic') level of meaning that is already present and active in the infant and that in the form of a welcoming or containing environment is already the expression not only of biology but also of culture. To simplify: in Freud it is as if it were a question of all or nothing, both before and after the acquisition of language. Why is that? Because we observe the development of the subject regarded according to the invention of a psyche separated from others and focusing on the functioning of its internal mechanisms, and not the transformations of a more complex system formed at least by a pair of two people (in actual fact, potentially comprising the whole human group, in the same way as an individual term takes on meaning within the totality of a linguistic system). It is interesting to note in this regard what little interest Bion has in Freud's second topography.

The psychic, and thus 'the truly psychical' which is the unconscious (Freud, 1938a, p. 286), can only come from the psychic. Again, however, we must be careful. It is not the same as saying that the external object is necessary to satisfy the motion of desire, and as such would indeed be interchangeable. No, one needs the mind of the other. There is a distinct difference. Freud (1911) maintains, however, the fiction of a child who grows by itself. He is aware of this and says so clearly. Nevertheless, he does not delve further into this aspect. Freud keeps to a psychological model based on the traditional notion of subject (as separate), however decentralized from the unconscious. Let us use a fiction, too. We take literally Winnicott's statement that there is no such thing as a child. If we were to give a graphic representation of a larger unit divided into two sub-units, the nature of the whole system would be evident. As such, one could not say that the symbolic order absolutely does not exist. We would say that it is present in one sub-system directly and in the other indirectly. The child as a sub-unit of the psychological field formed by the mother-child enters the symbolic order immediately. The child's unconscious, then, is not formed by an internal drive regardless of any outside influence, as if it were independent and purely biological, but is immediately immersed in society, from even before the ego is established as the central agency of the personality – in other words, as self-awareness.

One might then think of primal repression as a system of social laws passed on to the infant by the mother, who is their spokesperson, through the very means of interaction she has with the child from conception onwards. It would therefore not be repression that comes from self-awareness and *direct* subjection to the law. The establishment of a pre-symbolic semiotic order in the child precedes the symbolic order in the proper sense of the term. From this point of view, the inaccessible unconscious would also be indirectly influenced by the effects of repression – even before the repression was decreed by the now established critical agency of the subject itself. In some respects primal and secondary repression are the same thing, but in the first case the repressing agent is the mother's unconscious as a complement to the rudimentary conscious of the infant, in the second it is the infant's nascent superego.

Strictly speaking, then, we should not even regard the unrepressed unconscious as completely removed from any social determination, in line with the view that it has nothing to do with the word, but for the above reasons this is not possible. Again we come to the conclusion that the *concept of the unrepressed unconscious only makes sense from a one-person point of view. In reality, not even the repressed/cognitive/structural/inaccessible unconscious is original in the sense of not being touched by the Other and by culture.*

Binocular vision

What we have achieved, I hope, in this difficult but enthralling excursus is a binocular vision of the problem of the transition from body to mind. Looked at side by side, the metapsychologies of Bion and Freud give us a depth of vision that perhaps neither would be able to provide in isolation. Both Freud and Bion developed a theory of thinking and how this key transition occurs, but they do so in significantly different ways. One focuses on representation, the other on emotion. In the end, these are the two components of the psychical representative of the drive. Both strive to take account of access to the symbolic order, to the word. Both explain how the letters of the alphabet of peripheral sense impressions are rearranged in the brain to meet the functional needs of the organism and 'no longer topically' (Napolitano, 2010, p. 76), which is what would happen if they were based on a one-to-one relationship between body surface, the collecting station of all sensations, and the cerebral cortex. Freud does this using his drive theory, Bion with his theory of transformations. Since Bion comes along later, however, it is as if he took literally the Freudian metaphor of the poetry of the mind, and set off from that starting point to remedy the ambiguities and lacunae of drive theory.

The mechanisms that lead from the body to the word and from unconscious to conscious processes, or from primary to secondary processes, are all essentially the same. They are mechanisms of symbolization or abstraction that follow the same rules of 'neurological condensation' (Cambon, 2008, p. 71) described by Freud in his paper *On Aphasia*, rules which he then transposes onto the psychological level of description of dream work. Whether we talk of nerve bundles guided towards the cortex, of memory traces which produce images, thing- or word-representations, beta elements and alpha elements, the idea is always to simplify. The principle of identity that characterizes the secondary process can be seen as the culmination of a process of simplification-abstraction-categorization that is part of the associative activity characteristic of the primary process. Symmetry leads in the end to asymmetry, the infinite to the finite.

The essential point to grasp is that both the representation and the concept imply condensation. Very few delegates represent the populace of feelings and emotions in the parliament of consciousness. Compared to the natural tendency to simplification inherent to anatomical structures, what the word adds is the opportunity to take this process to its zenith thanks to an intersubjective agreement (for the most part, one that cannot be thematized or put in words) as to its meaning. Word representation provides a walkway that stops us from falling into the abyss of infinity and the infinite differences of things in nature. As Freud says, the word 'closes' the meaning, but since it is itself conveyed by what is called the signifier it can never 'close' it completely. In fact, in terms of meaning, it is polysemous and context-dependent. Thought comes into being in this fissure as the more or less successful attempt to bridge it.

8

THE GRID AND THE TRUTH DRIVE

> As the thing, as the other, the true dawns through an emotional and almost carnal experience, where the 'ideas' – the other's and our own – are rather traits of his physiognomy and of our own, are less understood than welcomed or spurned in love or hatred.
>
> (Merleau-Ponty M., *The Visible and the Invisible,* 1964)

Chatting about this and that to a friend, I let slip that I am thinking of writing something about Bion's Grid. All of a sudden, an expression somewhere between dismay and wry amusement appears on his face. Then he immediately associates *Grid* to the Italian word *grida* (yells). *Who* is yelling? What does this image express? Indeed, why is it that even among Bion scholars and his readers, the Grid is so infamous? Why is it seen as the pinnacle of Bion's frustrating tendency to indulge in abstract speculation? What actually is Bion's Grid, the 'notorious' Grid? A cross for his readers to bear? An ingenious invention? A harmless leisure occupation for the analyst? His Rubik's cube? And then, is it more like a periodic table of the elements, a Cartesian coordinate system, a naval battle game, a chessboard or a military map? Lastly, what is the meaning of the 'mysterious' column 2? Is it the column of lies or of dreams? Again, what can it tell us about the 'truth drive', which Grotstein identifies as the key principle of Bion's entire oeuvre?

In this chapter I shall attempt to answer these questions on the basis of the fascination and slight sense of annoyance that this instrument has always aroused in myself as well as others. In the first part, I shall examine the construction of the Grid. Allowing my imagination to roam freely, I shall tentatively offer a dynamic, in-relief representation of it. Precisely because it illustrates with such immediacy the compact dialectic that links the various concepts used by Bion, the Grid lends itself to the generation of new interpretative hypotheses. In the second part of my text, I shall consider the meaning of column 2. My basic thesis is that, given its felicitous reinterpretation by Grotstein as the dreaming column, it can throw light on a central aspect of Bion's theory of thought – namely, the concepts of truth and the 'truth drive'. For I believe that the Grid offers a fascinating perspective on the connections between dreams, knowledge and truth.

A degree of ambivalence towards the Grid is widespread. One is surprised at how casually it is sometimes dismissed or looked at askance, considering that Bion placed it at the centre of as many as two of his splendid books, *Elements of Psycho-Analysis* (1963) and *Transformations* (1965); that he devoted not inconsiderable space to it at the beginning of *Attention and Interpretation* (1970); and that he used it for the title of two other short but incisive essays. The first, 'The Grid', dates from 1963, even if it was not published until some years later, in 1997 (Bion, 1997). By a trick of fate in view of the reserve with which it was received in many quarters, it was written with the aim of creating a 'lingua franca' to help resolve the controversy between the London Kleinians and Freudians (Grotstein, 2002, 2007; Charles, 2002). The effort deployed in abstracting common elements from the key concepts of the most accredited psychoanalytic theories was intended to allow analysts of different schools to engage in a debate without allowing themselves to be overwhelmed by passion.

After all, Bion had no intention of constructing an nth theory, interested as he was in the theory of observation in psychoanalysis, but aspired instead to produce a meta-theory. He wanted to map out a common conceptual terrain. The only path that seemed to him to be negotiable, as with Propp in his study of the morphology of the folk tale, was to define the elements, objects and functions considered in various senses in the principal existing models. The second paper, on the other hand, dates from 1971, and was published in Brazil only in 1977 (Bion, 1977a).

However, let us now consider the construction of the Grid. For reasons of space, I shall assume basic familiarity with the fundamentals of Bion's thought.

The Grid

The Grid is composed of intersecting vertical and horizontal lines that make up a number of squares, as in a crossword puzzle. We thus have eight rows and seven columns, giving a total of 56 boxes (or 'containers' – Grotstein, 2007, p. 243). The horizontal rows are identified on the left, from top to bottom, by the letters A to H. Each letter relates to a key concept in Bion's theory of the mind; in order, these are β elements (A), α elements (B), dream thoughts, dreams and myths (C), pre-conception (D), conception (E), concept (F), scientific deductive system (G) and algebraic calculus (H). The seven vertical columns, on the other hand, bear numerals, to which the following categories correspond: definitory hypotheses (1), Ψ (2), notation (3), attention (4), inquiry (in the first 1997 version – that of the paper presented in 1963 – this column was called Oedipus) (5), action (6), . . . *n*. Each box (or 'drawer', if imagined in three dimensions) is thus identified by a capital letter and a numeral whenever a row intersects with a column.

The vertical axis expresses growing levels of complexity of thought, from the most concrete to the most abstract, and thus sums up within itself the phylogenesis and ontogenesis of the subject. In other words, by virtue of the work of removal of sensory and concrete elements and of abstraction (from Latin *abs-* 'away' and *trahere* 'to draw' – Webster, 1961, p. 8) from the β elements performed by the mysterious α function, a transition takes place from matter to α elements – that is, visual, auditory, acoustic, tactile and olfactory images or pictograms – then to dream thoughts and hence to concepts and numerals. This is a painstaking labour of subtraction of the differences between interdependent or contiguous terms, together with transference of other elements – the base level in my opinion being contact (in terms of rhetoric, metonymy, which is perhaps the most elementary psychological mechanism we are able to conceive) – and then analogy or metaphor. The column is therefore the vector of the assimilation or interpretation of sensible data, of digestion of quanta of reality (the thing-in-itself, O, the Divine, the infinite, etc.) that serves for the formation of thought.

Bion's basic idea is that, in order to become food for the mind, to enter into the anti-entropic process of autopoiesis of a living system, ultrasensible or infrasensible reality ('O') first needs to be 'cooked' – that is to say, rendered personal. I quote Grotstein (2007, p. 124):

> We are O and are terrified of it – thus the need for inward-directed 'sunglasses' that allow diminished illumination and disguise. O *is* the Real. What we believe we experience is a 'virtual reality' – a Reality that has become 'virtued' ('laundered') by the refractions of phantasy, imagination, illusion, and symbolization, leaving us with a 'cooked' 'Real' (O) suitable for our timid digestion.

The Grid's horizontal axis, on the other hand, specifies the *uses* that can be made of β elements at various levels of aggregation and complexity, from A1 to F1, or, in other words, of the various 'dishes' cooked in column 2. The area of definitory hypotheses is the supermarket where one goes shopping (the interface with O), while the area of column 2 (C2) is the restaurant's kitchen. Sometimes the raw foods we have bought cannot be used – that is to say, the β elements cannot be mentalized – and are ultimately evacuated in action or the body. They are therefore accommodated in A6. There are some β elements which C2 is unable to transform. For example, in row 1, the β elements, 'elements like an unpremeditated blow which is related to, but is not, thought' (Bion, 1977a, p. 3), are transformed into action without passing through thought or semantic memory; boxes 4, 5 and 6 are, after all, empty. However, we know from experience and intuition that they can be memorized in the filing systems of implicit memory as sensorimotor schemes, so that, strictly speaking, 'pure' β elements do not exist. Again according to Grotstein (2007, p. 46), an infant is born as a 'semiotic individual' and is already in possession of a rudimentary (hereditary) α function, along the lines of Chomsky's generative syntax (2007, p. 45). Grotstein sees β elements as α elements produced by this function but rejected by the mind and degraded, *impersonal and unclaimed* residues of experience. That would explain why, with regard to the β→α transformation, Bion reversed the alphabetical order of the letters.

The categories on the abscissa also express growing levels of sophistication and sum up phylogenesis and ontogenesis – this time, in use. At the most advanced level is action. Action is sometimes seen as the antithesis of thought, but this is not always a correct assumption. What makes the difference is whether the action is filtered through thought (to be found in the lower rows of the Grid) or remains confined within row A: in the latter case, the action would be unreflected or impulsive. It is a thought that constitutes at most a trial action, a pre-conception as compared with action that adaptively modifies the environment (Freud's 'specific action'), or an 'action' in the internal world whereby pre-existing behavioural schemes are modified on the basis of new experiences.

Grating

Bion suggested using the Grid to 'score' session data and to improve one's ability to observe those data. The idea that the Grid may have any practical use should in fact be immediately dismissed. Were we to try to label the facts of analysis during a session, we should be relinquishing the mental condition of negative capability suggested by Bion himself, the state of naivety or 'Faith' whereby the patient can be seen in each session as if for the first time (Bion, 1992). It would also be more difficult to find an authentic language (a language 'of achievement') for communicating intuition and using it in a disciplined way. The risk would be of identifying with the patient on the conscious level only, of understanding him rationally, and of confining one's analysis to the facts of material reality.

Aspiring to compress the complexity of the events of a session into a set of boxes is an enterprise doomed to failure. The vicissitudes of analysis are always overdetermined, multidimensional and ambiguous. They can be grasped only a posteriori, and never completely. Analysis necessarily involves a constant postponement of sense. Rather than that of 'polysemy', which after all will always include the expectation that the entire range of meanings can be known completely, the concept that most precisely expresses the manner in which sense is constructed in analysis, and in which it constantly 'slips away' without ever crystallizing, is Derrida's notion of 'dissemination' (1972). This coinage, derived from *sema* and *semen*, introduces a principle of contingency of meaning that imparts a radical dimension to Freud's concept of *Nachträglichkeit*: any text always generates new readings, even if not all of them are correct, because the context will inevitably be different each time.

Nor can the Grid be used as a tool for mental gymnastics on the part of the analyst *after* a session. Nothing arouses more boredom than papers claiming to schematize the course of a session by forcing the events that punctuated it into the categories of the Grid, which then acts, contradictorily, as a Negative Grid (see below). With regard to this aspect, Bion himself ultimately took a more pessimistic view. He often said that the problem with the Grid was the Grid itself. Furthermore, he held that any report was unfaithful, and would be even more so if a mechanical recording system were used. The fact is that Bion was acutely aware that the experience of analysis could be apprehended only aesthetically[57] (Bion, 1967; Ogden, 2007); I would add that it can be apprehended only in the subjective narration of the analyst, which is not on that account false, because it constitutes a redreaming of the session and hence a conscious *and* unconscious summarization of its *truest* aspects.

The most profitable use to which the Grid can be put, on the other hand, is to understand Bion and to build further on his theory. It could be seen, for instance, as the equivalent of Einstein's famous equation expressing the relationship between energy, mass and the speed of light. In other words, the Grid too constitutes the brilliant synthesis, which is not lacking in aesthetic qualities, of an extremely well-constructed theory, the true significance of which quite a few analysts find it difficult to grasp. As Bion himself points out, 'The visual image . . . has great power of lateral communication' (Bion, 1977a, p. 23). An overall consideration of the elements of psychoanalysis offered by the Grid reveals implicit and also surprising aspects of his thought – aspects that are less obvious when presented discursively.

If, however, the emphasis were placed on the unsaturated nature of the elements (concepts) contained in it, the Grid would appear to us as analogous to an abstract painting. In contemplating it, we could all discover in it significant figures standing out from a chaotic, indistinct background and could then subject them, as in examination of the record of a Rorschach test, to a process of consensual validation. Again, as with many non-representational paintings where the artist wishes to allow for as wide a range of interpretation as possible, many of Bion's concepts could be given the same label: *Untitled*.

In accordance with one of its own constitutive elements, the Grid can be regarded as a pre-conception awaiting various possibilities of realization – a theoretical device that is sufficiently 'open' and not merely 'technological' (Charles, 2002) because it facilitates the birth of new thoughts and insights. Hence Bion's suggestion of expanding some of its parts or of creating differentiated Grids. By virtue of its open structure, the Grid illustrates what Bion means by the concept of Faith. As indicated above, this does not imply any concession to mysticism, but only summarizes the mental attitude of someone who leaves himself time to allow the images from the always open workshop of unconscious thought to emerge. For Bion, Faith is a scientific concept or instrument, like Husserl's *epoché*. It is another name for the patience required of the analyst in waiting for a selected fact (an image, idea or emotion) to present itself and confer order on chaos, as well as for the trust that it will sooner or later present itself. Having Faith during a session means trusting the binocular (conscious/unconscious) vision of the psychoanalytic function of the personality (clearly, I am attempting here to apply this principle to the description and interpretation of the Grid itself).

It would also be interesting to compare the Grid with some of the more famous maps of the psyche drawn by Freud. Rather than compartments of the mind, the Grid represents activities, functions and transmutations. In Freud's diagrams of the first topography, the various contents are defined on the basis of the position they occupy in the compartments *Ucs., Cs.* or *Pcs.*, and transfers from one compartment to another must overcome the barrier of the two psychic censorships. The Grid's system of Cartesian coordinates, on the other hand, does not specify any content so definitively. Everything is more liquid and in motion. Instead of predefined psychic provinces, we see energy flows, as if in a 'primitive scheme of electrical switches, wires and so forth' (Bion, 1977a, p. 32); as we know, for Bion psychoanalysis belongs to the field of transformations.

However, the Grid offers only a static representation of these extremely dynamic phenomena. That is why it seems abstruse to Bion's readers. It would be less so if it could actually be seen 'working'. An animated model of the Grid would be needed to make this a reality. It would then be possible to display the rapid movements of subatomic particles of α elements from column to column and from row to row and back so as to produce 'idea atoms' (Bion, 1992) – perhaps in the form of a fabric of multicoloured lights, now flashing and sparkling, now continuous and about to merge almost imperceptibly into other hues, or, eschewing metaphor, into different degrees of transformation of emotions and thoughts (the contents of the Grid). It is like the headlights of a car that approaches and then disappears into the darkness, the flashing of a lighthouse at the entrance of a harbour, the trails of light of a firework – or Arnold Dreyblatt's installation (1998–1999) inspired by the 'mystic writing-pad', *The ReCollection Mechanism*, displayed at the IPA Congress in Berlin in 2007.

Bion was aware of the deficiencies of the Grid and he himself suggested an animated model of it. In one of his São Paulo lectures (Bion, 1990) and then in the *Tavistock Seminars* (Bion, 2005, p. 63), he writes: 'If you could turn the Grid edgeways on, then it would become nearer to being a grating; the space between these various categories would get smaller and smaller and smaller'. In the same way, we should be flexible enough to vary the vertices of observation and put things together in ways (imaginative conjectures) that may initially seem insufficiently controlled. The word 'grating', as opposed to 'Grid', is derived from a verb form and already suggests something more dynamic, as evidenced by Grotstein's (2007, p. 245) use of it to indicate how the alpha function acts – 'like a *grating* to sort out raw β-elements'.

Taken as a whole, the Grid could also be thought of as the 'scoring', in terms of a new metapsychology, of the film of psychic activity. Its operation could be seen as analogous to the neuroimaging of brain activity, displaying areas of the cerebral cortex in different colours according to the nature and intensity of the stimuli impinging on the senses; or to a second- or third-level abstract representation of the functioning of a mind at a given moment. This would, for example, resemble scenes of a science fiction film intended to portray the path of a nerve impulse by means of a kaleidoscopic, vertiginous sequence of frames.[58] A β element, an entity that still possesses the qualities of a thing while already belonging to the psychic order, would then be seen to enter the prism of the mind and to fragment into a fanlike pattern of light beams. These beams take various paths, some of them retrograde and collateral, interweaving and separating at supersonic speeds. In this way they convey an idea of the wiring, this time in concrete form, of the neural pathways on which, according to Freud (1891), the psychic processes of condensation are ultimately based. On each occasion there is the 'big bang' of the transition from the body to the mind, from the thing to the no-thing of the idea, from the material to the psychic. We observe the repetition of the quantum leap from the definitory hypothesis, which is still the locus of the concrete and of the symbolic equation (the idea of something awaiting verification, here perhaps in the sense of happening, is inherent in the concept of a hypothesis), to symbolic thought.

How these transformations are brought about remains an open question. If the Grid is thought of as the device that governs them, then the input of course consists of proto-emotions and proto-sensations. Sensory sparks are kindled by the friction of the body with O, the real, *das Ding* (Lacan, 1986), immediately feed into their circuits and reach their relays. The Grid shows in three dimensions what happens when, like an image emerging from a bas-relief, subjectivity springs out of the fine atomic dust of infrasensible or ultrasensible reality. It conveys an impression of the processes of transformation that give rise to the subject. The starting point is the notion that the distinction between subject and world is ultimately arbitrary. We lack an external – i.e. transcendent – view of things, even if we succeed in pretending that this is not the case. Our common sense is absolutely convinced of this. Yet perception is only a text – a *seeing-as*, according to Wittgenstein (Borutti, 1999).

Just as the futurists sought to show ingeniously and in every possible way in the field of art, there is between the body and its environment a mutual penetration, a continuous osmotic interchange of energy; the boundaries of the self stand out as dynamic states against the background of electromagnetic fields. The subject is a 'field of relations' (Merleau-Ponty, 1945); it comes into being by differentiating itself from the real and can never completely free itself from it. The real is like water to a fish or air to a bird. A modicum of identity with the real (of *truth*, understood as a balance between identity and difference) is absolutely indispensable to life. By portraying the interface with the real diagrammatically, the Grid obliges us to rediscover ourselves in continuity with the real, and to remember that we are part of it.

Bidirectionality

Another important property of the Grid is that it can be traversed in both directions, also from left to right and from bottom to top. A thought, action or dream can regain a concrete value, of emotional discharge, *even if it retains its appearance*. An α element can be partially destroyed and become a β element again, but with fragments of meaning still adhering to it. This is what happens, for example, when a dream is used to evacuate untransformed emotions, when a concept is reified, or when an element is de-personalized, deprived of what gave it meaning.

This possibility also helps us to define the nature of the elements situated in C1: at all levels, for instance, there are no actual α elements, dreams or concepts, etc., but β-agglomerates as proto-containers, precursors of α elements; instead of 'pure', unassimilated reality, there are projections of a reality that is beginning to be idiosyncratic, a reality that is already less formless, sense impressions ready to be transformed from C2 into something mental; or else, regressively, elements that retain only the semblance of a concept – i.e. false concepts. An example is transformation in hallucinosis, a phenomenon that describes how it is possible to have correct perceptions of reality which, however, are deprived of meaning because they are projected on to an infinite background and disconnected from each other.

C1 could be thought of as a semiotic (Kristeva, 1974), precategorial level of sense, which is for this reason still obscure or partial – the level described by Merleau-Ponty as inter-corporeal or intersensory, which therefore could be recorded only in the implicit, non-repressed or inaccessible unconscious (Bion, 1997).

Like the horizontal axis, the vertical axis too can be traversed in a retrograde direction, from bottom to top. This is a physiological fact. In general, α elements serve to know things and β elements to be ignorant of them – the latter being certainly no less important a function than the former. Bion (1992, p. 182) writes:

> Without α-elements it is not possible to know anything. Without β-elements it is impossible to be ignorant of anything: they are essential to the functioning of projective identification; any unwanted idea is converted into a β-element, ejected from the personality, and then becomes a fact of which the individual is unaware, though he may be aware of feelings of persecution stimulated by it.
>
> I reserve the term, 'knowledge', for the sum total of α- and β-elements. It is a term that therefore covers everything the individual knows and does not know.

With regard to the capacity to think, what matters is the curve showing the variation of the ratio of β to α over time. There is no need to confuse the bidirectionality whereby the rows and columns of the Grid can be traversed with what Meltzer (1986, 1987) calls the Negative Grid. In a mature mind, the possibility of traversing these vectors forwards and backwards is equivalent to the balanced functioning, described by Ogden (1989), of the various 'positions' (autistic-contiguous, paranoid-schizoid and depressive) whereby we confer a personal sense on experience.

The concept of the Negative Grid indicates that the free, progressive and regressive interplay of transformations performed by the α function is replaced by a *significant* and *stable* reversal, as when a group is in basic assumption mode. In other words, it is what happens when the dialectic of defences and ways of feeling and of being unconscious collapses into a single mode of functioning. With the Negative Grid, we are unequivocally in the field of pathology. So it is a matter not of negativization *within* the Grid, with which column 2 is concerned, but of negativization *of* the Grid itself. The prevailing links are –L, –H and –K, which deprive experience of its emotional colour, so that a delusional system becomes established in the personality (Meltzer, 1986).

Among other things, this ability of the Grid to become transmuted into –G need not always be a negative fact, because it expresses a psychic defence that becomes maladaptive only in the long term, only if not transformed into a more appropriate way of solving emotional problems. The onset of, for example, a symptom of hypochondria could be an indication of a negative container-contained transformation (-♀ ♂) – i.e. of a relative reversal of the process of symbolization or of a regression to the (autistic) use of symbols whose meaning has been emptied out. Overall, however, it would represent an attempt to re-establish contact with psychic qualities – a task required to reinstate a condition of adequate somato-psychic integration (Civitarese, 2011a, 2011b).

The interpsychic dimension in the Grid

The agent that effects the transitions from row to row and from column to column is the α function (and then the α-meta-function of the apparatus for thinking thoughts/dreaming dreams). In itself, the α function, as an empty concept, an x that stands for mental events of which we know little or nothing, thus presents itself as an intrapsychic concept. It becomes less mysterious only if referred to the mother-child relationship, which revolves around emotional attunement. At birth, an infant has a rudimentary consciousness but not its unconscious complement (Bion, 1967). The α function, which allows one to dream experience and to perform the task of construction/deconstruction of the contact barrier that separates and unites conscious and unconscious, is not yet established and operational, or else it too is present only in elementary form (Grotstein, 2007). '*Becom[ing]* conscious' (Bion, 1962, p. 15), in the sense of full consciousness of self (the ability to say 'I') is possible only if the unconscious too has been established and with it the capacity to be aware of oneself. For this to happen, the child's primitive α elements cannot dispense with the maternal reverie. Hence the α function cannot develop autonomously on the basis of biological maturation, which, however, it presupposes.

It may be wondered whether the interpsychic origin of the α function features in some way in the Grid. It would be a serious limitation if the thoroughly intersubjective nature of Bion's theory were not represented in it. The problem was stated by Bion (1990, p. 26) at one of his São Paulo seminars. A participant asks: 'Is it possible to show the model "mother-baby" on the Grid?' He replies: 'If it could be shown it would be by something in the area of transformations of visual imagery (C3), like saying, "I had a dream last night", describing in *words* something that was *seen* when off one's guard as in sleep.'

What might this mean? As usual with Bion, it is not easy to say. I construe it as follows. First of all, it could simply refer to the concept of reverie. Second, one might note that, unlike theories (accommodated in row F), according to this reply he places the concept of a model in row C (the row of dreams, myths and hallucinations); then, on a different, more specific level, which, with regard to the matter to which he is referring, Bion sees the mother-child *model* (as opposed with the real mother-child relationship) as equivalent to the reporting of a dream as opposed to the dream itself – that is, as the schematization of a phenomenon that is just as intangible as a dream, a phenomenon of which it is not possible to have direct knowledge. This concerns the shared experience of an unconscious, primitive and deep mode of communication which we explain on the metapsychological level by the interplay of projective (and introjective) identification and reverie. Just as an individual in the waking state confers sense on his dream images recorded in memory, recognizes them, names them and recounts them to himself or to someone else, so we recount the mother-child interaction by means of a scientific model. By this reply, Bion makes explicit the status he assigns to the concept of a model in general, but does not yet tell us *how* the mother-child model is represented in the Grid.

Another answer could also be given to the question put to him at the São Paulo seminar – namely, that the mother-child model is symbolized by the structure of the Grid itself. Let us consider this.

The Grid resembles a fractal[59] – that is, a geometrical figure with the property of identical repetition of itself on any scale. Overall, as if it were an ideogram of it, the Grid represents the selective membrane of the mind (thought) that is interposed between stimulus and action (*I*, which stands for *idea*, is the letter which for Bion denotes it in its entirety – 1963, p. 4). The action A depends on the value assumed by the stimulus S for the idea function I – that is, A = I (S). We thus have a pair of terms functionally separated/linked by a slash,[60] which symbolizes a contact barrier.

Close examination of the Grid shows that this structure is repeated at the dimensional level of rows and columns. The entire horizontal axis, broadly speaking, reflects the vertical axis. C1 is the reflection of the β category on the horizontal row: both refer to unmentalized psychic elements. The horizontal line between rows A and B separates β elements from pictograms (α elements), while that between B and C separates pictograms from dreams and thoughts. Crossing these frontiers – that is, transferring from β to α (intermediate elements between β and the 'sensory images' of dreams, myths, narrations and hallucinations), and then from α to dream thoughts and to thoughts or dreams proper – is equivalent to crossing those between C1 and C2 (transformations performed by the α function) and then between C2 and C3 (transformations performed by the apparatuses for thinking thoughts and for dreaming dreams). So, along the same lines, row C (dream thoughts/dreams/myths) could be seen as a reflection of column 2 (Ψ); row D (pre-conception) as a reflection of column 3 (notation); row E (conception) as a reflection of column 4 (attention); and row F (concept) as a reflection of column 5 (inquiry). In fact, boxes D, E and F (pre-conception, conception and concept) might perhaps be seen as a single group, in the same way as 3, 4 and 5 (notation, attention and inquiry). The rows and columns, too, can be seen as pairs of opposites linked dialectically by an interface that separates and unites them at one and the same time, represented graphically by the horizontal and vertical lines.

However, the same can also be said in general terms about the *internal* organization of the Grid's rows and columns, on an ever-decreasing scale. *The same essential structure*, that of a binary pair separated/joined by a slash (which is then tantamount to a function), is found not only, as we have seen, in the Grid itself and in the second-order filters represented by the rows and columns, but also in the third-order filters of the actual lines that define the boxes. From the largest to the smallest scale, the Grid as a whole, the columns, the rows and finally all the sides that define a box, can be seen as the slashes of an equal number of semi-permeable membranes, or 'contact barriers', which simultaneously divide and rejoin two terms, which are thus found to be dialectically opposed. What does this signify? It means that the two terms are not endowed with a fixed and autonomous meaning, but are defined only in relation to each other.

On the level of meta-theory (the theoretical level), this structure could be seen as reflecting the general principle of Bion's method of transcending the caesura and the manner in which, on the basis of this principle, he dialecticizes all the classical oppositions that define the analytic field of experience. The most telling example is the invalidation of the distinction between night dreams and waking dreams (waking dream thought), between *Cs.* and *Ucs.*, between the primary process and the secondary process, between the pleasure principle and the reality principle, etc. After all, if the upper part of the Grid broadly corresponds to the primary process and the unconscious and the lower part to the secondary process and consciousness, the two areas merge into each other without a clear line of distinction between them.

In terms of Bion's theory of thought, on the other hand, it would not be wrong to see in this obsessive *specularity* an allusion to the mirror function performed by the object for the infant psyche, which is mediated by the process of projective and introjective identification – a reflection which, once internalized, becomes the sense of existing, the capacity for self-reflection (for being two in one).

Hence the binary pair obtained by selecting any two elements of the Grid separated by the caesura of a slash (the side of any box) symbolizes, *both* in structure *and* in functioning, the mother-child relationship (the pair by antonomasia) and the model of it that we construct. This is essentially suggested by the fact that it is the only relationship model that can give an idea of the working of the container-contained mechanism which governs the passage from box to box at all levels, and of which the α function is an expression.

This structural persistence is found to reflect the constitutive duality (group nature) of every mind, *in so far as this is represented in the Grid itself.* Its syntax alludes on macroscopic and microscopic levels to the essentially interpsychic (bipersonal/multipersonal) nature of meaning, and to Bion's radically social/political theory of the birth of the psyche. Pursuing our fractal metaphor further, this dual/group-type level would appear as the natural continuation of what, on a larger scale, would be two or more Grids (G1, G2, G3 . . . G*n*) in a dialectical relationship with each other.

The contact barrier, seen not only as the filter interposed between unconscious and conscious, but also as the specialized surface governing the porosity of any 'container', describes the schematic anatomy of the mind (of the Grid/Idea). The container-contained mechanism (♀ ♂) represents its physiology. This is a concept which Bion (1963) 'abstracts' from the Kleinian theory of projective identification: scattered elements of experience become meaningful when they are combined in a container that confers a recognizable form on them. The relationship is dialectical and reversible in terms of the roles. The container too is modified by the contained. From another point of view, on a larger scale, each container may in turn represent a contained. A 'container' or a 'contained' is of course to be understood not as a psychic location but as a process. It is a matter of 'to contain or to be contained' rather than of inert, structurally fixed envelopes (Bion 1963, p. 7; Ogden, 2005).

Of all the concepts used by Bion to describe psychic transformations, the container-contained (♀ ♂) mechanism is the most general and abstract in scope, because it is the least common denominator of the Ps↔D oscillation, of the oscillation between negative capability and selected fact (NC↔SF), and of the PI↔ reverie circuit. For unlike these, the container-contained (♀ ♂) mechanism in its various forms (convivial, parasitic, symbiotic, reversed or negative) can be applied to both the intrapsychic and the interpsychic levels.

The container-contained (♀ ♂) mechanism is the factor that on each occasion governs the transition from one row of the Grid to another. That is why, at all levels, the slash is also the interface where turbulence is generated. Even when a contained encounters a container which is a perfect fit for it, so that they become *a unity*, in the same way as an antigen 'recognizes' an antibody, the process is never (entirely) painless: it always entails an interaction in which each term recognizes and at the same time negates the other, and vice versa. Being in unison is the outcome of a process of neg(oti)ation, involving the sacrifice of aspects of the self and, in a specular manner, of aspects of the other. In exactly the same way as for the purpose of categorization, and so that we can then recognize ourselves in the concepts we use, we need to obliterate the differences and emphasize the similarities between things (i.e. to abstract).

Upon each slash, the proto-emotions – a term that is of course not susceptible to unambiguous definition and denotes a range of states – record the noises of the battle for recognition between container and contained. Before being identified – that is, before being contained in an idea or clothed in a film of thought and hence used on the level of cognition and/or motivation because they express a movement of repulsion or attraction – they are the bearers of an excess. Emotions inform the mind about the state of its relations with the object (with the world). They display the balance of its cathexes. However, if untransformed, they are scattered in an immense mental space, so that the subject may in effect 'bleed to death in his own tissues' on account of a surgical shock (Bion, 1970, p. 12).

The secret painter of the mind

Of all the Grid's caesuras, I am for the present concerned mainly with column 2. My approach to the Grid is in fact inspired by Grotstein's reading of it (2007, p. 236):

> For me the contact-barrier is a cognate of α-function as well as its object. It corresponds, I believe, to Column 2 of Bion's Grid in so far as Column 2 is not only the *lie* column (*denial*) but also

> the *negation* column, which is necessary for differentiation of one object from another (secondary process). I see the contact-barrier, in other words, as the *continuation* of α-function.

Again:

> Column 2, to me, constitutes the *dreaming column – that is*, the *α-function column* – which must aesthetically alter (*quasi-falsify*) the β-elements from Column 1 (Definition Hypothesis) to make α-elements suitable for subsequent mentalizable portage through the rest of the Grid.
>
> (Grotstein, 2007, p. 249)

In agreement with Grotstein, I suggest that the 'mysterious' column 2 is the Grid's real theoretical treasure, because it is derived from the α function that coincides with the contact barrier.

The importance of column 2 is immediately obvious. What we observe is that before C2 thought does not exist, but after C2 all thought is 'false'! *In other words, in the Grid nothing has meaning before the passage of β elements into C2.* As we have seen, in C1 concepts too exist only in the form of connected agglutinations of β elements; they are not thoughts, but 'souls of thoughts' waiting to be actually dreamt; hence they are proto-concepts or pre-conceptions, like the bed of a river as opposed to the water that flows over it (but which could also *not* flow). In C1, things have *sense* (from the Latin *sentire*, to feel), but lack *significance* (*signum*, a sign) (i.e. meaning); all mental contents are concrete. The contradiction can be overcome only by imagining a linear progression from the communicative register of the semiotic to that of the semantic, from sense to significance (meaning).

Considered in these terms, C2 could be the column for the work of the negative, which extends over a continuous spectrum that includes repression, splitting, disavowal, foreclosure, rejection, negation and so forth (Green, 1998). In order to succeed, any process of mentalization must necessarily pass through column 2. Column 2 is the agent of *aesthetic* processing (of the treatment of sensation/*aisthesis* by thought/dreaming) which transforms O into a fictional truth – that is, a lie that is to a greater or lesser extent shared.

Any element in the first column, definitory hypotheses, results from schemes emerging from β elements,[61] swarms of sensations, which do not yet constitute thought; hence, in order to become thought, they must necessarily undergo the 'falsification' of the Ψ (*psi*) filter. It is not by chance that Bion, to denote this column, also uses the initial Greek letter of both *pseudos* (deception, lie, but also 'poetic fiction') (Derrida, 2005; Chantraine, 1999) and *psyche*. This is where the mind is born. Mind and mendacity (lying) have the same root in *mens* (López-Corvo, 2002, p. 309): 'You cannot let something become unconscious if α is not done to that something' (Bion, 1992, p. 139). Consciousness depends on the α function. The elements of column 1 become accessible to thought, dreaming, memory and attention only after passing through C2. Prior to this passage, they are β-configurations with different degrees of complexity, which, however, have not yet been dreamt. Perhaps β should be thought of as the base level of α. Pure β elements may perhaps not be able to exist – or else, as Grotstein says, they are degraded α elements or, conversely, according to Bion, rudimentary α elements.

Dreaming, as the unconscious psychological work of creating meaning (essentially, the α function), therefore, is not found in row C – it is there as a contained, but not as a function – but is present *at all levels* in column 2. For this reason, Grotstein (2007, p. 284) also defines it as the *column of dreams* ('*Column 2 constitutes a container-dreamer-thinker-function!*'). This idea is supported by a note by Bion himself (1963, 80n.): 'category C2 is intended to contain dream thought . . .'. This is the difference between row C and column 2. However, row C is important because, in the Grid, it ideally denotes the point of equilibrium between unconscious and conscious thought, between symmetrical and asymmetrical thought, between the primary process and the secondary process, between the pleasure principle and the reality principle, and between animism and abstraction.

The elements of row C, night dreams and waking dreams, as well as all gradients of dreaming, on the other hand, are produced by the apparatus for dreaming dreams, a kind of α-meta- or super-function (Ferro, 2006), whereas all the lower rows (D, E and F) have their origins in the apparatus for thinking thoughts: both functions make use of the dream thoughts produced by the α function (α elements). The acquisition of language could admittedly be accommodated between the α function and the apparatus (or apparatuses) for dreaming dreams and for thinking thoughts, but, after all, why should we make a radical distinction between the two psychic mechanisms? Could the analogy with the mathematical figure of the fractal not apply here too? The α function, the apparatus for dreaming dreams and the apparatus for thinking thoughts could be conceived of as increasingly complex levels of one and the same basic function, or ones applied to products of increasing sophistication (abstraction), even if Bion specifies that the *manufacture* and *use* of dreams could lead to two different systems.

The only real difference might be that, in order to cook O, some take as their starting point the raw food of semiotic language and others the precooked food of symbolic language, but both can be seen as expressing one and the same drive to simplify and/or categorize. All the psychic contents located to the right of column 2 are infiltrated by dreaming at any level of the progression from β elements to the most abstract thought and to action. Algebra too is infiltrated by dreaming, because it arises from the equating of the similar and the dissimilar. In nature, however, two equal things do not exist, unless the differences are disregarded. No two trees are identical. If I create for myself the concept of a 'tree' or I put two trees together, this means that I am metaphorizing one with the other, that I am transferring the properties of one to the other, that I am *obliterating* the differences – which, as we know, is the work of C2! Bion (1992, p. 71, my emphasis) writes:

> A child learning to walk is engaged in attempting to make conscious material unconscious; only when this is done can it walk. *The same is true of every piece of learning ever done* – its success depends on the central operations by which dream work is able to transform conscious material into unconscious material suitable for unconscious waking thinking.

Abstract thought too presupposes a series of unconscious processes and the neutralization of potentially confusing stimuli. This, after all, is the original sense of the mechanism of repression, imagined by Freud in the 'Project' (1895) along the lines of the physical elimination, as undertaken by the mother, of stimuli that might disturb the child. Knowing, transforming β elements into α elements, entails the capacity to forget, to pretend (in the sense of imagining, shaping or moulding), to relegate inessential elements of the figure to the background and to act as if they did not exist: 'A determination not to experience anything can be shown to co-exist with an *inability to reject or ignore any stimulus.* Sense impressions can be seen to have some meaning but the patient feels incapable of knowing what the meaning is' (Bion, 1962, p. 18, my emphasis).

Sense can only be conferred on things by virtue of a process of negation, of the hallucinatory element that inevitably infiltrates perception (Botella and Botella, 2001), just as exposed and unexposed frames alternate in the physical substrate of a film. Like a 'sieve' (Freud, 1895, p. 313), the α function retains elements that are useful for its purposes and rejects others.

Hence column 2 is effectively the hinge between the human, the real assimilated in dreaming and the capacity to be conscious of it, on the one hand, and, on the other, the pre-human element of the impersonal, formless and infinite O, or the dream of primary animal consciousness from which waking is impossible. *In the column of definitory hypotheses, there is as yet no mind, for its existence would entail the capacity to distinguish between self and not-self.* The constant conjunction of two facts, their linkage on this level by a bond of contiguity, *cannot yet be thought.* True symbolization does not yet exist. This is born with Ψ, with unconscious 'lying'. Dreaming does not make a mind except after column 2. Even before C2, however, there is a sense which pre-exists the establishment of an ego and which on the one hand passes to the child from the mother, in so far as she embodies his future α function as a component of the dyad, and on the other takes the form of innate psychophysical dispositions, pre-conceptions, primal fantasies, etc.

What is the truth for psychoanalysis?

However, is column 2 then the locus of the lie, in accordance with many authors' interpretations and as ambiguously suggested by Bion himself, or is it the locus of dreaming? Can liars be treated? And if all thought is false, what is the meaning of the proposition that the subject is moved by a 'truth drive'? Is this the engine of the Grid's functioning (what the Grid represents)?

A passage from the 'second' Grid essay suggests that Bion invented C2 in response to the view, expressed privately to him by Klein, that liars were unbeatable. He objected to her that, during an analysis, her own theory of projective identification 'could itself be presented in the course of analysis as a series of lying statements' (Bion, 1977a, p. 5). Considered in these terms, there would not be a single patient who does not lie in analysis. Even the distinction Bion draws immediately afterwards between (voluntary) lies and falsehood leaves the problem unresolved.

He himself recognizes that man's capacity to survive depends also on his capacity for illusion – broadly, for lying to himself and lying in general: 'It is difficult to accept real life because frustration is an essential feature of real life. In an extreme position it obstructs the development of thought' (ibid., p. 28). Again:

> man owes his health, and his capacity for continued health, to his ability to shield himself during his growth as an individual by repeating in his personal life the history of the race's capacity for self-deception against truth that his mind is not fitted to receive without disaster.
>
> (Bion, 1992, p. 192)

However, seemingly contradicting this assumption, Bion also writes that the capacity to survive depends on 'a constant supply of truth' (1992, p. 99), because truth is food for the mind. He thus sees the search for truth as a central drive, so that Meltzer even writes that his theory of the mind is 'epistemological', while Grotstein invokes a 'truth drive'.[62]

From this it may be deduced that in his clinical practice Bion applied a relative and not an abstract concept of truth. The analyst's standpoint is never that of a moralist, philosopher or historian, as he would otherwise use different investigative methodologies. In the same order as above, he would examine the correct interpretation in the language of catechistic precepts, evaluate the rigour of logical argument, seek documentary evidence, and so on. In analysis, on the other hand, it makes no sense to claim that truth is the absolute antithesis of a lie. Instead, truth should be defined on the basis of the specific parameters of the theoretico-clinical field of psychoanalysis, combined in the binary oppositions of conscious/unconscious, explicit/implicit and sustainable/unsustainable. Let us consider these in that order.

First, what matters is the subject's unconscious truth, because if there is psychic suffering, what he knows about himself must be insufficient: there is not enough food for the mind. As to the unconscious/conscious parameter, however, it is also the case that the 'liar's lie predicates the truth in disguise-like dreams' (Grotstein, 2007, p. 149). In some cases, lying may be the only, or the most effective, recourse of the patient to protect himself from anxiety and pain, as well as to make himself understood. The truth of O and the encounter with O (the anonymous, indeterminate and infinite reality that must be rendered meaningful in personal form by dreaming) is involuntarily expressed also in intentional lies. Like a dream, reverie or symptom (Ogden, 2001), a lie too is a metaphor, not a direct vision, of the subject's unconscious experience. For this reason, from the analyst's point of view, the problem of the lie can arise only as a symptom; it is at any rate not an insurmountable obstacle to the treatment.[63] Hence the parameter of conscious intentionality does not help us to resolve the contradiction between the need for truth and falsity of thought.

Whereas by definition we can have only explicit knowledge (a feeling or idea) on the conscious level, on the unconscious level a distinction must be made between explicit or representational 'truth' (the repressed unconscious) and its implicit-affective or non-representational counterpart (the inaccessible or non-repressed unconscious). Consequently, increasing the patient's area of truth may mean either helping him to accept knowing more about himself or learning to know how to do more things, even if he would be unable to say how – for instance, being better able to confront certain situations in emotional terms. This is an area in which the subject's ability cannot be based solely on ideas (which may, on the other hand, be adequate for other purposes and tasks in life).

The third parameter – sustainability/unsustainability – already evidenced at the beginning of the section with the quotations from Bion, is perhaps that which best expresses the specificity of his vision, which is that one's starting point should be an intersubjective psychoanalytic theory. The truth that interests Bion (ourselves) in analysis is the truth that feeds the mind and is adaptive with respect to external reality only when it is emotionally sustainable (and also compatible with the ecology of the internal world), only when it does not involve an excessive degree of frustration and does not 'obstruct the development of thought'. Otherwise the effect will be the opposite of that desired –

undermining instead of increasing the patient's capacity to dream and/or to think.

However, the notion of sustainability concerns what is true not only for the analyst but also for the patient. Conversely, a truth that arises only in the analyst's mind may be poisonous to the patient. In order to be the food that feeds the mind, the truth must be receivable – that is, shareable – which is the case when the patient is in possession of sufficient mental space to receive, recognize and assimilate it. Hence the need to introduce an intersubjective or social definition of truth as something involving common sense and arising from emotional unison, from the experience at the beginning of a child's life that creates the object first and foremost as something that is common to the senses. For a better understanding of the nature of this sharing, the model of the birth of thought (truth) in mother-child interaction can be used.

The truth drive

It is only by virtue of reverie (Bion) and the mother's capacity for holding and handling (Winnicott) that a newborn succeeds in emerging from a state of non-integration and in coordinating his senses in such a way that they confirm each other. It is the mother who makes up for the infant's immaturity with her own mind. What is true for the infant in perception, in the sense of 'common to the senses' – touch tells sight: 'Received loud and clear; what I am feeling corresponds to what you are seeing', and vice versa – stems from an infinite set of micro-experiences of emotional confirmation, unison and consensuality. These minimal emotional experiences (of sense) interweave to form the stuff of thought. The mother helps the child to confer order on the chaotic flow of stimuli in which he is immersed and so to speak passes on the method of so doing to him.

At the beginning of life in particular, this drive towards integration and the construction of a psychic space can obviously be fulfilled only on the basis of emotional unison, and not yet by intellectual agreement, because, if any type of categorization is already present, it is preverbal and prereflective, semiotic, affective and not yet truly conceptual in nature. At this stage, the emotions directly express the principle of value essential for survival, and they continue to do so throughout life, even when accompanied by logico-rational thought – because there will always be reasons of the heart or body which the mind cannot represent to itself but can only feel.

For this reason, it is in my opinion wrong to see truth and lies as absolute opposites. A more meaningful conceptualization is of a gradient extending from the truth of the minimum possible level of emotional accord and consensuality compatible with life to that of the maximum attainable degree of attunement with others and oneself. For the same reason, in analysis a truth other than unconscious, emotional, shared truth is of scant importance because, in accordance with its own model of psychic functioning and in terms of the declared aim of treatment, unconscious emotional life is the specific level of action of psychoanalysis.

So the answer to the first of the questions that began the previous section is that C2 can be both – that is, both the column of lies and the column of dreams – because, if it is seen as coinciding with the contact barrier or the α function, what matters is how it functions. If it functions well, the result will be the dream ('digestion') of reality, the shared lie of commonsense reality, the as-if of perception; if it works badly, there will be undreamt dreams (night terrors) or interrupted dreams (nightmares – Ogden, 2005) expressed in various symptoms and pathologies. These might also include intentional lying or an inauthentic, even if hyper-adapted, life or, at the limit, the use of factual reality for deception (Derrida, 2005).

As to the second question, on the basis of the foregoing the answer is yes, it is possible to treat liars. How? Just as in other situations, it is a matter of attaining emotional unison. 'Communication' (Strachey's translation of *Verständigung*, which literally means understanding or agreement – Freud, 1895, p. 318) allows the patient to increase his capacity to think and to achieve a higher degree of agreement, even with regard to material reality and the facts of his present and past life, so that he no longer needs to lie.

We now come to the final point, the truth drive. The concept of truth having been redefined as un/conscious, emotional and shared, and hence as something accommodated along a continuum and not as a rigid antithesis between truth and lies, a sense will be gained of the possible meaning of a truth drive: not, of course, the urge to appropriate in abstract terms a given system of true statements about reality, but the impulse to achieve ever greater degrees of emotional attunement with the other, which, it is important to note, also constitutes the foundation of thought-based communication, albeit only secondarily. Considered in this way, the contradiction between the intrinsic falsehood of thought and the truth (relative falsehood) that promotes growth of the mind is seen to be invalid, because it is now reduced to a quantitative rather than a qualitative factor.

So the truth drive is found to consist in the search for this special attunement with the other. This means that truth feeds thought. The same idea could of course also be expressed as the search for the object and the satisfaction of libido, or by other models. If Bion chooses to speak of truth, a term that should always be used with a degree of modesty, it is because his conception of it is social and relativistic, and because, I would say, it demonstrates better than any other term that the factor which promotes life and makes for development of the mind is the thirst for sociality. This in my view constitutes the specificity of the concept of the truth drive, and explains why Bion prefers it to the equivalent Freudian formulations.

The value of the concept of the truth drive (reformulated as the urge for emotional attunement) is not confined to the sphere of analysis, because it helps us to see that any type of truth recognized by a community – at the limit, including, too, the truths of science – is a particular case of communication, and also has its roots in emotional accord, in being-in-unison. Given the centuries-old tradition of contrasting the passions with reason and dreaming with waking, the idea that judgement concerning factual reality is ultimately rooted in emotional and 'oneiric' reality may seem bizarre, but, given the premises of Bion's theory, it is not. In moving on from 'somatic *emotional* categorization' (Grotstein, 2007, p. 276f.) – i.e. semiotic categorization – to the concept, all we are doing is getting to know reality by simplifying it and reducing it to a system of relationships (of 'invariants').[64]

To return to our original images, the Grid has a certain quality of 'tankishness' (Souter, 2009), which pervades all Bion's writings, so that it is in some respects like a military map, a naval battle or a 'psychoanalytic game'. It shares the difficulty and diabolical perfection of the Rubik's cube, the speculative character of the system of Cartesian coordinates, and the ingenious combinatorics of chess.

While as it were constituting a Mendeleev-type periodic table of the elements of psychoanalysis, the Grid has the inestimable epistemological, theoretical and technical merit of being, on the one hand, an effective representation of the continuity between the unconscious and the conscious – considering that, in order to be expressed, the position of every psychic event requires a parameter on the vertical axis (use) and another on the horizontal axis (thought) – and, on the other, a visually intuitive synthesis of dreams, knowledge and truth.

In particular, the importance of C2 is evident in the light of the foregoing, because it so to speak rules out from the beginning any absolute, metaphysical or positivistic conception of truth and enables us to grasp the scope of the seemingly contradictory concept in Bion's theory of the truth drive. Column 2 is the secret painter of the mind (Grotstein, 2007) – our inner Monet.

9

INTERMEDIARITY AS AN ESPISTEMOLOGICAL PARADIGM IN PSYCHOANALYSIS

> The relationship between the two people is an activity in two directions, and since one is concerned with showing that relationship, it is not a question of speaking about analyst and analysand; it is a matter of speaking about something *between* those two.
>
> (Bion, 1978–1980)

Zwischenreich zwischen

Pontalis stresses that Freud is 'a thinker of conflict more than of itermediarity' (2007, p. 316). In Freud, a binary mode of thought, made from the polar opposites of conscious/unconscious, primary thinking/secondary process, pleasure principle/reality principle, narcissistic libido/object libido, etc., coexists with a tripartite mode: for example, the three-way partition Inc-Prec-C of the first model or the *Ego-Id-Superego* structure of the second. Even though dualism was to prevail, along with the idea of psychic life as essentially based on the conflict of agencies, forces, quantities, desires, etc., Freud was acutely aware of the need for intermediary thinking or, since he preferred a more abstract term, intermediarity. It is indicative of this fact that very early on he coined the suggestive neologism *Zwischenreich* ('in-between realm' or 'halfway region'). The term appears as early as a letter dated 16 April 1896 to Fliess, his friend and correspondent in Berlin (Masson, 1985, p. 181), and yet it is not really clear in this instance what Freud was referring to. Masson, the editor of the correspondence, notes that according to Schur the expression alludes to the unconscious and the relationship between body and psyche, and that Fliess would use it later on in relation to bisexuality.

In 1912, in *Recommendations to Physicians Practising Psychoanalysis*, Freud uses this term again explicitly to indicate the transference, the halfway region which stands between illness and reality, with the clarification that the transference neurosis is only an 'artificial' illness. It contrasts with what is natural; it is made by art, is a surrogate, an expedient, an illusion. Thus the *Zwischenreich* is the site of infinite transformations, a 'gymnasium', a provisional and virtual one; but as Freud explains, this very fact makes it 'accessible to our intervention' (1914a). The term recurs in his writings on two other occasions, referring to the imagination and art (Freud, 1913, 1917b). We can catch another glimpse of his interest in the intermediate space from his writings on telepathy and on the processes of thought-transmission or thought-transference (*Gedankenübertragung*) which it would imply (Freud, 1921).

The history of psychoanalysis from Freud onwards is the story of the exploration of intermediate space. Confining ourselves to the principal authors: after Freud, for whom the *Zwischenreich* is first and foremost the halfway region of the transference and then of imagination and art, for Klein it is the area of play; for Winnicott, the potential/transitional space; for Lacan, the mirror stage and the stage of primitive alienation which establishes the subject according to how it is reflected in the gaze of the other; for Bion, 'O' – that is, the 'something between' patient and analyst which is the object of the analysis; for Green the 'third' in analysis; for Ogden (2004a) the 'intersubjective third' of the analysis.

I shall limit myself here to illustrating the most radical instance of this paradigm, represented by Ferro's concept of the analytic field (Ferro and Basile, 2009; Civitarese, 2008a, 2011a). But first I shall note the conceptions of intermediarity which we can find in Merleau-Ponty and Bion because they represent the foundation of the modern concept of the analytic field.

The ego-field of Merleau-Ponty

Merleau-Ponty is hardly ever cited in the psychoanalytic literature. And yet, together with Derrida, he is perhaps unique among great philosophers in entertaining a very close relationship with psychoanalysis in an 'intersubjective' circularity of projective and introjective exchanges. Like Derrida, he took a great deal from psychoanalysis, but he also gave much to it, both directly – helping to inspire of the concept of the field as first formulated by the Barangers (W. and M. Baranger, [1961–62] 2008) – and indirectly. Indeed nowadays new psychoanalytic theories have to take account of intermediarity and intersubjectivity, of implicit kinds of memory and of the inaccessible or foetal – and therefore not repressed – unconscious (Bion, 1997). Not all of this can be brought back into perception and consciousness because there is an embodied, not representational perception, a level of meaning that can be defined as semiotic but not yet semantic. For this reason Merleau-Ponty comes into the picture once more as a privileged interlocutor with psychoanalysis.

Lacan's critical dismissal of his ideas about the unconscious may have contributed to the scant attention he has received from analysts.[65] When I first read the pages of Merleau-Ponty's course on infant development, and saw how he referred to the psychoanalytic literature, there came a point where I too wondered 'What about the unconscious? Where did that end up?' – especially because Merleau-Ponty never even mentions something that, thanks indirectly to him, is an ever more central notion for us today: as Freud put it, the communication between unconscious and unconscious (Freud, 1912). Now, on the one hand it would seem that he accepted the Freudian idea of the unconscious, otherwise he could not have conceptualized, as he did, the distinction between emotional ambivalence, which is unconscious, and ambiguity, which is conscious; or between racism as a reaction formation, an expression of rigidity of character, a rejection of ambiguity, and projection. On the other hand, however, Merleau-Ponty was interested above all in the cognitive and procedural unconscious that is not repressed; in the intercorporeal, preverbal or presymbolic 'pre-communication' which precedes and then always accompanies linguistic or symbolic communication. This is not in fact the classical Freudian unconscious of the first model, which is a representational, repressed and dynamic unconscious.

For Merleau-Ponty, the ego is a field of intercorporeal relationships. The infant communicates with the world through the medium of its parents. From birth its perception of the world cannot be split off from sociality. Learning to speak means passing through a series of identifications and so is equivalent to constructing an affective grammar. If we see the psyche as isolated, this process remains inexplicable. Before communicating in words we communicate with the body. Intercorporeal communication precedes the linguistic/symbolic kind. The other is my own skin, notes Merleau-Ponty. The individual is immediately part of a 'system' or a 'field of relationships'. The body is impregnated with what it touches, sees, hears, tastes. The consciousness of one's own body is never, even when an ego has been established, the consciousness of an 'isolated block', but a postural schema that is not closed, arising from the position that it occupies at any moment in relation to the environment. It is also always a 'certain style of action' (Merleau-Ponty, 1962, p. 118). No one has provided us with more effective descriptions of this interpenetration of bodies than Merleau-Ponty: 'Husserl said that perception of others is like a "phenomenon of coupling". The term is anything but a metaphor,' he comments significantly (ibid.).

To emphasize this essential dimension of personal identity, Merleau-Ponty brings the distal senses (sight, hearing and smell) back to proprioception and touch. He elevates the latter two at the expense of the first three, seeing all perception as tactile perception. In this way he enables us to intuit how the subject may be part of a totality, of a system in which everything is in motion and in which every part interacts with every other part. Our current metaphors are revealing in this respect: we say the gaze *rests* on an object, or that words can caress, touch or wound, and so on. Touch is the sense of continuity, of being in touch, of syncretic sociality. The visible is reconnected to the invisible, the body (a concept that separates) to the flesh (which is a way of conceiving the continuity of the sentient/sensible). After all, all we need to do in order to experience depersonalization is hear ourselves recorded. The voice we hear normally is coloured by a 'tactile' sound that does not reach us in the same way as we hear sounds from outside, and never appears in a recording, but comes to us through the bones and flesh, and contributes to defining our sense of self.

It goes without saying that compared to the other senses, sight and hearing are the most closely linked to consciousness, because it is the word that makes consciousness possible by uniting itself with the image of the thing. And yet, even if it does not contain representations of the word but only representations of the thing, the unconscious in Freud is itself intimately linked to language. It is the negative of the conscious. It is the conscious from which words have been taken away. In Merleau-Ponty's contribution, however, we can read an intuition of what we now call the procedural, unrepressed unconscious. The intellect is brought back to its material and corporeal basis, but here too, as in the repressed unconscious, not outside the perimeter of 'existence'; that is, of the symbolic. The concept of existence in a philosophical sense would have no meaning if applied to animals since it implies self-consciousness, but if we follow Merleau-Ponty, the concept of the unconscious is extended to include the corporeal. The traces of the oldest traumas which could not be represented are imprinted in the body, but the shadow of the repressed also weighs on it. As Lacan asserts, we are caught in the net of the symbolic even before we are born.

In Merleau-Ponty, subjectivity begins to be organized in the pre-linguistic phase of the infant's development, when 'there is not one individual over against another, but rather an anonymous collectivity, an undifferentiated group life' (ibid., p. 119). All the varied bodily activities converge dynamically to construct the sense of space in which the subject moves – breath, posture, the sensitivity of the oral cavity, etc. – everything that analysts call the relationship with the breast. In the beginning the other is felt only as a sensation of bodily well-being or discomfort. Above all, this state-process of 'syncretic sociality' is never completed and never abolished. In a passage in *The Child's Relations with Others*, Merleau-Ponty gives the example of a child who disobeys his parents, grabs hold of a glass and then puts it down. Straight afterwards he hears the sound of another glass breaking. The child is immediately assailed by a feeling of anxiety, as if it had been his fault. There has not been time for any more elaborate thought process to unfold. Rather, it is as if the hand itself retained an implicit memory of the glass. This is the way in which a kind of magical bond (a transference) is set up between the representational order and the procedural order, between the forbidden act and the shattered fragments of the glass. Thus, on an entirely prereflective level, the repressed also throws its shadow over what the body signifies. Merleau-Ponty comments (ibid., p. 149),

> there is a sort of spatial syncretism: ie. a presence of the same psychic being in several spatial points, a presence of me in the

other and the other in me. In a general way, there is an inability to conceive space and time as environments that contain a series of perspectives which are absolutely distinct from one another.

In analysis we say that the analyst's interiority, like that of the patient, is a place in the analytic field.

Not only Merleau-Ponty's phenomenology but also his emphasis on the body owe much to psychoanalysis. Freud repeatedly affirms that the ego is a bodily ego. Even in 1938, in one of his last notes dated 12 July, he writes that the infant's *being* precedes its *having*, and that the primordial mechanism of possession is identification: 'I am the breast' (*Ich bin die Brust*): that is, the object (Freud, 1938b, p. 565), and that the consciousness of *having* only appears later, which implies a separation: 'I have it, there I am not it' (*Ich habe sie, d.h. ich bin sie nicht*) (ibid.). This extraordinarily condensed sentence seems to reiterate yet again the identity between ego and body. Not only that, it also implies that the ego is the other, culture, sociality, and that the first ego is a sensory ego. The first *Zwischenreich* (the first *between*) is 'an area of sensation of a soothing sort' (Ogden, 1994b, p. 174), the fine film which is created at the interface between the subject and the object. The object is not yet perceived as separate but its imprint has been felt: the expression 'I am the breast' conjoins intersubjectivity and corporeality in an inspired synthesis. In fact the theorizing imagination which runs throughout Freud's work is that of the 'poetry of the mind':[66] the images that populate the psyche are abstractions of the external perceptual afferents which gradually *condense* as the brain grows larger (Freud, 1891). Not to mention Melanie Klein and the most vivid and dramatic representation of the earliest unconscious fantasies, wholly based as it is on the body and on the fragmented body, and which in figurative art is so well illustrated by Cubism's deconstruction of the female body.

The fact is that, even as they lay out the foundations for undermining the positivist position and the single-person approach to psychology, both Freud and Klein are still moving within that horizon – hence the Derridean accusation of logocentricism, which is essentially the conviction that one can arrive at an ultimate truth about things. Their intersubjectivism is incomplete, and it could not be otherwise. Such was the epistemological context of their time. Merleau-Ponty's direct contribution to psychoanalysis is no more than tangential – and indeed comes via the Barangers – but his great value is that of having first dismantled the idea of the isolated subject. After Merleau-Ponty, thinking about the subject means thinking about the intermediate space. This concept of his offers psychoanalysis a theoretical framework on a more abstract level and with a broader reach, besides confirming the intuitions which it has drawn from clinical practice.

The proto-mental system

In one of my papers I have tried to show that Bion adopted the method, which could be defined as deconstructionist *avant la lettre*, of systematically going beyond the caesura of all Freud's binary oppositions (Civitarese, 2008b), including those between individual and group and between mind and body. A concept that places these two 'betweens' in a dialectical relationship both vertically and horizontally, and which I find especially useful for exploring the area of the intermediate in psychoanalysis – in some respects close to that of 'pre-communication' in Merleau-Ponty – is Bion's idea of the 'proto-mental system'. If the models of intermediarity in Lacan and Ogden make us look principally to the Hegelian theory of subjectivity filtered through Kojève's reading of it, what counted for Bion were Rickman (his analyst and then collaborator), Gestalt theory and Lewin's field theory (Civitarese and Ferro, 2013), besides of course the Freudian concept of communication between one unconscious and another.

In his work on 'basic assumptions' Bion (1961) develops the concept of unconscious fantasy within a group (and of course he considers the analytic couple as a group). For Bion, individuals are endowed with 'valencies' – a term taken from chemistry which indicates the readiness of atoms to bind with each other to form molecules – that is, the spontaneous and instinctive (unconscious, automatic and inevitable) capacity for setting up an emotional bond between one another in order to share a basic assumption and to act on that basis: 'behaviour in the human being that is more analogous to tropism in plants than to purposive behaviour' (ibid., p. 117). The basic assumption (which may be one of Pairing, Attack-Flight or Dependency) gives rise to 'mental activities that have in common the attribute of powerful emotional drives' (ibid., p. 146). It is 'the cement that binds the group' (López-Corvo, 2002, p. 53).

Valencies and basic assumptions express aspects of the individual's psychological functioning dictated by the 'proto-mental system'. Bion coins this concept, which is among his most speculative in that it 'transcends experience' (1961, p. 101), to explain the tenacity of emotional links which consolidate groups, joining the members in a common psychological situation, and to indicate a psychic dimension in which basic assumptions may be located during those moments when they are inactive. The proto-mental system is

> one in which physical and psychological or mental are undifferentiated. It is a matrix from which spring the phenomena which at first appear – on a psychological level and in the light of psychological investigation – to be discrete feelings only loosely associated with one another. It is from this matrix that emotions proper to the basic assumption flow to reinforce, pervade, and, on occasion, to dominate the mental life of the group. Since it is a level in which physical and mental are undifferentiated, it stands to reason that, when distress from this source manifests itself, it can manifest itself just as well in physical forms as in psychological.
>
> (Bion, 1961, p. 102)

There are extraordinary resonances between this passage from Bion and some pages of Merleau-Ponty's *Phenomenology of Perception*, which appeared only three years earlier.[67] The proto-mental system's lack of distinction between individuals and between physical and psychic naturally leads back to the ambiguous position of the drives in Freud's thinking, a 'borderline concept between somatic and psychic', just as the valencies recall the concept of libido (Fornaro, 1990, p. 55). But the essential point here is that 'proto-mental phenomena are a function of the group' (Bion, 1961, p. 103). The individual's proto-mental system is merely part of a vaster setting which is the proto-mental matrix of the group, and for this reason it cannot be studied in isolation from the group. As we have seen, Bion is in accord with Merleau-Ponty on this point: the subject cannot be thought of except as emerging from the innate intersubjective dimension of the proto-mental system, from the area of the 'first bio-psychic emergence' (Fornaro, 1990, p. 20). The psychic exceeds the physical limits of the individual; it is 'trans-individual' (ibid.). The (relative) lack of mind-body distinction in the individual is therefore correlated in some ways with the background of substantial (relative) lack of distinction occurring between individuals.

The analytic field

The field model is only one of the virtually countless models we could construct to represent human relations in terms of intermediarity. Other perspectives are always possible. We need not fall into the error of assigning an ontological value to a particular model, as Merleau-Ponty sometimes tends to do.[68] After all, the notion of subject is also a construct. It works well for a whole series of things, but however necessary it may be it is always a fiction. Think how it changed after Freud. The real point is a different one: asking oneself which model is more suited to describing a particular phenomenon because it tells us more, or does so more comprehensibly, makes new features emerge from it and fits it better to our purpose. This is what has happened with the introduction of the field concept into physics and of Gestalt into psychology.

For analysts, adopting an interpretation of the intersubjective events of the analysis is like DNA testing in the investigation of crimes (Civitarese, 2011c). The field may also be thought of as a new metaphor which, as Kuhn (1962) explains well, urges us to ask new questions, to look in new directions, to see old discoveries in a new light. Field theory is a new and profound theory of unconscious communication between individuals because, compared to other models, it implies a more radical idea of the unconscious and the way dreaming works in the session; it offers a more accurate description of how the analytic relationship works; and it modifies our ideas about the therapeutic factor in analysis and interpretation.

In a manner analogous to the electromagnetic and gravitational fields of physics, the vertex of the analytic field postulates that an invisible force field is set up between patient and analyst, powerfully influencing the interactions between them. These forces cannot be known directly but can only be deduced from their derivatives. Investigating the field's intermediate space helps us understand how communication occurs between one unconscious and another (Freud, 1912).

Once established, a field acquires a life of its own. It disregards the subjects which have given it life, in the sense that it is more than the sum of its constituent parts. Viewing the objects found there, we would be unable to say which belonged to which subject.[69] We could do so according to the manifest text – who had said or done what – but not according to the latent text. The asymmetry of the unencrypted text is lost in the unconscious text. The deep structure of the analytic dialogue is quite different from the superficial structure.

But what is the field made of? A psychic field is derived from the encounter between reciprocal identifications, both introjective and projective. The subjects absorb and emit 'psychic' radiation. Obviously these are psychological processes which occur in the analyst's and patient's minds when each is connected to the other like two dynamic systems interacting in real time. One could say that the field does not exist outside the two minds, but actually this is not the case. It is part of everything that furnishes the place where the physical people are, as a possible source of stimuli, such as the more or less subtle actions that each makes to compel the other to receive projective identifications. Both halves of the couple in fact try unconsciously to imprint a certain shape on reality with their own transferences or, in Bion's language, with their own transformations in hallucinosis. Externalizing their own fantasies (unconscious schemata or scenarios, narratives which combine more elementary representations) is a way of making reality familiar, and therefore knowable and bearable, in a dialectic between identity and difference, assimilation and accommodation.

Unlike Merleau-Ponty's postulated Ego-field and Bion's protomental area, the concept of projective identification takes on a powerful explicatory value since it renders 'tangible', as it were, the channels of communication through which this unconscious and shared psychological area can be established.

It makes us 'see' how the psychic reconnects itself to the sensory-tactile and through which concrete and indispensable points of contact the processes of inter-individual psychic influence occur.

In order to distinguish between simple psychic projection, an exclusively intrapsychic process, and projective identification, an interpsychic process, Grotstein (2005) invented the concept of 'projective transidentification'. We could speculate that projective identification and projective transidentification are the same phenomenon, after all, varying only in intensity: from the change that happens in the subject's mind to the extension of this change into unconscious behaviours that have the aim of influencing the other and forcing him into the role of container.

The field is pervaded by forces of attraction and repulsion caused by the collision between bundles of particles of projective identification heading in opposite directions. Every place in the field exercises a gravitational force on any object which may be in the field. The interactions can be weak, or very weak, and therefore difficult to observe, or they may be strong. However, things are also invested with projections, transference and magical thinking. In essence, an object (of whatever kind) is unconsciously assimilated to the object of love or hate. Obviously there will be differences in the way one reacts to inanimate objects compared to people, because they have less of the special reactivity that we have towards our likenesses, which we now know to be based on specific neurophysiological functions.

The personality is the result of the work carried out by several functions: for example, the mind's alpha function, of which dream thought is a central element. That is, we have innate structures which nevertheless need favourable environmental conditions for their development, and which act as the apparatus for symbolization. A primary law of the field is that unconscious communication can neither be prevented nor controlled. A second law is that this dream-thought is active both by night and day. A third law of the field is that the higher the 'temperature' (the emotional engagement, the passion) of the relationship, the more intense the forces in the field. Holding sessions in close proximity and taking a long time over treatment has the aim of raising this temperature to an optimal level. For Freud, this point is the trigger for the transference neurosis.

The symmetry↔symmetry oscillation in the analytic field

The relationship between patient and analyst is not asymmetrical in an absolute sense because is it not possible to determine each participant's contribution. It is certainly asymmetrical on the manifest level, but not necessarily on that of unconscious communication. There are those who fear that the model of the analytic field implies the disappearance of the subject as a concept. This is a groundless fear. Both the viewpoint of the subject and that of the dynamic interaction are merely models, conventions, not the thing itself. They are perspectives in continuous evolution which we transpose onto reality in order to know something to which we have no direct access. Even here we can see continuity or discontinuity: intersubjectivism is not opposed to the concept of the subject but integrates it. In fact, even if only from a partial perspective, the subject is ousted for a second time, and in a more radical way, from the house of the ego; not only is it pushed back towards the unconscious, but the individual unconscious is itself brought back to sociality.

The therapeutic relationship is asymmetrical because the patient has the space he needs for speech; the analyst is a professional and, what is more, should have been well taken care of in his own analysis. Pathological projective identifications normally go from patient to analyst. Nevertheless, there are occasions when the asymmetry is temporarily interrupted or inverted; otherwise we would not speak of negative reverie or negative therapeutic reactions. The analyst must identify them because, if they become chronic, they can do harm instead of good.

The distinction between symmetry and asymmetry, however artificial, allows us to describe two modalities of functioning in a single process. The secondary process tends to claw back the asymmetry continually, but does so while making use of unconscious thought and symmetrical communication. However, this cannot be taken for granted. It requires work. The only things which can, or should, be taken for granted are the external elements of the relationship: responsibilities, intentions, methods, levels of personal suffering, etc.

There are consequences to conceptualizing the intermediate space in this way. For a start, interpretation is no longer directed at the patient in order to change something in him, but to improve the narrative capacity of the field, understood as a two-way un/conscious narrative. If it seems that one is *addressing the patient, from this vertex one does so only as a place in the field.* What matters is the improvement of the general level of the text which analyst and patient are composing and reciting together on the way.

Every intervention therefore aims to increase the capacity of the couple to dream the problem which could not hitherto be dreamed. In general, an unsaturated or transference interpretation expands the oneiric capacity of the field a great deal more than a 'closed' interpretation. If this is successful, the room is better 'oxygenated', the patient breathes more easily and the analyst is also changed by the encounter.

This is the goal on which the analyst bases his choice of opportune interventions, whether they are intended to make the patient aware of his own unconscious dynamics, or are simply openings for discussion or punctuations of the dialogue. To orient himself he follows the patterns of the conversation, the characters appearing in the session. These act as the thermometer that measures the emotional temperature of the field, the fluctuating needle of emotional unison and the relevant band of oscillation (Ferro, 2010). They give information about the state and quality of oneiric functioning in the field: that is, the system's capacity to carry out a specific un/conscious psychological task of transforming the emotions. Analysis is no longer the struggle between good and evil, as it is in Freud between reason and the demonic drives seething in the unconscious, but one between meaning and the absence of meaning, between the capacity or incapacity to use the poetic-creative-productive-aesthetic potentialities of the unconscious.

Piazza Armerina

A. tells me that his father is originally from Piazza Armerina, in Sicily. Curious, without wanting to dwell on it, I ask him if he has ever been there. He tells me no. The session goes on. Only towards the end, twenty minutes after I had asked my question, I suddenly realize that Piazza Armerina could stand, DOES STAND!, for *piazza d'armi*, for a place where weapons are displayed or where one shows oneself armed; in other words, ready for a fight. A. is very afraid of conflict, and hardly ever dares to express his own point of view on things. It has always been the case that he tends for the most part to adapt himself mimetically to the views of others. I'm struck with amazement. Something that I already knew about him, and indeed about us, unexpectedly feels true. It is a truth made up of knowledge and emotion. In the apparent 'talking-as-dreaming' (Ogden, 2007) of my 'tourist's' question, without knowing it, I had elicited a truth which now became available for psychological growth. What could have presented itself from the start as a banal association, re-emerging after the subterranean work of the un/conscious, then took on the qualities of reverie. That is, it was the fruit of conscious, but above all unconscious, psychological work, by means of which we give a personal meaning to experience; something very close, when it is authentic, to aesthetic experience.

I could have used an insight like this in various ways. From the intrapsychic viewpoint, if the opportunity had arisen, I could have commented on what *his* avoidance meant, and thereby said something about how *his* mind works. Or from an intersubjective viewpoint I could have wondered why it was still not possible to live in the here and now with contrasting ideas, affections, etc. In the first case I would obviously have explained his inclination to avoid conflict in terms of a need to be in unison with others and not to feel in danger. In the second case I would have supposed that *both of us* would feel in danger in different ways if we had entered into conflict or if we had too quickly abandoned a certain symbiotic mode, as if a powerful coupling fantasy might pervade the emotional field. I feel that this second idea is truer, even if it can be integrated with the first, because it is the fruit, as Bion would say, of something which has happened under our very eyes; of *passion*, being available to take on the burden of the other's unconscious, and one's own, in a radical way; and of *myth*, the possibility that all of this might be successfully rendered as a meaningful narrative.

From the vertex of the analytic field, 'visiting' Piazza Armerina (among other things, the diminutive '–ina' suggests something infantile, weapons as toys) is an opportunity not to decode a meaning that applies only to the other and hence objectifies him, but to make metaphorical the reality of the emotional experience shared in a given moment. The presupposition is that, when we grant dream-thought space to do its work, we obtain a much more authentic, rich (ambiguous) view of reality. With regard to the analytic field, a transformation from non-sense to sense is achieved; from beta to alpha; from rational thought to aesthetic experience. On an unconscious level one could not say who had contributed to the narrative, or how, whether A.'s story or my question had done more; his memories or mine, still very vivid, of the visit to the ruins of the beautiful Roman villa at Piazza Armerina and its famous mosaics. I could also have been influenced by the memory of the account I read a few months later in the newspaper, about acts of vandalism which had ruined it beyond repair. So it could be said that patient and analyst are continually engaged in composing their own mosaics: would we be able to say that one piece is more important than another? Isn't it the differentiating game of shapes and colours that counts?

The halfway region as a symbolic area

If we were now to ask ourselves what can intermediarity be related to, the only answer I would feel able to give is that language is the connectivity which creates the halfway region. As human beings we are nodes in a network that we share only with other human beings. We are members of a highly specialized system in which the principle of meaning holds sway. Could we say that an unconscious communication exists between two chairs or two animals? Speaking of unconscious communication means speaking of language. Lacan saw this clearly when he postulated the subject as the fruit of a radical alienation; but it is already in Freud. It is true that in the Freudian unconscious there are only representations of things and not of words, but the unconscious – I repeat – is constructed by the taking away of language. Conscious and unconscious experience are two sides of the same coin.

A child who had been brought up by a robot and never learned to speak would not have a reflective consciousness and therefore no unconscious either:[70] whereas, even if it is not yet speaking and does not have an ego capable of thinking thoughts, the normally raised infant from the start absorbs fragments of meaning from the mother and preserves them without knowing it. In this way, the repressed (the Norm, the Law, the Ego Ideal) acts in him like an interposed person and is also present in non-verbal communication.

The problem of the unconscious is difficult to grasp if it is studied as an individual and not a social phenomenon. Neuroscientists who insist on identifying precisely when the first sparks of consciousness appear end up in the swamp of byzantine nominalist distinctions because they do not consider the social dimension in which individual development takes place from the start of life. If we do not begin with the dyad, we have too narrow a view of the equivalence between language and self-consciousness. We struggle to see the mother as the unconscious complement of the baby's rudimentary consciousness. If we only consider the baby, before it has a reflective consciousness and can therefore learn to speak, the concept of repression has no meaning. If we consider the baby *and* the mother, then their intercorporeal interaction based on motor-sensory schemata, and the consequent laying down in them both of procedural memories, are forever under the shadow of the repressed. This is why the intermediate space is the realm of language, culture and the unconscious, or rather the un/conscious.

The case for a psychoanalysis of intermediarity

The objective of analysis is to explore and modify states of consciousness-subjectivity. This can be done from different perspectives and using different paradigms. Emphasizing the isolated subject privileges a single-person approach to psychology which points to a vertical paradigm where what matters is the identification of certain and unequivocal elements. Hence I must objectify the other's subjectivity. If instead I place myself in a horizontal, intersubjective perspective, and try to grasp the other's subjectivity using my own, I must give up that kind of objectification. I have to accept that I am part of the relational game and cannot get out of it by lifting myself up by my own pigtail like Baron Münchausen.

Even if, for practical purposes, we can continue to see in the dynamic evolution of the field the interaction between two isolated subjects, the analytic field necessarily dissolves this model and imposes the renunciation of any attempt to investigate the origins of the field's dynamic elements. As when reading a novel with two authors, for example *The Sunday Woman* by Carlo Fruttero and Franco Lucentini, a reader would never know who had contributed a certain line or word. What counts is that the story works, that it is gripping and moving, and that in the end the narrative threads are tied up. Just as good literature is food for the mind, so in the same way the psychoanalytic narrative expands the psychic container and increases the capacity to think. Obviously there are no restrictions on the narrative genres, whether literary or psychoanalytic: Kleinian, Freudian, Bionian, Winnicottian, etc.

In clinical practice this model interacts dialectically with the single-person model of the subject and with the one I would define as 'weak subjectivity'. By this expression I mean a model of working in which the interaction is read in terms of the field – that is, every event in the analysis is seen as jointly generated by the couple – but in practical terms one treats it as if it consisted in the dialogue of two distinct interlocutors, as if the analyst were unconsciously responding to what the patient had just finished saying and vice versa.

On this theoretical basis we can understand that, starting with Bion, and still more with the developments of post-Bionian thought, we can speak on behalf of a change of paradigm in the sense indicated by Kuhn (1962). For example, it can be misleading to use classical concepts of transference and countertransference to define the characters in the analytic field because they presuppose an arrangement in which analysand and analyst are standing 'face to face' as two positive subjectivities, pure, complete, separate; each in some way totally 'external' to the other. On the contrary, the foundation of the analytic relationship is 'the simultaneity of the dialectic of oneness and twoness, of individual subjectivity and intersubjectivity' (Ogden, 1994b, p. 74n.).

In a theoretical framework inspired by a one-person psychoanalysis, even the concept of projective identification would be used in an a-dialectical and essentially solipsistic way. If instead we think of subject and object as places in an intersubjective field, we realize, as Ogden says (2005), that when a patient enters analysis, he loses his mind. He reconnects with the proto-mental area. He sets up a communication that engages him at a profound level and which can be channelled in order to repair dysfunctional regions of his internal group life, and to re-launch the conversation that the various parts of his mind are constantly holding among themselves, forever seeking better ways of thinking about the current emotional problem. (We should, however, consider terms such as unconscious thought, dreaming, thinking, etc. as roughly equivalent.)

Freud uses the term *Zwischenreich*[71] to designate the intersection of two intermediate areas which lay the foundations for the subject: the horizontal plane of the transference understood as the something that stands between past and present and between patient and analyst; and the vertical plane of the drives, of that which stands between body and psyche. It is therefore the area of the symbolic.

Psychoanalysis devotes obsessive attention to this because it is precisely there that we play the game of becoming, or ceasing to be, human beings. The artificiality of the halfway region, from the transference to its more radical and intersubjective version as field, consists in this. Here artificial does not mean false, but relates to sociality and to culture, the mode through which we adapt nature to our human needs.

10

BION'S *EVIDENCE* AND HIS THEORETICAL STYLE

> I'm not interested in writing short stories. Anything that doesn't take years of your life and drive you to suicide hardly seems worth doing.
>
> (Cormac McCarthy, 2009)

> The experience in reading that Bion is imagining . . . may incite murderous feelings in the reader.
>
> (Ogden, 2005)

'"I remember my parents being at the top of a Y-shaped stair and I was there at the bottom . . . and . . ." That was all' (Bion, 1976, p. 312). These are the opening words – a quotation from a patient – of 'Evidence', an eight-page paper that Bion wrote three years before his death. The Italian translation of the expression *Y-shaped stair* (*scala a forma di Y*) fails to render the significant fact that, in English, *Y-shaped stair* could also be understood as *why-shaped stare* – i.e. *a look in the form of a 'why?'* This is how Bion immediately reformulated the patient's words to himself.

In the Italian version, a note at the bottom of the page explaining the double meaning (the pun) is supplied by Bion's daughter, Parthenope, living at the time in Turin. Just as Bion's patient looked up the stair at his parents, so she looks up at her father from the bottom of the page.

Immediately, we become immersed in a climate of ambiguity: who is speaking? What is the actual scene? Is it the (realistic) scene of the patient's memory or the fantasmatic one of the addition to the text by Bion's daughter (fantasmatic in that it is transfigured into the first)? True, there are quotation marks, but they are not enough to dispel doubt.

The patient offers no associations. Some things, however, occur to Bion. We have barely reached the sixth line and already he surprises us with one of his typical throwaway phrases: 'I am supposed to be the analyst' (1976, p. 312). Just like that, between brackets. Like a thought that emerges from the preconscious. What does he mean by 'supposed to be'? Is he perhaps *not* the analyst? And the patient he has just told us about – is he not the patient? And if Bion is not the analyst, then who is he? Any father? And what kind of father was he to Parthenope? What kind of daughter was Parthenope to Bion?

Bion is struck by the ambiguity of the expression the patient uses, but says nothing. 'After a while the patient went on, and I started producing what seemed to me to be fairly plausible psycho-analytic interpretations' (p. 312). Again, what is meant by 'producing' (the term suggests mechanical activity and routine) and 'seemed'? And why 'fairly plausible'?

We recognize Bion's unique style. Like a Brechtian actor, he plays the role of the analyst, then he steps to one side and shows us what he is doing. The world is a stage, he seems to be telling us, and I, all of us, we are merely players. Between roles and people, and between words and things, there is no correlation.

At this point, the reader may begin to wonder what 'evidence' or what truth such a sceptical author might want to talk about. Among other things, in English, the word *evidence* is much closer to the concept of truth than the Italian *evidenza* because it also means *proof* – in particular, in legal language – as well as *trace, sign*. So far the author has done nothing but disappoint our expectations as readers, exasperating us and reversing our natural perception of things.

Bion continues to play around with the idea of something Y-shaped. He imagines the figure turning into a funnel or a cone, and finally into the shape of a breast – for an analyst, something 'fairly plausible' (p. 312). Less ordinary, however, is the path he takes to gets there. Although going by the name of free association, it is more like a daydream. What he does is describe how the image gradually forms in his mind. He did not find this 'fairly plausible' thing by looking for it in memory and desire; actively suspended, memory and desire give it to him while he is in a state of passivity.

Meanwhile, this digression has given zealous servants of the psyche the chance to tap into unconscious psychological work. Here ends the 'patient's' first session. Bion uses neither an invented name nor an abbreviation for him; throughout, he simply calls him *the patient,* as if to maintain an aura of mystery about his identity or to be able to abstract some general truth from a particular case.

About the next session, he writes, 'I seemed to be killing time with conventionally acceptable interpretations' (1976, p. 313). Conventional, but acceptable – so he decides to communicate them to the patient. The patient responds: 'Yes, that's right. But you've been a very long time about it' (p. 313). As you can see, we are in a play by Beckett. The Irish playwright was in fact in analysis with Bion, and at times it would be difficult to say who is imitating whom (Anzieu, 1999); after all, what does it matter how long he has taken?

However, the patient's remark chimes in surprisingly well with Bion's comment about killing time. It is unclear here whether Bion, by reporting the answer, wants to emphasize, with a hint of annoyance, the patient's ingratitude, or simply to be seen in a distorting mirror of self-irony so as to share with the reader the sense of emptiness he feels at his efforts to come up with something that sounds significant. His 'killing time', to which the patient responds by telling him that 'you've been a long time about it', means the words that say something true – and that are thus food that nourishes and nurtures the mind – came too late. It is agony for the patient.

In fact, thinking does not come from the mere absence of the object, but from his return after an absence that was bearable. For this reason, however, *killing time* here stands for *killing new thoughts,* subjectivity itself. When the patient says, 'that's right, but . . .', this actually reminds Bion that a truth that does not involve feeling together, moving at the same pace, living in unison, is not a truth. But how then can one communicate so as to be on the same wavelength as the patient (or, likewise, how can one write so as to be in tune with the reader)?

As we can see, Bion continually distances himself from himself. He shows how constantly dissatisfied he is when measuring himself against the ideal image he has of himself as an analyst and as a person. While Freud writes using a rhetorical style that constantly struggles to convince a critical reader, Bion struggles with himself.

He suffers in his own flesh the conflict between the pleasure principle and the reality principle, between desire as the expression of the phantasy and material reality, between patient and analyst. He becomes – as expressed in the recommendation he makes to everyone – the O of the patient. In some ways, it is hard to work out who is the analyst and who is the patient; rather, one gets the impression of two subjects immersed in a common field of interactions ceaselessly buffeted by waves of emotional turmoil.

For Bion, O is the ultimate, ineffable, unknowable reality, or even the 'inexpressible truth of one's experience' (Ogden, 2008, p. 17). It is close to Lacan's concept of the Real and to Kant's *thing-in-itself. Becoming* O means that we cannot know it rationally but that we can approximate it through experience. In session, *becoming the O of the patient* would mean apprehending the emotional truth of what is going on unconsciously in the analytic field, entering a state of passivity in order to be receptive to reveries, to the products of our unconscious psychological work. So O/*being* is opposed to K (knowledge)/*knowing,* which indicates an intellectual understanding. Ideally, in clinical work, the analyst should continuously go through the sequence of O → K → O → K, a process I would reformulate as a constant oscillation between immersion and interactivity (see Civitarese, 2008c).

When we read Bion, we are far removed from the position of superiority of the classical Freudian analyst who cultivates an objective view of things. Here, multiple, dynamic, and reciprocal identifications, change roles and positions constantly in an endless game of variations in points of view.

By presenting himself in this way, Bion is not trying to get around the matter of truth. The key question he poses can be summed up as follows: what evidence has the patient provided and what evidence can be garnered from the analyst's associations, from what he has seen or believes he has seen?

When interpreting, the analyst merely engages in imaginative guesswork. Emotions can be guessed at; when they are evident to the senses, or clearly legible in the body, it is already too late. Language has no words to describe emotions. One needs rather to be a painter or a musician, or at least to have their means of expression.

In these initial remarks, Bion comes across as an extremely serious author – responsible, anti-narcissistic, a writer for whom writing means struggling to solve a problem that obsesses him, and who is both intellectual and emotional. Then he changes register and (by dint of imagination) also place. As in a reverie, he remembers the lesson Freud learned during his period of study in Paris, when he was the one to question his master with a *why-shaped stare*. In his obituary notice for Charcot, Freud emphasized that the master had taught him we must keep on observing an unknown phenomenon until some pattern emerges. But in analysis, he added, 'we are not supposed to use our senses in physical contact with the patient' (1976, p. 313), as a doctor of physical medicine might do.

Elsewhere Bion says that the analyst's interpretation should be the fruit of sense, myth and passion. There is no contradiction between these propositions because, for Bion, using the senses means getting rid of the sensual realities of pleasure that are to be found in the memory of the past and in the future and in perception, and dealing instead with present reality. He is thus referring to a particular use of the senses; namely, what occurs when the analyst is in a state of hallucinosis that is inverse and symmetrical to that of the patient, whose hallucinosis is orientated towards internal reality completely.

This state of formal regression of thought (Botella, 2012) is used to see what the patient sees, his (invisible) hallucinations. It is a way of bracketing off material reality and intuiting what comes closest to being a 'fact' of analysis, an emotion or a feeling.[72] In analysis, what is truly important is not the patient's biography as certified by official documents, but his person (subjectivity). What matters is if he comes back every day: 'The problem, in a sense, is that of trying to make it worthwhile for the patient to come again another day' (Bion, 1976, p. 313). This is a trite thing to say, but Bion is never trite. He is suggesting that if the patient is to return, he should receive something that is not a matter of sensual or material gratification. What then? Truth, food for thought, as previously noted; but what is this truth? How can we grasp it and, above all, how can we communicate it?

Bion gives an indirect explanation, again drawing on the words of Freud, looking up at him from below, as if Freud were his father ('"I remember my parents being at the top of a Y-shaped stair and I was there at the bottom . . . and . . ." That was all' – clearly the leitmotiv of the text; 1976, p. 312). Bion quotes a famous passage in which Freud (1926) calls into question the caesuras (the discontinuity) between life in the womb and birth: 'There is much more continuity between interuterine life and earliest infancy than the impressive caesura of the act of birth would have us believe' (p. 138).

Bion draws forth a whole way of thinking from this passage. Transcending the caesura of binary oppositions that structure the theoretical and technical field of psychoanalysis can be seen as his general principle of method (Civitarese, 2008b). It is significant, therefore, that he should comment that Freud stopped there, seeing himself as the child who surpasses the father.

Earlier, Freud (1914b, p. 22) noted:

> I learnt to restrain speculative tendencies and to follow the unforgotten advice of my master, Charcot [this time it is Freud looking up at his father from below]: to look at the same things again and again until they themselves began to speak.

It is hard not to be reminded of another famous phrase of Freud's, '*Saxa loquuntur!*' – translated from the Latin by Strachey as 'stones talk!' (Freud, 1999 [1896], p. 192n.) – as well as of his comment in relation to Dora: 'He that has eyes to see and ears to hear may convince himself that no mortal can keep a secret. If his lips are silent, he chatters with his fingertips; betrayal oozes out of him at every pore' (Freud, 1905, pp. 77–78). This is, Bion explains – in the very act of acknowledging the legacy he has inherited from Freud – what he means by his injunction to the analyst to eschew memory and desire when listening to the patient.

The truth must speak for itself; it must impose itself. The mind must be as far as possible a *tabula rasa*. More precisely, it is the idea that one must suspend voluntary attention and veil consciousness in order to listen to the poetic truth of the unconscious.[73] Then, as Ogden (2003) writes, 'The unconscious speaks with a quality of truthfulness that is different from, and almost always much richer than, what the conscious aspect of ourselves is able to perceive and convey' (p. 603).

What Bion means can be made immediately clear in a practical example. It is a matter of taking risks – for example, the risk of taking oneself seriously if one thinks that a given patient is not married when in fact he is, or that the date of birth on his birth certificate does not count. What matters is the moment when one is born, and the two do not necessarily coincide. That is the kind of sensoriality needed in analysis. Thinking this way, however, exposes one to the risk of appearing crazy. The idea that a person may have a memory of his life in the womb was not commonly held at the time Freud expressed it. According to Bion (1976), psychoanalysis is revolutionary because of its idea (which he calls 'disturbing', p. 314) that nothing can be 'forgotten in the sense of really disappearing' (p. 314). But what is revolutionary here is that Bion takes this concept of Freud's to its logical extreme.

In the meantime, however, we realize that there has been an imperceptible shift between the planes of investigation; or rather, a deeper and more personal plane has emerged. Beneath the question of 'what is truth in analysis?' we can now make out the truth of the relationship with the parents and in particular with the father. It will be noted that, throughout the text, what Bion does is to place before us the central figure of the relationship of the child with the father. The *why* brings to mind Christ's 'Father, why have you forsaken me?' from the Gospels, and 'Father, don't you see I'm burning?' in one of the most poignant dreams described by Freud (1900, p. 509). The *why* also recalls Freud's own father, Jakob; in the dream Freud had after his father's death, Freud begs him to close his eyes ('you are requested to close the eyes' (Masson, 1985, p. 202), Freud says in describing the dream in a letter to Fliess). Furthermore, the *why* makes us think of Freud himself in silent contemplation of Moses, in the Basilica of St Peter in Chains in Rome. All these inevitably bring to mind the curiosity of Oedipus and that of the child, imbued as it must always be with guilt and helplessness.

Beneath the technical-theoretical problem of truth in analysis lies the Oedipal fantasy – yet there is more. We read 'a why-shaped stare' – a Y, a cone, a breast. But the Y is composed of three segments. After Freud had to come the other segment of the Y: Melanie Klein, his mother, his analyst. Bion looks to his analytic parents with an eye in the form of a Y ('why-shaped stare'). What is taking place here, as we can see, is a deep-seated unconscious identification with the patient, with the child he himself had been, with his daughter, with Freud, with Charcot. It is as if he were living simultaneously in an infinite number of possible worlds, something which raw sense perception would belie.

Where does the patient end and the analyst begin, asks Bion elsewhere, but here he asks this while showing himself in the act of becoming the O of the patient. He is the one who is projecting onto the patient his anxieties about his daughter; his doubts as father and analyst, the residues of transference onto the masters. Or is it the patient who is prompting thoughts and feelings of countertransference in him? This is not, however, how Bion would write it. He would go beyond this caesura and write '(counter-trans)-ference' (Bion, 1977a, p. 56) to indicate, in the very way the word is written, that what matters is something between analyst and patient, the intervening space.

After studying Freud, and in his development of the speculative idea that he had first articulated and then stepped back from, Bion leans on Klein to support his hypothesis of the existence of a foetal 'psychic' life. He again picks up the formidable idea of projective identification: the powerful fantasy of getting rid of something of one's own, something one unconsciously rejects, so as to put it into the other. Could this mechanism underlie the formation of an 'archaic mentality, unconscious thought . . . which is extremely active' (Bion, 1976, p. 314)? As a person might ask his father and mother to explain where he came from, so Bion takes from Freud and Klein fragments of theory that obsessively refer back to the archaic life of the foetus, to the point of assuming there is a completely physical mechanism of projective identification: *what matters is the moment of being born.*

Assuming, however, that all this makes sense, then we would have something that *does not* happen and that cannot be seen from outside but whose effects are very powerful. Again, what evidence do we have of such a process? If an analyst went around saying that an adult patient shows remnants of foetal life (which is what he does!), in the same way as a surgeon readily diagnoses a tumour of embryonic origin, he would not be taken very seriously.

When necessary, Bion does not spare analysts his sarcastic barbs, because nothing infuriates him more than the whitened sepulchres of psychoanalytic institutionalization. Thinking of an imaginary patient, he describes him as follows: 'He prides himself on being grown up and on not believing in that sort of psycho-analytic rubbish' (1976, p. 315). Yet he is not in the habit of absolving himself completely: it is not clear, at least at first glance, what he is talking about, the patient or the analyst, who of course has become a caricature, who has become grown up and part of the establishment, or in other words has allowed his thinking to become rigid.

While the surgeon has his instruments, the analyst has to fall back on words; he can use only everyday, debased, impoverished words. For this reason, he should develop a personal vocabulary. *Personal* suggests a lot more than what one might expect at first sight. The word reflects the analyst's entire subjectivity – his person, in fact. It is not a question of choosing a few effective words or efficacious formulaic expressions, but rather of forging a personal style.

Bion thus distances himself from the abstract language of science and draws our attention to the performative nature of the text itself. It is obvious that the author's intention is not only to illustrate the concepts but also to put them to work. If truth in analysis and the way of telling the truth coincide, since the mode of expression allows one to play with the possibility of emotional sharing, the truth then becomes a question of aesthetics. And asking oneself 'what language the full-term foetus speaks or understands' (1976, p. 316) becomes a rhetorical way of couching the problem of the ineffable in radical terms, since it is related to the inaccessible or non-representational unconscious (Civitarese, 2013c). This becomes a way of hyperbolically expressing the concrete, intercorporeal quality of human communication. For the full-term foetus, there might be only a musical language, a being contained within a tactile-sonorous housing, a stream of sensations that are rhythmically ordered but continually exposed to disorder. But, we might ask, is this not the constant challenge of writing and style – namely, how to talk to our 'foetal' or embryonic or somatopsychic elements?

Clearly, if we were artists, it would be easier. Leonardo and Shakespeare would know what to do. And even philosophers understand what to do – for example, Francis Bacon. About halfway through the text of 'Evidence', Bion quotes from *Novum Organum*:

> There are two ways, and can only be two, of seeking and finding truth. The one, from the senses and particulars, takes a flight to the most general axioms, and from these principles and their truths, settled once for all, invents and judges of intermediate axioms. The other method collects axioms from senses and particulars, ascending continuously and by degrees, so that in the

> end it arrives at the more general axioms; this latter way is the true one, but hitherto untried.
>
> (Bacon quoted in Bion, 1976, p. 316)

Note the metaphor implied in this passage, which revolves around verticality (down/up). The centripetal movement of attraction that runs through the text brings us back once again to the 'why-shaped stare' that we met at the beginning. The true method views (humbly) the *whys* from the bottom upwards (in accordance with the logic of induction). In addition, Bion found in Bacon (or rather, he was inspired by Bacon to find?) the psychic transformations he had described himself, from beta to alpha, and the dream thoughts that give rise to the concept – from sensory experience to ideas, along a continuum without any rigid caesuras.

But what is the point of invoking this procession of fathers, of yoking together Shakespeare and Bacon? Here again, by way of explanation, Bion transcends the gap that separates art from philosophy by quoting another eminent philosopher, Kant: 'Thoughts without content are empty, intuitions without concepts are blind' (Kant, 1781, p. 86). He reformulates this idea:

> When I tried to employ meaningless terms – alpha and beta were typical – I found that 'concepts without intuition which are empty and intuitions without concepts which are blind' rapidly became 'black holes into which turbulence had seeped, and empty concepts flooded with riotous meaning'.
>
> (Bion, 1977b, p. 229)

It is important, then, that there should be a mixture of dream thinking and logical-abstract thinking, so as to redeem unreflection through reflection, to graft intuitions onto concepts and concepts onto intuitions.

At the level of manifest discourse, this is the heart of 'Evidence' (1976), the point of convergence towards which all its lines of force are moving: the problem of truth and which truth receives its first unveiling in psychoanalysis. Neither mystical/aesthetic nor scientific/philosophical thought can give us the truth. The former is lacking in concepts, the latter in emotions/feelings. The former is wholly unconscious, the latter wholly conscious. But truth in analysis has to do with the ability to make sense of personal experience. In *Transformations* (1965), Bion explains that 'something seems real [we might also say 'true'] only when there are feelings about it' (p. 77).

Those analysts who stop up their holes with theories are like amnesic patients who invent false memories to fill voids: 'If you are at all tired and more than usually ignorant, it is useful to reach out for the nearest paramnesia that is handy, the nearest psychoanalytic theory that you find lying about' (Bion, 1976, p. 317). The sense of disillusionment with which Bion dismisses theories as paramnesias, on a par with history and voluntary memories, is amazing. Of course we know that he can afford to do so only because he has a more all-embracing theory. The value of this theory, however, is that it takes its own weakness and turns it into strength, in the same way that Freud sublimates the crisis of an ego that is no longer master in its own house into ethical responsibility.

The problem is how to forge a language that can describe things accurately. Artists are clearly at an advantage because 'they can resort to the aesthetic as a universal linguistic' (Bion, 1976, p. 317). In describing the trial of Socrates, for example, Plato

> points out what a great disadvantage it is that in spite of the fact that Socrates and Phaedrus can apparently talk very accurately and precisely, they are actually using extremely ambiguous terms . . . If we consider that there is a thing called a mind or a character, is there any way in which we can verbalize it which is not a complete distortion? The mathematicians talk about 'quantum intermediacy', something unknown in between . . . look at it [my hand] from one side: there is a psycho-somatic complaint; turn it round: now it is soma-psychotic. It is the same hand, but what you see depends on which way you look at it, from which position, from what vertex – any term you like. But does one look at a character from any direction at all?
>
> (Bion, 1976, pp. 317–318)

Having established the assumptions underlying his argument, Bion goes on to suggest that we abandon ourselves to imaginative conjecture:

> a flight into fantasy, a kind of infancy of our own thought. I can imagine a situation in which a nearly full-term foetus could be

> aware of extremely unpleasant oscillations in the amniotic fluid medium before transferring to a gaseous medium – in other words, getting born. I can imagine that there is some disturbance going on – the parents on bad terms, or something of that sort.[74] I can further imagine loud noises being made between the mother and the father – or even loud noises made by the digestive system inside the mother. Suppose this foetus is also aware of the pressures of what will one day turn into a character or a personality, aware of things like fear, hate, crude emotions of that sort. Then the foetus might omnipotently turn in hostility towards these disturbing feelings, proto-ideas, proto-feelings, at a very early stage, and split them up, destroy them, fragment them . . . I can imagine the foetus being so precocious, so premature that it tries to get rid of its personality to start off with, and then . . . he may preserve a mind at the deeper level, which knows nothing about that, but which might nevertheless have well-established feelings of guilt.
>
> (Bion, 1976, p. 318)

The theme of deep-level guilt reverberates here like a warning signal. Similarly disturbing is the reference to 'sub-thalamic fear' – an expression specially coined by Bion to refer to fear unrestrained by a higher level of the mind. What is he driving at? The answer is not long in coming, because Bion finally decides to show us his cards. And the cards are tinged with darkness:

> I remember [a patient] . . . who was quite articulate, in fact articulate enough to make me think that I was analysing him rather well. Indeed the analysis did go extremely well, but I was beginning to think that nothing was happening. However, the patient checked all that. After a session he went home, sealed up all the crevices throughout his room, turned on the gas, and perished. So there was my highly successful analysis – a very disconcerting result indeed, and no way of finding out or learning for myself what exactly had gone wrong, excepting the fact that undoubtedly it had gone wrong.
>
> (Bion, 1976, p. 319)

Bion blames himself for having been unable to feel this 'primordial', 'physical' fear that had broken out again and led the patient to suicide. As he was analysing him 'well' and the analysis seemed highly successful, the patient took his own life. This brief sequence of statements condenses a deadly brew of conflicting and violent emotions.

A veritable *coup de théâtre*. In an impressive crescendo, Bion takes us on a journey of discovery: from the theme of what is true in analysis to the truth that the helpless child seeks in the sphinxlike eyes of the mother, or when faced with the spectacle of the hideous monster invented by Klein, the phantasy of the combined parental figure, and finally on to the phantasy of death evoked by the suicide of his patient. This phantasy foreshadows and finally brings to pass his own death which, as he described in his memoirs, had already occurred on the battlefield of Amiens.

Thus, writing, reading and analysis converge in the same place: all are significant if they involve an experience of truth, the ability to learn from experience. As Bion writes:

> The practising analyst must wait for the analytic system to evolve . . . for an evolution to take place so that O becomes manifest in K through the emergence of actual events. Similarly, the reader must disregard what I say until the O of the experience of reading has evolved to a point where the actual events of reading issue in his interpretation of the experiences. Too great a regard for what I have written obstructs the process I represent by the terms he becomes the O that is common to himself and myself [*sic*].
>
> (Bion, 1970, p. 29)

This brief but very intense passage helps us realize that the question of language and style in analysis is a matter of life and death. Bion also makes this clear in 'Evidence':

> Supposing we are in fact always dealing with some kind of psychosomatic situation. Is it any good talking to a highly articulate person in highly articulate terms? Is it possible that, if feelings of intense fear, self-hatred, can seep up into a state of mind in which they can be translated into action, the reverse is true? Is it possible to talk to the soma in such a way that the psychosis is able to understand, or vice versa?
>
> (Bion, 1976, p. 319)

Now, talking to the soma (the foetus) is what makes this style – it is the how, not the what, and the semiotics, not the semantics of the expression. Sometimes, understanding the language of the body and speaking to the body (knowing, for example, that the setting, as Winnicott says, is the maternal womb) may be the factors that either save a life or cause it to be lost.

On more than one occasion, I have found myself wondering whether I would have become interested in psychoanalysis had Freud not been the writer he was. The thought has always been somewhat disturbing, suggesting as it does that what has always impassioned me about psychoanalysis has been something extrinsic – in other words, not the *thing* itself. But in actual fact this is not the case, because writing in analysis is not ornament, not the mere vehicle of concepts. It is the truthful transposition of the thing, almost the thing itself. A type of psychology that seeks to account for the private, subjective world of the individual strives to combine insights and concepts; mind and body could not be expressed at a lower level.

It is no coincidence that the great authors of psychoanalysis, those who nourish our love for this discipline, are all great writers, although they differ enormously in style. Through style they convey the understanding they have attained of the mind, of humanity and existence. The theory is in the writing; it does not precede the writing because it is a theory of how to see a mind, touch a character, smell an emotion. In philosophy, the same constraint of necessity that binds concept and expression is found in the 'literary' style of Derrida, a writer unsurprisingly steeped in Freudian thought and often misunderstood – and here misunderstanding is something sought, desired and regarded as productive.

In the same way that the metaphors we use direct the gaze of the researcher, so, too, does the style. Freud does not discover the unconscious; he writes it. He discovers and invents it at one and the same time in the act of writing it. Analysis as theorizing and as treatment is a textual practice – with texts as people and people as texts. The style is the body, emotions, history – everything specific to a given person. The body (the music) of writing comes before the concept, the idea; it is the unconscious of the text.

In 'Evidence' (1976), Bion offers us a unique opportunity to see him at work in his clinical practice (his style): in the story-dream of a patient, he reconstructs two sessions that are all the more true for being imaginary. It is not 'verbal exactitude' (Bion, 1965, p. 20) that counts. A psychoanalytic text 'should stimulate in the reader the emotional experience that the writer intends . . . and the emotional experience thus stimulated should be an accurate representation of the psychoanalytic experience (O) that stimulated the writer in the first place' (ibid., p. 32).

An analytic text also demonstrates how to re-create psychoanalysis in oneself, namely, in one's personality, which is, according to Ogden (2009), what every analyst should do. We come to admire the maddening beauty and fragile power of Bion's style as central factors in his thinking. As a writer, Bion carefully avoids an academic style, which is namely what he pillories in his last 'literary writings' in *A Memoir of the Future* (1991), where the dangerous character of satanic jargon comes onto the scene. The style is not dry or impersonal: it is interwoven with emotions. He speaks in the first person and like all great writers is not afraid of appearing naked. He deploys an expressive minimalism that is designed to lend maximum brevity, simplicity and concision to his style.

'Evidence' (1976) is pervaded by a tone of bitter and sceptical wisdom. It is grief work. What Bion expresses in this text is sarcasm and pity towards himself, and sorrow and rage towards a patient who has committed suicide. It is atonement in the sense of unison/identification (at-one-ment) and expiation, a coming together of anger and despair. 'Evidence' is a painful meditation on a dramatic personal and professional failure, which, due to the extraordinary fascination of the text, is transformed – as in Philip Roth's novels – into a sense of awe at the beauty of human existence and indignation at the horror that all this must end.

Bion's systematic doubt, so characteristically present in this text, does not resolve itself in a sophisticated intellectual exercise – as in Descartes, where deep down there lies a sense of vertigo and fear, albeit apparently under control; it is pure emotion, taking stock of his life, and the life of a man who carries within himself the terrible experience of war. Evidence is something that is there but cannot be seen; it is the evidence of a person's death, the evidence of death. We all need to take shelter from this evidence behind some form of lie. The other side of the lie is truth: that which can be shared emotionally with the other and that can thus become the vital fullness and joy of existence.

In Bion's style, human matter and thought merge in an inimitable style. The body joins with the mind, and ideas become musical again; they become *sensuous* (Carbone, 2008). Bion becomes his patient and suffers the patient's inner turmoil in the same way that a mother who hears her baby crying *lives* its pain. 'Evidence' is structured in such a way that, as Benjamin (1955) says in his reflections on Nikolai Leskov's *The Storyteller*, what gives meaning to a story is the death of the protagonist (especially if it is exemplary).

The final section of 'Evidence' retrospectively illuminates the whole paper, doing so by opening up a dizzying array of perspectives. As in the phantasmagoric transmutations we find in dreams and poetry, Bion is father, son, person, man, analyst and patient. As Vitale writes (2005), underlying psychoanalytic thinking is the image of the apocalypse. The revelation will come to pass at the end of the world – the imminent becomes immanent. 'Evidence' is an apocalyptic text, but also the apocalypse of meaning since it strongly reaffirms the circular temporality of Freud's *Nachträglichkeit*.

The end of this paper prompts us to go back and reread the beginning, and so on, as in life itself. Why else would we be so hungry for stories? After all, every symbol, every word comes into being under the aegis of the (albeit tolerable) absence of the object – an absence that does not kill but establishes temporality. The return of the object rewrites the absence and transforms it a posteriori into symbol-truth.

As a whole, the text of 'Evidence' is a text-symbol whereby Bion mourns – for his analytic fathers and mothers, for his daughter, for the patient. Make no mistake: underneath his bitter sarcasm lie harrowing experiences and nostalgia for the beauty of life. In Rilke's words, it is terror of the kind we are able still to bear.

POSTSCRIPT

From Freud's *Italienreisen* to the Pavia School: on the history and current state of psychoanalysis in Italy

In Galileo's observatory: the past

'[T]his traveling in Italy is not so completely without difficulties as one might expect' (Freud, 1999 [1896], p. 1253):[75] the sentence is taken from a letter Freud (1999 [1896]) wrote to his wife Martha on 7 September 1886. Only recently tracked down by Harold Blum (1999), director of the Sigmund Freud Archives of the Library of Congress, Washington, DC, the letter was written while Freud was staying at Torre del Gallo, a tower located close to Florence which Freud believed was also called Torre di Galilei, in reference to Galileo, who spent the last years of his life in the adjacent villa. In it, Freud (1999 [1896]) mentions the difficulties of travelling by rail, how wonderful the food is, the beauty of the places he has visited and the pervasive presence of works of art. They are to be found almost everywhere. 'The memorials stand around in half-dozens on the street', he writes; they stun the visitor, making him feel 'the whole dizziness of southern beauty' ('*der ganze . . . Schwindel südlicher Schönheit*') (ibid., pp. 1253–1254), an expression which in some way suggests the 'Stendhal syndrome' that in the contemporary view affects tourists particularly susceptible to aesthetic emotions. Equally prophetic is Freud's fascination with the observation tower used by Galileo – a scientific figure one can easily imagine him identifying with. Part of the house had been converted into a museum, and Freud decided to stay there with his brother Alexander, renting three rooms from the owner of the building: 'The whole magnificence will only last another three days. On Friday morning we'll telegraph our trip home, a trip during which we will probably atone for all our sins' (ibid., p. 1255).

Freud's ironic expression associating Italy with sin and guilty pleasure is suggestive and gives some indication of Freud's way of looking on Italy as a place of the unconscious. Antoinette and Gerard Haddad (1995) have argued that Italy must have played a special role in the discovery of the unconscious and the Oedipus complex, both of which occurred during the years of Freud's self-analysis and his first trips to Italy. For Freud, the land of beauty and sensuality represented the forbidden place of the mother's body. The expression AMAR ITALIA, a condensed fusion of the names of Freud's wife Martha and his mother Amalia, and the long-standing inhibition that kept Freud away from Rome (read backwards, the Italian name becomes AMOR, i.e. 'love'; Freud would also spend whole days in a kind of trance studying the topography of Rome) appear to support their idea.

Yet, in spite of the great love or passion that Freud felt for Italy in a mixture of 'Grand Tour' and incestuous fantasies, as evidenced by his numerous trips there (no fewer than twenty!), the penetration of psychoanalysis into the 'Bel Paese' was not at all easy, indeed 'not so completely without difficulties' ('*nicht so ganz ohne Beschwerden*'), due to several specific concomitant factors. First of all, Catholic culture, which – similarly to the way it treated the revolutionary theses of Galileo – for a long time blacklisted psychoanalysis on account of Freud's materialism, the Darwinian imprint of his thinking and his so-called pan-sexuality; then there was the philosophical idealism of Benedetto Croce, the greatest Italian philosopher of the last century, and of his pupil Giovanni Gentile, who disparaged psychology and the positivistic spirit that informed scientific research, preferring instead aesthetic and historical knowledge; and furthermore the organicistic orientation of psychiatry at the time, dominated by Cesare Lombroso, founder of criminal anthropology, who sought in somatic features the stigmata of 'mental degeneration'. Later, the spread of psychoanalysis was hindered by the general cultural isolation imposed on society by the Fascist era, during which initial ambivalence turned ever more into intolerance; then, after the Second World War, psychoanalysis was also repudiated by many of the political and cultural forces inspired by Marxism, which regarded it as bourgeois, irrational and abstract.

In the light of all this, it is soon clear why the gateway for psychoanalysis in Italy was Trieste – a border town, Central European, Slavic and Italian, German, but with a significant Jewish presence, an integral part of the Austro-Hungarian Empire, whose port it was until 1918. And, again, one can see as a presage of the future the presence there of a very young Freud, third-year medical student at the University of Vienna who spent four weeks in 1876 at the recently established Experimental Zoological Station on a scholarship to do research on the gonads of eels, which became the subject of his first scientific publication.

Trieste was the home town of Edoardo Weiss, the man who brought the 'plague' of psychoanalysis to Italy. Weiss, who came from a Jewish family, as did almost all the leading Italian analysts, was born in 1889. He studied medicine and psychiatry in Vienna, where he met Freud and was analysed by Paul Federn, later becoming a member of the IPA (1913) and the Vienna Psychoanalytic Society. To give an idea of the climate that reigned in Trieste: it was here that Joyce lived for 16 years, until July 1920 when, at the age of 38, he left the city where he had written and published all his early works and where he drafted the first episodes of *Ulysses*. We know that James Joyce met Edoardo Weiss's brother, Ottocaro, and Italo Svevo (Ettore Schmitz). He started giving Svevo English lessons in mid-1907, going on to become his close friend. Svevo was the author of *Confessions of Zeno* (1923), one of the masterpieces of world literature inspired by psychoanalysis, which would later serve as a model for Giuseppe Berto's novel *Il male oscuro* (*Dark Illness*) and Philip Roth's *Portnoy's Complaint*. Finally, Trieste was home to one of the greatest Italian poets of the first half of the twentieth century, Umberto Saba, who was deeply influenced by his encounter with psychoanalysis and his analysis with Weiss in Via San Lazzaro 8.

Weiss's *Elements of Psychoanalysis,* with a foreword by Freud, was published in 1931. Weiss was also responsible first for re-establishing the Italian Psychoanalytic Society (SPI) on 1 October 1932, in Rome, one of whose honorary members was Levi-Bianchini (who had helped found it in Teramo, Abruzzo, in 1925), and three years later for having it affiliated to the IPA. The new association enjoyed only a short life. After two years, in 1934, the *Rivista italiana di psicoanalisi* (*Journal of Italian Psychoanalysis*) had to discontinue publication, as reported by Jones (1953, p. 219), apparently after direct intervention by the Catholic Church. In 1938 the race laws were introduced, psychoanalysis was condemned as 'Jewish science' and the association was disbanded. Psychoanalysis in Italy ceased to exist in the period from 1939 to 1945, the year the country was liberated from Nazi occupation. In 1939, like many other European analysts, Weiss was forced to flee to the United States, ending up in Chicago, where he lived until 1970, working for a long time with Franz Alexander.

The society was reorganized and officially reconstituted in 1947. The previous year the first congress had been held in Rome on the subject of 'Aggression' (!). The *Rivista di psicoanalisi*, the official organ of the society, began publication again in 1955. To give an idea of the situation in terms of numbers: in 1964 the SPI had 27 members and an almost equal number of associate members. Today the total number is about a thousand, taking into account the various categories of members and candidates.

The leading figures in Italian post-war psychoanalysis were Weiss's students: Nicola Perrotti, originally from Abruzzo, and Emilio Servadio from Rome. Further figures included the Venetian Cesar Musatti, Alessandra Wolff Stomersee and Princess Tomasi di Lampedusa. I have deliberately mentioned the regional origin of some of the early Italian Freudians because the question of 'the province' and 'provincialism' offers a compelling key to understanding the paths of development – the 'journeys', so to speak – taken by psychoanalysis in Italy.

One of these paths started from as far away as Russia: Alexandra Tomasi di Lampedusa, the daughter of a high official of Tsar Nicholas II, spent the first 20 years of her life in St Petersburg, trained at the Berlin Psychoanalytic Institute directed by Karl Abraham and in 1934 moved to Palermo, the city of her second husband, the author of *The Leopard*, the novel that was made into the famous film by Luchino Visconti. With this charming cosmopolitan figure located at the opposite end of the peninsula from Trieste, Palermo became another 'psychoanalytic province', an environment where outstanding analysts would develop, including Francesco Corrao, to whom goes the credit for introducing Bion and opening the way to the study of groups.

In the second half of the last century, psychoanalysis in Italy grew not only in numbers, as I have already pointed out, but also culturally. Increasingly, Freudian theories began to make themselves felt in society almost to the point of becoming 'fashionable', managing to overcome considerable resistance, although never completely (perhaps this would not even have been desirable, if we take this fact as a sign of their persistent radical nature and effectiveness). For a certain period, the influence of ego psychology was overwhelming, on a par with its dominant position in the United States. Over time other influences were added. Many analysts received their training in London, and went on to introduce the ideas of Melanie Klein and Anna Freud. Groups that took their inspiration from Lacan were formed. Bion and Meltzer then held seminars in Italy that left their mark. Matte-Blanco moved to Rome from Chile in 1966 and became an influential figure. In the 1960s and 1970s, there persisted, however, a certain aristocratic attitude that led the SPI to isolate itself not only from the world of universities and psychiatric institutions but also from other societies as well as from the IPA (Albarella, 1997).

A room with a view: the present

As already mentioned, on the whole, Italian psychoanalysis was, and in part still is, provincial, in the sense that it has paid a high price for its abiding cultural and linguistic insularity (a factor not to be overlooked), and this has led it to translate and import much from abroad and export very little – hardly anything, in fact, with the exception of very few names. However, at the same time a situation was created where various styles and models coexisted and have succeeded reasonably well at entering into dialogue with each other and establishing an atmosphere of basic tolerance and respect. Of course, sometimes appearances might suggest otherwise, judging by the harshness of certain debates at conferences and scientific seminars. From this point of view, psychoanalysis in a country marked by its provincial geography, and not centralized in its capital, not monolithic, can prove to be an asset, in the same way as Italy enjoys the great heritage offered by the gentleness, life wisdom and variety of its many provinces. Kleinians, Winnicottians, Bionians, Lacanians . . . the map is both broadly based and highly structured. So what about the Freudians? The fact is that, to paraphrase Benedetto Croce, we cannot not call ourselves Freudians.

The fact is that the reference to Freud is always crucial, both because psychoanalysis can only be apprehended as a genetic phenomenon, and because psychoanalytic thinking is inherently dialectical and paradoxical and cannot set aside any of the polarities that maintain its network of concepts in a state of tension. The difference is between those who regard Freudian theories as strict doctrine and those who believe that true allegiance to Freud is best demonstrated by respectful infidelity – in other words, by being faithful to his creativity and courage. We must not forget that on the occasion of his trip to America with Jung, Freud had talked of bringing the plague. I believe that the kind of psychoanalysis that is rigid in its certainties and utterly normalized, that loses its spirit of radical criticism of the constitution of the subject, the Cartesian *cogito*, as well as towards its own inevitable ideological colouring, loses the right to be considered truly alive.

In the meantime, the overview I have just outlined has already changed or is in the process of changing. For several years now, there has been a steady growth in the number of Italian authors whose contributions have appeared in international journals. The language gap is seen as less of a problem. Italians are not just translators of thoughts elaborated elsewhere but are also becoming exporters of psychoanalysis. There are, for example, regular scientific meetings with psychoanalytic societies in French-speaking countries, as well as with the English and Argentine associations. The EFP conferences, which in recent years, thanks to the invaluable work of David Tuckett, have been a great success and are fashioning an original model of exchange and dialogue, enjoy the increasing participation of Italian analysts. The *International Journal of Psychoanalysis* publishes more and more contributions representing all the psychoanalytic regions of the world, including Italy, as do other major national magazines. *De facto* there has been a remarkable degree of openness and curiosity. After a period of crisis the impression is now one of a vibrant response to attacks from other scientific theories.

Also in terms of structure the SPI is becoming less elitist and hierarchical. There is a widespread feeling of challenges to be met: the difficult engagement with the university world, the possibility of psychoanalysis playing an ever-increasing role in care services, dialogue with neuroscience – there is great interest in the discovery of mirror neurons (Gallese, 2006) and the concept of the non-repressed unconscious (Mancia, 2006) – and with other psychoanalytic or psychotherapeutic schools, some of which, following in the wake of a necessary but hasty legal recognition of psychotherapy despite the ritual invocation of Freud, do not always appear to have the acceptable credentials to ensure a rigorous training path and even seem unable to offer much from the scientific point of view.

There is one theoretical development which in my view remains true to the radical nature and the spirit that characterized Freud and on which I focus both because it is the closest to my own way of thinking and because it began to be recognized internationally as an Italian 'product'. I refer to the concept of the analytic field as elaborated by Antonino Ferro. Starting from an obvious Kleinian matrix, from Bion and from the contributions of the Argentinean school of Willy and Madelaine Baranger, Robert Langs and Nissim Momiglian, Ferro (1992, 1996) has developed a so-called bi-personal model of psychoanalysis, now identified by many with the 'Italian Bionians' (Kernberg, 2011) or as the Pavia School.

Why Pavia?

What makes Pavia so special is the fact that its university, founded in 1361, is one of the oldest in Europe as well as being among the most distinguished especially in the field of medical studies. This explains the fact that so-called Pavia analysts are for the most part anything but 'Pavesi' in origin. For example, Ferro is from Palermo, my own region of origin is the Abruzzo and, with some exceptions, other colleagues come from various parts of Italy. In addition to being a popular place to study medicine, further enhanced by the presence of historical colleges founded as early as the sixteenth century to provide lodgings for deserving students, Pavia is also distinctive in having a School of Psychiatry most of whose lecturers and professors were (and are) analysts. Clearly, this explains why Pavia became a particularly fertile ground for the development of psychoanalysis. But when we come to speak of a Pavia School, this is certainly not to be equated with the entire range of psychoanalysis in Pavia, which until a few years ago had Milan as its point of reference. What is meant is a smaller handful of students and scholars drawn together by the teachings of Ferro. Over the years, the members of this group have included not only the present writer, but also Maurizio Collovà, Giovanni Foresti, Pierluigi Politi, Fulvio Mazzacane and Elena Molinari. Among later additions are Mauro Manica, Violet Pietrantonio and Luca Nicoli. The scientific activity of this group is documented not only by the many papers these analysts have published individually in various national and international magazines, but also by a number of books, some already translated with others in the process of being translated into other languages. To mention a few: *Sognare l'analisi* (To Dream Analysis), *Psicoanalisi in giallo* (Psychoanalysis as a Detective Story), *Psicoanalisi Oggi* (Psychoanalysis Today), *Psicoanalisi Oggi II* (Psychoanalysis Today II).

If the central mentor has been Ferro, it is also true that individually we have been through a range of different experiences – for example, some have worked with severe psychiatric patients – and have followed various training paths. As I mentioned, the Psychoanalytic Centre in Milan has represented a point of reference for all of us. Milan is a large centre with numerous members where, as throughout Italy, 'many languages of psychoanalysis are spoken'. In this respect we are very different, for example, from French psychoanalysis, which, whether rightly or wrongly, appears to us to be very hierarchical and monolithic. Even though I think with Rome Italy can boast the most beautiful capital city in the world as its real and spiritual capital, for historical reasons the country has many capitals. These were real capitals of real states until the unification that was achieved only recently compared to other European nations. As I have already pointed out, a great propensity to import and to translate knowledge, wedded to a certain provincialism and to the objective difficulties linked to the spread of the language, made Italian analysts consumers rather than producers of psychoanalysis. Recently things have changed somewhat. Italian psychoanalysis has begun to circulate in the world and its liveliness and creativity have begun to enjoy growing appreciation. This was reflected in the feeling of surprise I felt when I was requested to enlighten readers more about the so-called Pavia School. Why? Because now articles and books are widely available in the world's principal languages and some of us are engaged in the intense international activity of supervision and teaching.

I do not think it would make much sense here to retrace the theoretical tenets of the so-called theory of the analytic field – an expression that serves as a label for the Pavia School. This is what this book does, and so I would refer the reader to the various chapters and to the now many books that deal with this subject. To recall at least some of the main features of this way of understanding analysis, and of course at the risk of some simplification,

I would say that it is a matter of fully expanding certain classical Freudian principles which we can now at last fully appreciate: the unconscious as a psychoanalytic function of the personality; the inaccessible unconscious; dream work as an activity of symbolization; the systematic principle of doubt; the model of how the mind develops starting from another mind and the quality of its ability to engage in reverie; the reformulation of the goals of therapy (no longer translating the unconscious into the conscious but creating/generating the unconscious); the emphasis on psychic containers rather than on content; the centrality given to psychic transformations and the clarification of these transformations with the help of the various theories of narratology.

The reference to Bion remains central; his clinical insights are dazzling, although even I would find it hard to imagine a set of tools borrowed from Bion for clinical practice that had not first been filtered through the original, constant and passionate work of Meltzer, Ferro and Ogden; only thus have they become truly useful. This is in my view a characteristic feature of the analytic field model. While not simple, over time it has honed a series of extraordinarily versatile tools, readily understandable and easily communicable. What is their purpose? To expand the analyst's receptivity to the facts of the analysis and thus also his ability to help the patient make sense of personal experience. While it is true that the distinguishing mark of this type of psychoanalysis lies in its theoretical nature, it still privileges the moment of clinical engagement as the setting where analysts who as it were speak different languages are able to communicate profitably and more easily, and to verify the added meaning that certain theoretical tools enable us to acquire.

The future (of an illusion?)

In selecting the titles of the three sections into which this postscript is divided I was thinking of the tropes of vision and gaze as a way of suggesting implicitly what I believe to be the essential characteristics of psychoanalysis: the courage to seek the truth and the practice of science as personified by Galileo; the centrality of clinical practice, symbolized by a consulting room that has at least one window on the society within which it operates (and here the reference was to the title of E.M. Forster's wonderful novel, partly set in Florence); the prescience of Freud (which led him to write in a letter to Weiss dated 1 November 1923 that he had no doubt that in Italy the future would belong to psychoanalysis, but his correspondent would have to wait quite a while; Weiss, 1970), but also the intrinsically self-reflective and self-deconstructive attitude that typifies psychoanalysis, an attitude that is necessary if analysis is to avoid becoming an *illusion* of science.

We cannot know what the future holds for us but we do know what problems are still awaiting adequate solutions. In future, psychoanalysis may be more present in the universities, and it may become more open to the world outside the various local centres in psychiatric institutions. We must contend with neo-biologistic psychiatry and the uncritical view of its progress, as well as with the desire for a counter-reformation in the field of mental health care, and with the urge to return to weakened forms of custodialism. We must continue with the democratic transformation of the psychoanalytic institutions, to come up with answers to the problem formulated so cogently by Kernberg (1996, 2012) in his classic works on the ways in which the creativity of students is stifled and psychoanalytic institutions are demoralized, namely solutions to the problem of dysfunction in the training of analysts, and promote the more active participation of members in the life of psychoanalytic societies.

To return to the future of Italian psychoanalysis: while the contention may appear presumptuous, I believe that no other contributions can rival those of the Pavia School in terms of vigour, originality and in the meantime also of diffusion. The paradox in this context is that what is now called Italian psychoanalysis, by which is meant Bionian analysis, is very much in the minority in Italy. Perhaps for this reason and again with regard to the future, it would be more interesting at this point to mention what happens outside Italy. As the Romans said, no one is a prophet in his own country. Beyond the borders of Italy, the impression is that there is a huge interest in a psychoanalysis that at least tries to keep up with the times, that is above all not afraid of the new, not afraid of looking in as yet unexplored directions and competing with the other disciplines that seek to treat and alleviate mental suffering.

NOTES

Chapter 1

1 If, following Winnicott (1947, p. 197), we think of the setting as 'the analyst's lap or womb', then they may appear in the sensations and rhythms of this 'body'.
2 'a surprising and at first incomprehensible phenomenon . . . This has occurred both in dreams immediately after the construction had been put forward and in waking states resembling phantasies' (Freud, 1937, p. 266).

Chapter 2

3 The definition of dream would always need to include waking.
4 See Bion (1965, p. 73): 'Meaning is a function of self-love, self-hate or self-knowledge. It is not logically, but psychologically necessary.'
5 See, for example, Schneider (1992, p. 32).
6 See ibid., pp. 33–34.
7 Translator's note: this is an allusion to the saying 'Un traduttore è un traditore' – 'A translator is a traitor.'

Chapter 3

8 I discuss a shorter version of this vignette and from a different perspective in Civitarese (2011a).
9 The clinical material in this and the following vignette was presented to me during my supervision of Rosamaria Di Frenna.
10 I would like to thank Elisa Marchi for allowing me to use this clinical material, which she brought to her supervision.

11 In philosophy, other interesting ideas useful for our discussion come from Merleau-Ponty. As Vanzago writes (2014),

> The fundamental thesis that emerges from Merleau-Ponty's analyses can be summed up in the statement that primordial bodily subjectivity is not univocal but plural. In other words, there is no separate and original *ipse* that is placed in relation to other subjects, but rather a relational structure into which different subjectivities find themselves immersed from the beginning . . . This form of intersubjectivity, however, is based on the situation of intercorporality and primordial indistinction, on which it feeds without ever overcoming it definitively. This remains true at every stage of the development of the subject, so that even the most complex structures of intersubjectivity maintain a core of initial syncretic intercorporality.

And further:

> Language is something much deeper and more vital than the mere shell of thought. Merleau-Ponty maintains that Freud is right when he says that there is an investment in language . . . The spoken language, moreover, amplifies and picks up already existing intercorporeal communication. Body and language are like strings moving puppets and which invisibly attract talking subjects to each other.

It is clear how reflection on the sub-categorical and the 'radical antisubjectivism' (Lanfredini, 2014) which characterize Merleau-Ponty's thinking are invaluable in giving a solid foundation to a theory of the analytic field.

Chapter 4

12 Translator's note: this is the subtitle given to *Second Thoughts* in its Italian version.

13 Translator's note: the wordplay and associations which are so important in this account are impossible to reproduce in English. S. says that when her dog welcomed her home, 'mi ha fatto le feste!' 'Fare le feste' for someone, besides meaning 'hold a party for them', is also a euphemism for 'wipe them out', 'waste them', 'do away with them', etc. Hence, we are told later in the account that 'the celebration of the dog' had become 'celebrate someone' in the sense of 'gun them down'. The box at the theatre holds four seats, two in front, two behind. The rear seats offer an inadequate view of the stage. *Orson Welles' Roast* is a one-man show written by Michele De Vita

Conti and Giuseppe Battiston, and performed by the latter in Rome in 2011, in which Welles gives a 'eulogy to contrariness'. The English word 'roast' is used in the title to indicate a rant, part panegyric, part invective. Non-intendo = 'I don't understand'.

Chapter 5

14 For Nietzsche (1882, pp. 297–298) the very act of becoming conscious relates to intersubjectivity:

> The whole of life would be possible without it, as it were, seeing itself in a mirror . . . *For what purpose*, then, any consciousness at all when it is in the main *superfluous*? . . . I may now proceed to the surmise that consciousness has developed only under the pressure of the need for communication.

What is more, etymologically, conscious comes from the Latin *cum-scire*, which means 'know together'.

15 See Freud (1923, p. 56):

> It is not only a helper to the id; it is also a submissive slave who courts his master's love. Whenever possible, it tries to remain on good terms with the id; it clothes the id's *Ucs.* commands with its *Pcs.* rationalizations; it pretends that the id is showing obedience to the admonitions of reality, even when in fact it is remaining obstinate and unyielding; it disguises the id's conflicts with reality, and, if possible, its conflicts with the super-ego . . . it only too often yields to the temptation to become sycophantic, opportunistic and lying, like a politician who sees the truth but wants to keep his place in popular favour.

16 See Stocker (2006, p. 82): 'There is always a lurking sense in Freud of the presence of truth in the unconscious, even if his discussion of the unconscious provides the tools to overcome that.'

17 See also Derrida's *Writing and Difference* (1967a, pp. 211–212):

> The unconscious text is already a weave of pure traces, differences in which meaning and force are united – a text nowhere present, consisting of archives which are *always already* transcriptions. Originary prints. Everything begins with reproduction. *Always already:* repositories of a meaning which was never present, whose signified presence is always reconstituted by deferral, *nachträglich*, belatedly, supplementarily*:* for the *nachträglich* also means *supplementary*. The call of the supplement is primary, here, and it hollows out that which will be reconstituted by deferral as the

> present. The supplement, which seems to be added as a plenitude to a plenitude, is equally that which compensates for a lack . . . Let us note: *Nachtrag* has a precise meaning in the realm of letters: appendix, codicil, postscript. The text we call present may be deciphered only at the bottom of the page, in a footnote or postscript. Before the recurrence the present is only the call for a footnote. That the present in general is not primal but, rather, reconstituted, that it is not the absolute, wholly living form which constitutes experience, that there is no purity of the living present – such is the theme, formidable for metaphysics, which Freud, in a conceptual scheme unequal to the thing itself, would have us pursue.

18 See Freud (1895, p. 300): 'memory is represented by the differences in the facilitations between the Ψ neurones'.

19 See Derrida (1967b, p. 324n.):

> This does not, by simple inversion, mean that the signifier is fundamental or primary. The 'primacy' or 'priority' of the signified would be an expression untenable and absurd to formulate illogically within the very logic that it would legitimately destroy. The signifier will never by rights precede the signified, in which case it would no longer be a signifier and the 'signifying' signifier would no longer have a possible signifier. The thought that is announced in this impossible formula without being successfully contained therein should therefore be stated in another way; it will be clearly impossible to do so without putting the very idea of the sign in suspicion, the 'sign-of' which will always remain attached to what is here put in question. At the limit, therefore, that thought would destroy the entire conceptuality organized around the concept of the sign (signifier and signified, expression and content, and so on).

20 The unconscious is the edge, the margin, the *parergon* (Derrida, 1978) that gives meaning to the conscious and receives meaning from it. The slash symbolizes the frame of the canvas, the edging of content.

21 Proof of this functionalist approach can be seen in the fact that López-Corvo's dictionary of Bionian concepts has no entry for the unconscious as a psychic place, but only one for the conscious and the relationship between conscious and unconscious. On the same wavelength, the whole of Bion's theory has been seen as coming from Freud's *Formulations on the Two Principles of Mental Functioning* (1911). Just as Freud talks of principles, so Bion speaks of functions

of the mind and elaborates a theory of psychic functions rather than contents. He sees the unconscious as a function of the personality, an innate grammar that serves to deal with and digest emotional experience. In its turn, the unconscious, as a function, depends on a series of factors, each of which could in itself be a function, that is, include a constant and a variable part. For example, a person's mood can be permanently influenced by his digestive function, which in turn depends on factors (or on other functions located on a lower hierarchical level). Likewise, the capacity to dream 'O', to give meaning to experience, could depend on the function performed by the un/conscious (by what we call unconscious), and this in its turn will depend on several factors which have generated or generate adequate 'realizations'. The un/conscious-as-alpha-function-as-dreaming is not the same in all individuals! It will have developed more or less according to the Ψs which ξ has encountered in the course of its development (but also depending on what one has eaten for dinner). So we have the personality in its entirety which depends on various functions. Only one of these is what we call un/conscious (others are, for example, somatic states, etc.).

22 See Fornaro (1990, p. 161) for the Bionian formula conception = pre-conception as a function of an emotional experience, in other words, $C = \Psi (\xi)$.

23 See Bion (1962, p. 89): 'Alpha-function is a factor of Ψ' (psycho-analytic function of the personality), so it is a ξ, the non-saturated element in Ψ.

24 Bion does not make a clear distinction between alpha function, what he initially called dream work alpha, and dream work proper, but it is easy to see that between the two terms there is a relationship as between a detail and the totality of the figure in a fractal. The only real distinction he makes is from the overall direction of Freud's *Traumarbeit*. For Bion dream work does not destroy meaning; it creates meaning. In fact, as Opatow (1997) points out, already in Chapter VII of *The Interpretation of Dreams* one can see a shift of emphasis from the content of the dream to dream rhetoric.

25 Other terms are more or less interchangeable: inaccessible unconscious (Bion, 1997), primary repressed unconscious (Bollas, 1987), pre-reflexive unconscious (Stolorow and Atwood, 1992), non-representational world (Bucci, 1997), procedural or cognitive unconscious, affective unconscious (Riolo, 2009), structural unconscious (Bonfiglio, 2010).

26 Avzaradel (2011) has written an interesting paper on the construction of the mind which takes Chinese ideograms as its starting point.

27 The auroral experience that the subject has of the object is autistic in form (the imprint of things on the skin).

28 On what happens when this mirroring function is defective, see Lemma (2010, 2013).

29 On this point, see this extraordinary passage in Heidegger (1927, p. 298):

> Strictly speaking, meaning signifies the upon-which of the primary project of the understanding of being. Being-in-the-world that is disclosed to itself equiprimordially understands the being of innerwordly beings together with the being of the being that it itself is, although unthematically and not yet diffferentiated in its primary modes of existence and reality. Every ontic experience of beings, the circumspect calculation of things at hand as well as the positive scientific cognition of things objectively present, are always grounded in the more or less transparent projects of the being of the beings in question. But these projects contain an upon-which from which, so to speak, the understanding of being is nourished.

30 The expression container/contained, which is an abstraction of the Kleinian concept of projective identification, is not sufficiently dynamic. It would be better to say 'contain/be contained' (Bion, 1963, p. 15).

31 See Bion (1992) for a description of how we arrive at algebra by passing through an infinite series of operations of abstraction which start with the formation of the alpha element. And further (ibid., p. 55): 'it is similarly thanks to the operations of α that it seems obvious that 2+2 = 4. If α has not operated, it is probable that it would not be "obvious" at all'.

32 As Westen writes (1999, p. 1070), '*preconscious* processes often operate by principles of association – a characteristic of primary process thinking ascribed only to dynamically unconscious processes . . . Thus, the distinction between primary and secondary process thinking needs to be recast'. Basically, unconscious and preconscious processes function on the basis of the same laws of association. There are unconscious affects which direct the action. The link Freud set up between primitive and instinctual needs to be loosened: 'Freud's concept of primary process . . . confounds a mode of cognition (associative thought) with a primitive form of motivation' (ibid., p. 1097).

33 Throughout her excellent work, Judith Butler has taken this notion to its extreme consequences. With her idea of 'performativity' she sees the body as increasingly conditioned by culture.

34 Bion's position is efficaciously anti-dualistic. The concept of the proto-mental system corresponds to what Heidegger calls *Dasein*

('existence', 'being in the world'). Equally, it is difficult to think of a more effective critique of Cartesian dualism and the representation of the subject as isolated in its *ipséité* (individuality) than the pages in *Being and Time* that address this theme. The theoretical profile of an undifferentiated and unthematizable background of pre-comprehension of the world which Heidegger's captivating and impassioned rhetoric insists on and constantly comes back to is something we find again in the Bionian idea of a state of indistinction between individual and group which gives rise to basic assumptions, powerful and obscure emotional germinations that condition the lives of groups.

35 See Peltz (2015) on the surface/depth dichotomy.

36 See Freud (1895, p. 318):

> At first, the human organism is incapable of bringing about the specific action. It takes place by *extraneous help* when the attention of an experienced person is drawn to the child's state by discharge along the path of internal change. In this way this path of discharge acquires a secondary function of the highest importance, that of *communication* [*Verständigung*], and the initial helplessness of human beings is the *primal source* of all *moral motives*.

And further (ibid., p. 366):

> Speech-innervation is originally a path of discharge for Ψ, operating like a safety-valve, for regulating oscillations in $Q\acute{\eta}$, it is a portion of the path to *internal change*, which represents the only discharge till the *specific action* has been found. This path acquires a secondary function from the fact that it draws the attention of the helpful person (usually the wished-for object itself) to the child's longing and distressful state; and thereafter it serves for *communication* and is thus drawn into the specific action.

Freud comes back to this question in *Formulations Regarding the Two Principles in Mental Functioning* (1911, p. 219n.):

> it will rightly be objected that an organization which was a slave to the pleasure principle and neglected the reality of the external world could not maintain itself alive for the shortest time, so that it could not have come into existence at all. The employment of a fiction like this is, however, justified when one considers that the infant – provided one includes with it the care it receives from its mother – does almost realize a psychical system of this kind.

When the objection is made that intersubjectivistic models are in danger of eliminating the subject, this overlooks the fact that they are *models* and nothing more. Both the subject-as-isolated and as seen in close relationship with the other or the group are simply notions that flow from adopting a certain fiction. Both express nothing other than points of view cut out from the chaos of infinite and unknowable reality.

37 See Kojève (1947, pp. 210–211) to understand what is implied by the operation of abstraction:

> Now, the concrete real is dialectical. Abstractions are not . . . Let us consider a *real* table. This is not *Table* 'in general', nor just *any* table, but always *this concrete table* right here. Now, when 'naive' man or a representative of some science or other speaks of *this* table, he isolates it from the rest of the universe: he speaks of *this* table without speaking of what is not this table. Now, *this* table does not float in empty space. It is on *this* floor, in *this* room, in *this* house, in *this* place on Earth . . . To speak of this table without speaking of the rest, then, is *to abstract* from this rest, which in fact is just as real and concrete as this table itself . . . is therefore to speak of an *abstraction*, and not of a *concrete reality*. And what is true is relation to space is also true in relation to time. *This* table has a determined 'history' and not some other 'history', nor a past 'in general' . . . In short, what exists as a *concrete reality* is the spatial-temporal *totality* of the natural world: everything that is *isolated* from it is by that very fact an *abstraction*, which exists as isolated only in and by the *thought* of the man who thinks about it.

38 See Borutti (2006, pp. 21–22):

> One can understand the metaphorical thought that lies at the basis of the fiction through that which Wittgenstein calls 'seeing as': 'seeing as' is knowing how to see connections, being able to see something '*as something else*' and to bring out the form against a ground of similarities and differences. 'Seeing as', seeing things in a set of relations, establishing connections between heterogeneous objects and contexts, is the expression Wittgenstein uses to refer to the metaphorical core of the poietic character of languages, that is, their capacity to project worlds of objects: 'I observe a face, and then suddenly notice its likeness to another. I see that it has not changed; and yet I see it differently. I call this experience 'noticing an aspect' [*Aspekt*]. 'But what I perceive in the dawning of an aspect is not a property of the object, but an internal relation between it and other objects'.

39 See Garroni (1966, pp. 14–15):

> The fact is that – *from an epistemological point of view* – one cannot demonstrate *by definition* the 'goodness' of paradigm in itself, *as a*

paradigm. A certain set of assumptions becomes a paradigm for a number of different reasons, not always easy to analyze or isolate. It can happen because of their non-contradictoriness and compactness (demonstrable only up to a certain point); because they permit the construction of a theory that is simple and elegant but also powerful (explanations that are clearly more 'aesthetic' than cognitive); because such a theory proves to be adequate according to certain criteria and leads to some applications being regarded as valid by scientists and also – but not always on the basis of the same criteria – by other members of society; because these assumptions and/or obtainable applied results are considered 'convincing', 'correct', 'good', 'advanced', 'interesting', and so on. Obviously, all these reasons have their habitat not in science itself, or in epistemology, but in the organization of society as a society of scientists, as a society-class, as society as a whole – that is to say, in its political, economic, ethical and (in the elevated sense) cultural and also psychological structures (both in terms of social and individual psychology).

40 See Derrida (2006), *The Animal That Therefore I Am,* for the section on Lacan and the difference between instinct and drive.

41 See *Attention and Interpretation* by Bion (1970, p. 35), where the oscillation between truth and omniscience is deducible from the three forms of 'respect' that Bion lists: respect for truth, for omniscience, for both (in this case, however, it is respect for omniscience masked as respect for truth; in other words there is no theory or model that cannot be used for *not* knowing).

Chapter 6

42 The alpha function must alphabetize the moment, but the moment also comprehends the memory of the past and the future: the now is the most intimate image of the past (Benjamin, 1966). Bion makes it clear that he wishes to 'reserve the term "memory" for experience related to conscious attempts at recall – expressions of a fear that some elements, "uncertainties, mysteries, doubts" – will obtrude'.

43 *Remembrance of Things Past, The Prisoner*, p. 73.

44 See LeDoux (1996).

45 See Rossetti (2008, p. 29): 'the continuity of dream-work alpha during wakefulness clearly has its origins in the concept of unconscious fantasy'.

46 Freud's double censorship sets up a closed frontier between two states that can only be breached. Bion's caesura not only separates but also unites; it filters selectively. In the same way, dream work (Freud)

hides/destroys meaning, which has then to be restored in the original text, while dream work (Bion) generates meaning/ambiguity.

Chapter 7

47 See Bornedal (2010, pp. 274–275):

> Freud's thing presentation is neither arbitrarily nor conventionally determined: rather, it refers back to a *perceived thing, a represented reality*, and especially (albeit not exclusively) to a *visually perceived thing* as its necessary *nodal point*. However, there is no one-to-one relationship between *thing-representation* and *perceived thing*; the thing-*presentation* is not simply a copy or a mirror-image of the thing (it is not like a projection into the mind of the real 'thing'), since to Freud, the *thing-presentation* is open-endingly referring to all possible *associations* emanating from the 'thing' as a nodal point. A *thing-presentation* then consists of an indefinite number of atomic impressions stored as memory in or as memory-traces, existing in some non-specific more or less loose connection with the apparent actual thing.

48 This passage is often quoted in relation to drives. Equally often the context is not specified. It comes in a letter Freud wrote to Einstein which also talks about the constructions of science as 'mythical'.

49 *Instinct* is the term Stratchey used to translate *Trieb*, a decision that has led to much debate.

50 See Denis (2014) on the concept of the phylogenetic schema.

51 See Damasio (1994) on the theory of somatic markers.

52 Ranchetti (Freud, 2005, p. 54) translates *Ansatzmöglichkeit* as 'a potential beginning' (*un inizio potenziale*) instead of 'potentiality' (*potenzialità*).

53 It is worth comparing this translation in the Standard Edition with Freud's original text. Here is the translation: 'there are no unconscious affects as there are unconscious ideas. But there may very well be in the system *Ucs.* affective structures which, like others, become conscious' (p. 178). In German: 'gibt es also keine unbewußten Affekte, wie es unbewußte Vorstellungen gibt. Es kann aber sehr wohl im System *Ubw* Affektbildungen geben, die wie andere bewußt werden' (GW, p. 277).

54 One could reply that it would then no longer be 'psychic'. But here the problem is different. We would have to rethink not only the concept of the unconscious but also the concept of representation (Barile, 2013). Whether the affect can be unconscious or not depends on the idea we have of the unconscious. There can be no repressed

affect in the repressed unconscious, while it can exist in the unrepressed conscious; if, that is, by affect we mean something that is of the order of a sensory-motor schema of a provision or emotional background that organizes experience and that, although not representational, is already an expression of sociality. We would not know how to identify such a state; we can only postulate its existence. It would be unconscious without being repressed, but it could also *be repressed*. We could also imagine preverbal complex interactions in which some modes of experience are actively encouraged and others are hindered or excluded. When we talk about something, we feel, or feel consciously, then the affect has been shifted to the surface of consciousness by the representation. It has already become a high-level affect.

55 See Bion (1963, p. 22) for his definition of the β element: 'the earliest matrix from which thoughts can be supposed to arise. It partakes of the quality of inanimate object and psychic object without any form of distinction between the two. Thoughts are things, things are thought; and they have personality'. The analogy with Freud's definition of the drive as something between the somatic and the psychic is quite evident.

56 According to Bornedal (2010), hallucination indicates the direction in which the subject should look for the object.

Chapter 8

57 See Bion, who states (1967, p. 120) that the presentation of a case history is a story like any other: 'If the narrative were a work of art it might be reasonable to regard it as more nearly representative of truth than any literal transcription.'

58 For example, in the second and third parts of *The Animatrix*, 'The second renaissance', by Mahiro Maeda, 2003.

59 In fractals, the same structure is repeated at difference scales in accordance with the principle of 'self-similarity'. The most common example is a tree. The Grid's resemblance to a fractal should not of course be taken literally, but in my view deserves to be emphasized. If the Grid as a whole is considered to be like a contact barrier that separates and joins two adjacent areas, the same can be said of each row or column, as well as of each side that defines a box (which must filter whatever enters and leaves it). A box as a whole, too, separates and unites its two neighbours (above and below). The 'form' that is repeated is therefore in particular a function (but ultimately also a form).

60 The English word *slash* onomatopoeically suggests both the 'cut' and the 'spark' of contact.

61 Bion (1997, p. 30f.) defines β elements as non-thoughts, bizarre objects, 'gross darkness', '"a tale told by an idiot, full of sound and fury, signifying nothing" – zero, O', negative numerals, 'infra-red' and 'ultra-violet', rhythm-like, 'the sort of thing the musicians know about'.

62 See Grotstein (2007, p. 52): 'I put forth the notion that beneath the hidden order that runs through the entirety of Bion's works lies the concept of a *truth drive* and that all the ego's defence mechanisms are principally counterposed to the irruption of unconscious truth rather than of libido and aggression'. According to Grotstein, Bion himself had mentioned the concept of a truth instinct to him in 1979.

63 At the risk of repeating myself, I should like to expand further on this point. In accordance with a post-Bionian model of the analytic field (Ferro, 1992; Civitarese, 2008a), which must in my view be linked dialectically to a model of the subject in isolation, I listen to anything a patient tells me – not in the form of ongoing monitoring, but allowing myself to be 'surprised' by this perspective – as a product of the unconscious communication between minds. From this – but only this – point of view, the problem of the falsehood or veracity of his words does not arise for me. If his being a liar reflects an unconscious conflict in him, how can I treat him otherwise than by helping him to be more authentic, and hence not to have to hide behind intentional mendacity? Not even someone who lies on purpose is in control of his own unconscious, whereas a person who espouses virtue and truth at all costs might, depending on the circumstances, be expressing sadistic impulses or a false self. If I had a child who constantly lied to me, I might well conclude that I need to reinstate a seemingly lost communication, of which systematic recourse to falsehood is a symptom. I would therefore not confuse conscious communication with the profound, unconscious communication of emotional attunement.

64 See Grotstein (2007, p. 218): 'Thus, truth is the invariant, and emotion is its vehicle or container'.

Chapter 9

65 See Fielding (1999, p. 185): 'Lacan . . . concludes, however, that while there are "a few whiffs of the unconscious to be detected in his notes [which] might have led him to pass" into psychoanalysis, Merleau-Ponty's phenomenology is ultimately dependent upon a Cartesian ego and an abstract eye, and is accordingly, incompatible with psychoanalysis.'

66 See Freud (1891, p. 53):

> We can only presume that the fibre tracts, which reach the cerebral cortex after their passage through other grey masses, have maintained some relationship to the periphery of the body, but no longer reflect a topographically exact image of it. They contain the body periphery in the same way as . . . a poem contains the alphabet, i.e., in a complete different arrangement serving other purposes, in manifold associations of the individual elements, whereby some may be represented several times, others not at all. If it were possible to follow in detail the rearrangement [*Umordnung*] which takes place between the spinal projection and the cerebral cortex, one would probably find that the underlying principle is purely functional, and that the topographic relations are maintained only as long as they fit in with the claims of function.

67 I recall that the article by Bion and Rickman on tensions in groups, which aroused the enthusiasm of the young Lacan ([1947] 2001), is from 1943. It is difficult to speculate about reciprocal influences between Merleau-Ponty and Bion. What is clear is that one was well versed in the psychoanalytic literature and the other in that of philosophy.

68 Some authors read his philosophy as a metaphysics of the body (Reynolds, 2004).

69 See Ogden (2004a, p. 168):

> The task is not to tease apart the elements constituting the relationship in an effort to determine which qualities belong to whom; rather, from the point of view of the interdependence of subject and object, the analytic task involves an attempt to describe the specific nature of the experience of the unconscious interplay of individual subjectivity and intersubjectivity.

70 It could naturally be debated whether a rudimentary form of self exists in animals. It might be based on mechanisms such as mirror neurons. But without language, these mechanisms could not of themselves make a consciousness, not even in humans. The risk, as always, is of thinking that more sophisticated knowledge of the neurophysiological substrate will be able to 'explain' the how and why of inter-human communication (that is, of language as a higher level of psychic organization), when in fact it is no more than an obvious and necessary precondition.

71 See Freud: 'Die Übertragung schafft so ein Zwischenreich zwischen der Krankheit und dem Leben, durch welches sich der Übergang von der ersteren zum letzteren vollzieht' (GW, 1914, p. 135)

('The transference thus creates an intermediate region between illness and real life through which the transition from the one to the other is made'; 1914a, p. 154 *SE*). The repetition of the preposition 'between', which is already present in the compound noun *Zwischenreich*, seems to us like a symptom of the effort Freud is making to penetrate this conceptual area.

Chapter 10

72 'Sometimes I think that a feeling is one of the few things that analysts have the privilege of seeing as a "fact"' (Bion, 1976, p. 317).

73 'I know that in writing I have to blind myself artificially in order to focus all the light on one dark spot, renouncing cohesion, harmony, rhetoric, and everything which you call symbolic, frightened as I am by the experience that any such claim or expectation involves the danger of distorting the matter under investigation' (Freud, 1916, p. 45). The resonance of Freud's metaphor with Oedipus's gesture of expiation for having wanted to know what he did wrong becomes deafening; it amounts to saying that one pays a price for the truth.

74 See the exhilarating opening to Laurence Sterne's *Tristram Shandy* (1759–1767), in which the protagonist traces back the misadventures of his life to an accident that happened during the copulation that led to his conception. At a critical moment, his mother had asked his father whether he had remembered to wind the clock.

Postscript

75 'Das Italienreisen ist nämlich nicht so ganz ohne Beschwerden, wie man sich's erwartet' (Freud, 1999 [1896], p. 1253).

Bibliography

Agamben, G. (2006) *Che cos'è un dispositivo*? Rome: Nottetempo.

Aisenstein, M. and Gibeault, A. (1991) The work of hypochondria – a contribution to the study of the specificity of hypochondria, in particular in relation to hysterical conversion and organic disease. *International Journal of Psychoanalysis,* 72: 669–680.

Albarella, C. (1997) Note sulla crisi della psicoanalisi. A proposito di due recenti pubblicazioni. *Rivista di Psicoanalisi,* 1: 103–118.

Anzieu, D. (1999) *Beckett.* Paris: Gallimard.

Avzaradel, J.R. (2011) On the construction of thinking. *International Journal of Psychoanalysis,* 92: 833–858.

Bachmann, I. (1972) Word for word. In *Three Paths to the Lake.* New Jersey: Homes and Meier, 1989.

Barale, F. (2008) Alle origini della psicoanalisi. *Rivista di Psicoanalisi,* 54: 129–148.

Baranger, M. and Baranger, W. ([1961–1962] 2008) The analytic situation as a dynamic field. *International Journal of Psychoanalysis,* 89: 795–826.

Barile, E. (2013) *Pensare Damasio. Due o tre cose che so di lui.* Milan: FrancoAngeli.

Barthes, R. (1984) *The Rustle of Language.* Berkeley and Los Angeles: University of California Press, 1986.

Benjamin, W. (1955) *1913–1926, Vol. 1: Selected Writings.* Boston, MA: Harvard University Press, 2004.

Benjamin, W. (1966) *Sul concetto di storia.* Turin: Einaudi, 1997.

Bernstein, J.S. (1975–1976) The autistic character. *The Psychoanalytic Review,* 62: 537–555.

Bion, W.R. (1948) Experiences in groups: I. In *Experiences in Groups and Other Papers.* London: Tavistock, 1961.

Bion, W.R. (1961) *Experiences in Groups.* Hove: Routledge, 1991.

Bion, W.R. (1962) *Learning from Experience.* London: Tavistock.

Bion, W.R. (1963) *Elements of Psycho-Analysis.* London: Heinemann.

Bion, W.R. (1965) *Transformations: Change from Learning to Growth*. London: Tavistock.

Bion, W.R. (1967) *Second Thoughts: Selected Papers on Psycho-Analysis*. London: Heinemann.

Bion, W.R. (1970) *Attention and Interpretation*. London: Tavistock.

Bion, W.R. (1976) Evidence. In *Clinical seminars and other works*. London: Karnac, 1994, pp. 312–320.

Bion, W.R. (1977a) *Two Papers: The Grid and the Caesura*. London: Karnac, 1989 (Rio de Janeiro: Imago).

Bion, W.R. (1977b) The past presented. In *A Memoir of the Future*. London: Karnac, 1991, pp. 219–426.

Bion, W.R. (1978–80) *Discussioni con W.R. Bion. Los Angeles/New York/São Paulo*. Turin: Loescher, 1984.

Bion, W.R. (1978) *Four Discussions with W.R. Bion*. Perthshire: Clunie Press.

Bion, W.R. (1990) *Brazilian Lectures*. London: Karnac (São Paulo, 1973; Rio de Janeiro/São Paulo, 1974).

Bion, W.R. (1991) *A Memoir of the Future*. London: Karnac.

Bion, W.R. (1992) *Cogitations*. London: Karnac.

Bion, W.R. (1997) *Taming Wild Thoughts*. London: Karnac.

Bion, W.R. (2005) *Tavistock Seminars*. London: Karnac.

Bion, W.R. and Rickman, J. (1943) Intra-group tensions in therapy: their study as the task of the group. *Lancet*, 242: 678–682.

Bleger, J. (1967) *Symbiosis and Ambiguity: A Psychoanalytic Study*. London: Routledge, 2012.

Blum, H.P. (1999) Reflections on Freud's Letter from Florence, September 7, 1896. *Journal of the American Psychoanalytic Association*, 47: 1249–1252.

Bollas, C. (1978) The aesthetic moment and the search for transformation. *The Annual of Psychoanalysis*, 6: 385–394.

Bollas, C. (1987) *The Shadow of the Object: Psychoanalysis of the Unthought Known*. London: Free Association Book.

Bonaminio, V. (2009) *The Psyche Indwelling in the Body: States of Integration*. The Thirteenth Annual International Frances Tustin Memorial Lectureship. The Psychoanalytic Center of California, Los Angeles.

Bonfiglio, B. (2010) Inconscio strutturale, funzioni dell'analista e verbalizzazione. *Rivista di Psicoanalisi*, 56: 821–838.

Bornedal, P. (2010) *The Surface and the Abyss. Nietzsche as Philosopher of Mind and Knowledge*. Berlin: De Gruyter.

Borutti, S. (1999) *Filosofia delle scienze umane: Le categorie dell'antropologia e della sociologia*. Milan: Mondadori.

Borutti, S. (2006) *Filosofia dei sensi. Estetica del pensiero tra filosofia, arte e letteratura*. Milan: Raffaello Cortina.

Borutti, S. (2010) *Leggere il Tractatus logico-philosophicus di Wittgenstein*. Pavia: Ibis.

Botella, C. (2012) Per un ampliamento del metodo freudiano [Toward a broadening of the Freudian method]. Paper presented at meeting of Associazione Studi Psicoanalitici, October, Milan.

Botella, C. and Botella, S. (2001) *The Work of Psychic Figurability: Mental States without Representation*. London: Routledge, 2004.

Bucci, W. (1997) *Psychoanalysis and Cognitive Science: A Multiple Code Theory*. New York: The Guilford Press.

Cambon, F. (2008) *De quoi est fait l'inconscient*. Paris: Epel.

Carbone, M. (2008) *Proust et les idées sensibles*. Paris: Vrin.

Carbone, M. (2011) *La chair des images: Merleau-Ponty entre peinture et cinema*. Paris: Vrin.

Chantraine, P. (1999) *Dictionnaire étymologique de la langue grecque*. Paris: Klincksieck.

Charles, M. (2002) Bion's Grid: a tool for transformation. *Journal of the American Academy of Psychoanalysis,* 30: 429–445.

Civitarese, G. (2004) Symbiotic bond and the setting. In *The Intimate Room: Theory and Technique of the Analytic Field*. London: Routledge, 2010, pp. 22–49.

Civitarese, G. (2008a) *The Intimate Room. Theory and Technique of the Analytic Field*. London: Routledge, 2010.

Civitarese, G. (2008b) 'Caesura' as Bion discourse on method. *International Journal of Psychoanalysis,* 89: 1123–1143.

Civitarese, G. (2008c) Immersion versus interactivity and analytic field. *International Journal of Psychoanalysis,* 89: 279–298.

Civitarese, G. (2010) Do cyborgs dream? Post-human landscapes in Shinya Tsukamoto's *Nightmare Detective* (2006). *International Journal of Psychoanalysis,* 91: 1005–1016.

Civitarese, G. (2011a) *The Violence of Emotions: Bion and Post-Bionian Psychoanalysis*. London: Routledge, 2012.

Civitarese, G. (2011b) Lipocondria e l'esilio. In V. Egidi Morpurgo and G. Civitarese (eds), *L'ipocondria e il dubbio. L'approccio psicoanalitico*. Milan: FrancoAngeli.

Civitarese, G. (2011c) Il riparo della quasi-morte e l'analista come detctive degli incubi. In A. Ferro and al., *Psicoanalisi in giallo. L'analista come detective*. Milan: Raffaello Cortina.

Civitarese, G. (2012) *Losing Your Head: Abjection, Aesthetic Conflict, and Psychoanalytic Criticism*. Lanham, Maryland: Rowman and Littlefield, 2015.

Civitarese, G. (2013a) Bion's 'Evidence' and his theoretical style. *Psychoanalytic Quarterly,* 82: 615–633.

Civitarese, G. (2013b) *The Necessary Dream: New Theories and Techniques of Interpretation in Psychoanalysis*. London: Karnac, 2014.

Civitarese, G. (2013c) The inaccessible unconscious and reverie as a path of figurability. In H. Levine, D. Scarfone and G. Reed (eds), *Unrepresented States and the Construction of Meaning: Clinical and Theoretical Contributions*. London: Karnac, 2013, pp. 220–239.

Civitarese, G. and Boffito, S. (2012) Stile e sovversione nella psicoanalisi postmoderna. State of Mind – Il giornale delle scienze psicologiche. Available at: www.stateofmind.it/2012/05/stile-sovversionepsicoanalisi-postmoderno/ (accessed 11 November 2015).

Civitarese, G. and Ferro, A. (2013) Metaphor in analytic field theory. In M. Katz (ed.), *Metaphor and Fields: Common Ground, Common Language, and the Future of Psychoanalysis*. New York: Routledge, pp. 121–142.

Cogliani, M. (2004) La musica delle emozioni e il contenitore di risonanza. In F. Oneroso and A. Gorrese (eds), *Mente e pensiero. Incontri con l'opera di Wilfred R. Bion*. Naples: Liguori, pp. 143–177.

Conrotto, F. (1995) Pulsione o relazione: una opposizione irriducibile? *Rivista di Psicoanalisi*, 41: 583–609.

Damasio, A. (1994) *Descartes' Error: Emotion, Reason, and the Human Brain*. London: Penguin Books.

David, M. (1966) *La psicoanalisi nella cultura italiana*. Turin: Boringhieri.

de Azevedo, A.A. (2000) Substantive unconscious and adjective unconscious: the contribution of Wilfred Bion. *The Journal of Analytical Psychology*, 45: 75–91.

De Lillo, M. (2005) *Freud e il linguaggio. Dalla neurologia alla psicoanalisi*. Lecce: Pensa Multimedia.

de Saint Aubert, E. (2012) 'Voir, c'est imaginer. Et imaginer, c'est voir': perception et imaginaire chez Merleau-Ponty. *Chiasmi International*, 14: 257–281.

Denis, A. (2014). I disturbi del pensiero a partire dagli schemi verbali filogenetici. *Rivista di Psicoanalisi*, 60: 63–81.

Derrida, J. (1967a) *Writing and Difference*. London: Routledge, 2001.

Derrida, J. (1967b) *Of Grammatology*. Baltimore, MA: Johns Hopkins University Press.

Derrida, J. (1972) *Dissemination*. Trans. B. Johnson. London: Continuum, 2004.

Derrida, J. (1978) *The Truth in Painting*. Chicago: Chicago University Press, 1987.

Derrida, J. (1992) 'To do justice to Freud': the history of madness in the age of psychoanalysis. In *Resistances of Psychoanalysis*. Stanford, CA: Stanford University Press, 1998, pp. 70–118.

Derrida, J. (1997) *Psyche: Inventions of the Other, Vol I and II*. Stanford, CA: Stanford University Press, 2007.

Derrida, J. (2005) History of the lie. Prolegomena. In *Futures of Jacques Derrida*. Stanford, CA: Stanford University Press, pp. 65–98.

Derrida, J. (2006) *The Animal That Therefore I Am*. New York: Fordham University Press, 2008.

Derrida, J. (2008) *Adesso l'architettura*. Milan: Scheiwiller.

Dreyblatt, A. (1998–1999) *The ReCollection Mechanism. Installation.* Available at: www.dreyblatt.de/html/art.php?id=97 (accessed 30 October 2010).

Edelman, G. (1989) *The Remembered Present: A Biological Theory of Consciousness*. New York: Basic Books.

Emanuel, R. (2012) An application of Bion's theory of thinking and transformations in hallucinosis: an experience of supervision with Dr Donald Meltzer. *Journal of Child Psychotherapy*, 38: 284–301.

Fedida, P. (1972) L'hypochondrie du rêve. *Nouvelle Revue de Psychanalyse*, 5: 225–239.

Ferro, A. (1992) *The Bi-Personal Field: Experiencing Child Analysis*. London; New York: Routledge, 1999.

Ferro, A. (1996) *In the Analyst's Consulting Room*. London: Routledge, 2002.

Ferro, A. (2002) *Seeds of Illness, Seeds of Recovery*. London: Routledge, 2004.

Ferro, A. (2006) *Mind Works: Technique and Creativity in Psychoanalysis*. London: Routledge, 2009.

Ferro, A. (2008) The patient as the analyst's best colleague: Transformation into a dream and narrative transformations. *Italian Psychoanalytic Annual*, 2: 199–205.

Ferro, A. (2009) Transformations in dreaming and characters in the psychoanalytic field. *International Journal of Psychoanalysis*, 90: 209–230.

Ferro, A. (2010) *Torments of the Soul: Psychoanalytic Transformations in Dreaming and Narration*. London: Routledge, 2015.

Ferro, A. and Basile, R. (eds) (2009) *The Analytic Field: A Clinical Concept*. London: Karnac.

Ferro, A. and Civitarese, G. (2015) *The Analytic Field and Its Transformations*. London: Karnac, 2015.

Fielding, H.A. (1999) Envisioning the other. Lacan and Merleau-Ponty on intersubjectivity. In D. Olkowski and J. Morley (eds), *Merleau-Ponty, Interiority and Exteriority, Psychic Life and the World*. Albany: State University of New York Press, pp. 185–199.

Finelli, R. (2005) Le tre logiche della 'Vorstellung' nella filosofia della mente di S. Freud. In M. De Lillo, *Freud e il linguaggio. Dalla neurologia alla psicoanalisi*. Lecce: Pensa Multimedia, pp. 9–36.

Fornaro, M. (1990) *Psicoanalisi tra scienza e mistica. L'opera di Wilfred R. Bion*. Rome: Edizioni Studium.

Freud, S. (1888) Some points for a comparative study of organic and hysterical motor paralyses. *SE* 1: 157–172.

Freud, S. (1891) *On Aphasia: A Critical Study*. New York: International Universities Press, 1953.
Freud, S. (1950 [1892–1899]) Extracts from the Fliess papers. *SE* 1: 175–280.
Freud, S. (1895) A project for a scientific psychology. *SE* 1: 293–397.
Freud, S. (1900) The interpretation of dreams. *SE* 4: 1–338; 5: 339–625.
Freud, S. (1905) Three essays on the theory of sexuality. *SE* 7: 123–246.
Freud, S. (1911) Formulations on the two principles of mental functioning. *SE* 12: 215–226.
Freud, S. (1912) Recommendations to physicians practising psycho-analysis, *SE* 6: 109–120.
Freud, S. (1913) The claims of psychoanalysis to scientific interest. *SE* 13: 163–190.
Freud, S. (1914a) Remembering, repeating and working-through. *SE* 12: 145–156.
Freud, S. (1914b) On the history of the psycho-analytic movement. *SE* 14: 1–66.
Freud, S. (1915) The Unconscious. *SE* 14: 159–215.
Freud, S. (1916) Letter from Freud to Lou Andreas-Salomé, May 25, 1916. *The International Psycho-Analytical Library,* 89: 45.
Freud, S. (1917a) A metapsychological supplement to the theory of dreams. *SE* 14: 217–235.
Freud, S. (1917b) Introductory Lectures on Psychoanalysis. *SE* 16: 241–463.
Freud, S. (1920) Beyond the pleasure principle. *SE* 18: 1–64.
Freud, S. (1921) Psychoanalysis and telepathy. *SE* 18: 173–194.
Freud, S. (1923) The ego and the id. *SE* 19: 1–66.
Freud, S. (1926) Inhibitions, symptoms and anxiety. *SE* 20: 75–176.
Freud, S (1937) Constructions in analysis. *SE* 23: 255–270.
Freud, S. (1938a) Some elementary lessons in psycho-analysis. *SE* 23: 279–286.
Freud, S. (1938b) Findings, ideas, problems. *SE* 23: 299–300
Freud, S. (1986) The aetiology of hysteria. *SE* 3: 187–221.
Freud, S. (1999 [1896]) A letter from Freud to Martha Freud. *Journal of the American Psychoanalytic Association*, 47: 1253–1255.
Freud, S. (2005) *Scritti di metapsicologia (1915–1917).* Trans. M. Ranchetti. Turin: Bollati Boringhieri.
Gallese, V. (2006) Mirror neurons and intentional attunement: commentary on Olds. *Journal of the American Psychoanalytic Association,* 54: 47–57.
Garroni, E. (1966) Introduzione. In AA.VV., *Il circolo linguistico di Praga. Le tesi del '29*. Milan: Silva, pp. 7–35.
Green, A. (1995) *Propedeutica. Metapsicologia rivisitata* [Propaedeutics: Metapsychology Revisited]. Rome: Borla, 2001.

Green, A. (1998) The primordial mind and the work of the negative. *International Journal of Psychoanalysis,* 79: 649–665.

Groddeck, G. (1977) *Meaning of Illness: Selected Psychoanalytic Writings Including Correspondence with Sigmund Freud.* New York: International University Press.

Grotstein, J.S. (2000) *Who Is the Dreamer Who Dreams the Dream? A Study of Psychic Presences.* London: Karnac.

Grotstein, J.S. (2002) Commentary on 'Bion's Grid: a tool for transformation' (ed. M. Charles). *Journal of the American Academy of Psychoanalysis,* 30: 447–450.

Grotstein, J.S. (2005) Projective transidentification. *International Journal of Psychoanalysis,* 86: 1051–1069.

Grotstein, J.S. (2007) *A Beam of Intense Darkness: Wilfred Bion's Legacy to Psychoanalysis.* London: Karnac.

Haddad, A. and Haddad, G. (1995) *Freud en Italie: Psychanalyse du Voyage.* Paris: A. Michel.

Heenen-Wolff, S. (2013) 'Translation' and 'transformation' in the analytic situation: Freud – Bion – Laplanche. *International Journal of Psychoanalysis,* 94: 437–451.

Heidegger, M. (1927) *Being and Time: A Translation of Sein und Zeit (1953).* New York: State University of New York Press, 1996.

Herrera, M. (2010) *Representante-representativo, représentant-représentation, ideational representative*: which one is a Freudian concept? On the translation of *Vorstellungsrepräsentanz* in Spanish, French and English. *International Journal of Psychoanalysis,* 91: 785–809.

Jones, E. (1953) *The Life and Work of Sigmund Freud, Vol 3.* New York: Basic Books, 1957.

Kant, I. (1781) *Critique of Pure Reason.* Trans. F. M. Müller. London: Penguin Books.

Kernberg, O.F. (1996) Thirty methods to destroy the creativity of psychoanalytic candidates. *International Journal of Psychoanalysis,* 77: 1031–1040.

Kernberg, O.F. (2011) Divergent contemporary trends in psychoanalytic theory. *The Psychoanalytic Review,* 98: 633–664.

Kernberg, O.F. (2012) Suicide prevention for psychoanalytic institutes and societies. *Journal of the American Psychoanalytic Association,* 60: 707–719.

Klein, S. (1980) Autistic phenomena in neurotic patients. *International Journal of Psychoanalysis,* 61: 395–402.

Kojève, A. (1947) *Introduction to the Reading of Hegel, 1947–1969.* New York: Basic Books.

Kristeva, J. (1974) *Revolution in Poetic Language.* New York: Columbia University Press, 1984.

Kristeva, J. (1980) *Powers of Horror: An Essay on Abjection*. New York: Columbia University Press, 1982.

Kristeva, J. (2000) *Melanie Klein*. New York: Columbia University Press, 2002.

Kuhn, T.S. (1962) *The Structure of Scientific Revolutions*. Chicago: University of Chicago Press, 1996.

Lacan, J. ([1947] 2001) La psychiatrie anglaise et la guerre. In *Autres écrits*. Paris: Seuil, 2001, pp. 101–120.

Lacan, J. (1966) *Écrits: The First Complete Edition in English*. New York: W.W. Norton and Company, 2007.

Lacan, J. (1986) *The Seminar of Jacques Lacan. Book VII. The Ethics of Psychoanalysis*. 1959–1960. New York: Norton, 1992.

Lanfredini, R. (2014) Essere una cosa che sente: il sotto-categoriale in Maurice Merleau-Ponty. *Rivista di Psicoanalisi,* 60: 433–453.

Laplanche, J. (2005) I Tre saggi e la teoria della seduzione. *Rivista di Psicoanalisi,* 51: 849–862.

Laplanche, J. and Pontalis J.-B. (1967) *The Language of Psycho-Analysis*. New York: W.W. Norton, 1974.

Le Guen, C. (2008) *Dictionnaire freudien*. Paris: PUF.

LeDoux, J. (1996) *The Emotional Brain: The Mysterious Underpinnings of Emotional Life*. New York: Simon and Schuster, 1998.

Leiris, M. (1934) *L'Afrique fantôme*. Paris: Gallimard, 1988.

Lemma, A. (2010) *Under the Skin: A Psychoanalytic Study of Body Modification*. London: Routledge.

Lemma, A. (2013) Whose skin is it anyway? Some reflections on the psychic function of necrophilic fantasies. *Rivista di Psicoanalisi,* 59: 283–304.

López-Corvo, R. (2002) *The Dictionary of the Work of W.R. Bion*. London: Karnac, 1970.

Lyotard, F. (2011) *Discourse, Figure*. Minneapolis: Minnesota University Press.

Mancia, M. (2003) Dream actors in the theatre of memory. *International Journal of Psychoanalysis,* 84: 945–952.

Mancia, M. (2006) Implicit memory and early unrepressed unconscious: their role in the therapeutic process (How the neurosciences can contribute to psychoanalysis). *International Journal of Psychoanalysis,* 87: 83–103.

Mangini, E. (2009) On primal repression. *The Italian Psychoanalytic Annual,* 4: 53–69, 2010.

Masson, J.M. (ed.) (1985) *The Complete Letters of Sigmund Freud to Wilhelm Fliess, 1887–1904*. Cambridge, MA/London: Belknap Press/Harvard University Press.

McCarthy, C. (2009) Hollywood's favorite cowboy. Interview of novelist Cormac McCarthy by J. Jurgensen, 20 November. *Wall Street Journal*. Available at: www.wsj.com/articles/SB10001424052748704576204574529703577274572 (accessed 11 November 2015).

Meltzer, D. (1978) *The Kleinian Development 3*. Strath Tay: Clunie.

Meltzer, D. (1986) *Studies in Extended Metapsychology*. London: Karnac, 2009.

Meltzer, D. (1987) Il modello della mente secondo Bion: note su funzionc α, inversione della funzione alfa e griglia negativa. In C. Neri, A. Correale and P. Fadda, *Letture Bioniane*. Rome: Borla, pp. 76–83.

Meltzer, D., Bremner, J., Hoxter, S., Weddell, D. and Wittenberg, I. (1975) *Explorations in Autism: A Psycho-Analytical Study*. London: Karnac.

Merleau-Ponty, M. (1945) *Phenomenology of Perception*. London: Routledge and Kegan Paul, 1962.

Merleau-Ponty, M. (1962) The child's relations with others. In *The Phenomenology of Perception and Other Essays*. Evanston, IL: Northwestern University Press, 1964.

Merleau-Ponty, M. (1964) *The Visible and the Invisible*. Evanston, IL: Northwestern University Press, 1968.

Napolitano, F. (2010) Prefazione. In S. Freud (1891), *L'interpretazione delle afasie. Uno studio critico*. Macerata: Quoadlibet, 2010, pp. 5–7.

Nietzsche, F. (1882) *The Gay Science: With a Prelude in Rhymes and an Appendix of Songs*. New York: Random House, 1974.

Ogden, T.H. (1989) *The Primitive Edge of Experience*. Northvale, NJ: Aronson.

Ogden, T.H. (1994a) The concept of interpretive action. *Psychoanalytic Quarterly*, 63: 219–245.

Ogden, T.H. (1994b) *Subjects of Analysis*. London: Karnac.

Ogden, T.H. (2001) *Conversations at the Frontier of Dreaming*. Northvale, NJ: Aronson.

Ogden, T.H. (2003) What's true and whose idea was it? *International Journal of Psychoanalysis*, 84: 593–606.

Ogden, T.H. (2004a) The analytic third: implications for psychoanalytic theory and technique. *Psychoanalytic Quarterly*, 73: 167–195.

Ogden, T. H. (2004b) An introduction to the reading of Bion. *International Journal of Psychoanalysis*, 85: 285–300.

Ogden, T.H. (2005) *This Art of Psychoanalysis: Dreaming Undreamt Dreams and Interrupted Cries*. London: Routledge.

Ogden, T.H. (2007) On talking-as-dreaming. *International Journal of Psychoanalysis*, 88: 575–589.

Ogden, T.H. (2008) Bion's four principles of mental functioning. *Fort Da*, 14B: 11–35.

Ogden, T.H. (2009) *Rediscovering Psychoanalysis: Thinking and Dreaming, Learning and Forgetting.* London: Karnac.

Opatow, B. (1997) The real unconscious: psychoanalysis as a theory of consciousness. *Journal of the American Psychoanalytic Association,* 45: 865–890.

Palmier, J.-M. (1972) *Guida a Lacan.* Milan: Rizzoli, 1975.

Peltz, R. (2015) What is deep? *Rivista di Psicoanalisi,* 61: 645–662.

Pontalis, J.-B (1972) La pénétration du rêve. *Nouvelle Revue de Psychanalyse,* 5: 257–272.

Pontalis, J.-B. (1988) *Perdere di vista.* Rome: Borla, 1993.

Pontalis, J.-B. (2007) Penser l'intermédiaire. In F. Gantheret (ed.), *Le royaume intermédiaire. Psychanalyse, littérature, autour de J.-B. Pontalis.* Paris: Gallimard, pp. 313–320.

Pozzi, M.E. (2003) The use of observation in the psychoanalytic treatment of a 12-year-old-boy with Asperger's syndrome. *International Journal of Psychoanalysis,* 84: 1333–1349.

Propp, V. (1928) *Morphology of the Folktale.* Eastford, CT: Martino Fine Books, 2015.

Quignard, P. (1995) *Rhetorique speculative.* Paris: Gallimard, 1997.

Racalbuto, A. (1994) *Tra il fare e il dire.* Milan: Raffaello Cortina.

Racalbuto, A. (1997) *Pensare. L'originario della sensorialità e dell'affetto nella costruzione del pensiero.* Available at: www.sicap.it/merciai/bion/papers/racal.htm (accessed 11 November 2015).

Racalbuto, A. (2003) Pulsione e relazione: inconciliabilità o integrazione? In E. Mangini (ed.), *Lezioni sul pensiero post-freudiano. Maestri, idee, suggestioni e fermenti della psicoanalisi del novecento.* Milan: Led Edizioni.

Reynolds, J. (2004) *Merleau-Ponty and Derrida: Intertwining Embodiment and Alterity.* Athens, OH: Ohio University Press.

Ricoeur, P. (1965) *Freud and Philosophy: An Essay on Interpretation.* Trans. D. Savage. New Haven: Yale University Press, 1970.

Rilke, R.M. (1995) *Ahead of All Parting: The Selected Poetry and Prose of Rainer Maria Rilke.* Ed. and trans. S. Mitchell. New York: Random House.

Rimbaud, A. (1873) *A Season in Hell and Illuminations.* New York: Random House Inc., 2005.

Riolo, F. (2009) Lo statuto psicoanalitico di inconscio: prospettive attuali. *Rivista di Psicoanalisi,* 55: 11–28.

Riolo, F. (2011) Transformations in hallucinosis. *Italian Psychoanalytic Annual,* 5: 107–120.

Rizzuto, A. (1990) The origins of Freud's concept of object representation ('Objektvorstellung') in his monograph 'On Aphasia': its theoretical and technical importance. *International Journal of Psychoanalysis,* 71: 241–248.

Rossetti, M. (ed.) (2008) *Mito, mitica e filosofia nel pensiero di Bion.* Venice: Cafoscarina.

Sandler, J. (1976) Dreams, unconscious fantasies and 'identity of perception'. *International Review of Psychoanalysis,* 3: 33–42.

Sandler, J. and Sandler, A. (1983) The 'second censorship', the 'three box model' and some technical implications. *International Journal of Psychoanalysis,* 64: 413–425.

Sbarbaro, C. (1914) *Pianissimo.* Venice: Marsilio, 2001.

Schneider, R. (1992) *Brother of Sleep.* New York: Overlook, 1992.

Semi, A. (2001) *Introduzione alla metapsicologia.* Milan: Raffaello Cortina.

Souter, K.M. (2009) The 'War Memoirs': some origins of the thought of W.R. Bion. *International Journal of Psychoanalysis,* 90: 795–808.

Sterne, L. (1759–1767) *The Life and Opinions of Tristram Shandy, Gentleman.* Ware, Hertfordshire, UK: Wordsworth Editions, 1996.

Stocker, B. (2006) *Derrida on Deconstruction.* London: Routledge.

Stolorow, R.D. and Atwood, G.E. (1992). *I contesti dell'essere. Le basi intersoggettive della vita psichica.* Turin: Bollati Boringhieri, 1995.

Symington, J. and Symington, N. (1996) *The Clinical Thought of Wilfred Bion.* London: Routledge, 2002.

Tustin, F. (1986) *Autistic Barriers in Neurotic Patients.* London: Karnac.

Vanzago, L. (2014) La psicoanalisi ontologica di M. Merleau-Ponty. *Rivista di Psicoanalisi,* 60: 455–468.

Vitale, S. (2004) 'Si prega di chiudere gli occhi'. Il pensiero selvaggio della cattedrale. In F. Oneroso and A. Gorrese (eds), *Mente e pensiero. Incontri con l'opera di Wilfred R. Bion.* Naples: Liguori, pp. 45–82.

Vitale, S. (2005) *La dimora della lontananza. Saggi sull'esperienza nello spazio intermedio.* Florence: Clinamen.

Webster's (1961) *Third New International Dictionary of the English Language.* London: Bell.

Weiss, E. (1970) *Sigmund Freud as a Consultant.* Piscataway, NJ: Transaction Publishers, 1991.

Westen, D. (1999) The scientific status of unconscious processes: is Freud really dead? *Journal of the American Psychoanalytic Association,* 47: 1061–1106.

Winnicott, D.W. (1945) Primitive emotional development. In *Through Paediatrics to Psycho-Analysis.* London: Karnac, 1975, pp. 3145–3156.

Winnicott, D.W. (1947) Hate in the countertransference. In *Through Paediatrics to Psycho-Analysis.* London: Tavistock, 1958; Hogarth, 1975, pp. 194–203.

Winnicott, D.W. (1949). Mind and its relation to the psyche-soma. In *Through Paediatrics to Psycho-Analysis.* London: Hogarth Press and

The Institute of Psychoanalysis, 1975; reprinted London: Karnac, 1992, pp. 243–254

Winnicott, D.W. (1956) Primary maternal preoccupation. In *From Paediatrics to Psychoanalysis*. London: Hogarth, 1987, pp. 300–305.

Winnicott, D.W. (1989) *Psychoanalytic Explorations*. Cambridge, MA: Harvard University Press.

INDEX